The Fragile Self

The Fragile Self: The Structure of Narcissistic Disturbance and Its Therapy

Phil Mollon, Ph.D.

Adult Psychotherapist and Head of Clinical Psychology Service
Lister Hospital, Hertfordshire

Foreword by
Malcolm Pines

JASON ARONSON INC.
Northvale, New Jersey
London

© Whurr Publishers Ltd. 1993
1994 hardcover edition—Jason Aronson Inc.

Library of Congress Cataloging-in-Publication Data *pending*

ISBN: 1-56821-234-8

Manufactured in the United States of America. Jason Aronson Inc. offers books and cassettes. For information and catalog write to Jason Aronson Inc., 230 Livingston Street, Northvale, New Jersey 07647.

Foreword

More than 10 years ago, Phil Mollon and I were both on the staff at the Tavistock Clinic. I had both the opportunity and the privilege to supervise some of his psychotherapeutic work with individuals and with groups. We found that we each had a keen interest in the concepts of the self at a time of increasing interest in the psychoanalytic literature on the psychodynamics of normal and pathological self states. This had come about through the clarification of such diagnostic entities as borderline personality, borderline states and narcissistic personality disorders, and as a result of the fact that psychotherapists were recognising how much of their everyday work was concerned with such patients, with whom it was, more often than not, difficult to conduct therapies.

Although British psychoanalysts and psychotherapists were well versed in home-grown schools of psychoanalysis, such as the object relations school (Winnicott, Balint and Fairbairn), the Kleinian approach (Rosenfeld, Segal, Bion, and later Steiner), the Anna Freud approach (Sandler, Holder and Dare), they were not as well acquainted as we were with the extensive and intensive writings of North American workers. In this respect, Mollon and I stood out from our Tavistock Clinic colleagues and were regarded with some suspicion. There was a a right language and a right technique – and we were on the wrong side! This applied particularly to me because I spoke not only from a psychoanalytic viewpoint but also from a group analytic one.

This group analytic viewpoint takes the social nature of the human being as its basis, and concepts such as mirroring are intrinsic to it. The group analytic approach incorporates aspects of both psychoanalysis and social psychology, and the work of Cooley and George Herbert Mead is part of the group analytic frame of reference.

During our time together, Mollon formulated many of his ideas about the fragile self and I was impressed with his sensitive understanding of the patients from whom he derived these ideas. His work has now been incorporated into this book which is a welcome and notable addition to the world of literature. The majority of writings on the self have come from North America; not much of substance has been published, in this country, in book form, although there have been notable theoretical and clinical contributions. Mollon has studied in depth and, in my view, has produced a masterly integration of the British and American work. In fact, he has done more than that: in his taxonomy of self-disturbance he has made a distinct contribution to the understanding of these clinical states. This book is important because Mollon also shows, through his sensitive clinical illustrations in the form of case studies, how much help we can give some of our patients through our understanding of the processes of self-development and through applying these to our work. Like Mollon, I have had many patients who steadily work towards and achieve a greater stability and coherence of self through such understandings.

Psychoanalytic psychotherapy is a fascinating and difficult art, but it can be made more difficult than need be if inappropriate theories and techniques are used. It often seems that therapists are irresistibly drawn to dramatic and powerful theories of pathology which then lead to prolonged and painful struggles with their patients, often ending in impasse and disillusionment. They should instead turn their attention to the approach outlined by Mollon and they will, I believe, find their work less difficult and more humane; in turn, their patients will find their experiences more rewarding.

Malcolm Pines
March 1993

Preface

What is an example of disturbance in the experience of self? Consider a person in a state of severe embarrassed self-consciousness. The person is looking on the self from what is anticipated as the other's position. This is a necessary capacity for adequate social intercourse and relatedness to others. On this depends the ability to take account of the other's point of view and compare that with one's own. It is the basis of the possibility of empathy. But for the pathologically self-conscious person, the capacity to remain conscious of one's own position is lost. The differentiated consciousness of self and other collapses. The experience of self implodes, the person is mentally paralysed and wishes to disappear. The ensuing sense of shame is catastrophic.

Mutual embarrassment of self and other arises from derailed intercourse. We expect adequate social performance from one another and when these expectations are disrupted then embarrassment is the result. It is not widely recognised, for example, that schizophrenic patients can experience intense shame and embarrassment and self-consciousness. This is because they have an awareness of being somehow different from others and of being unable to give an adequate social performance – a highly complex skill which requires the processing and organisation of large amounts of interpersonal information regarding the other's response to oneself, and the subtle attunement of one's own behaviour to this. The shame and related 'narcissistic affects' of self-consciousness and embarrassment compounds the primary schizophrenic disorder, which may have, at least partly, a biological basis.

There are a number of interrelated disturbances of self in the example of embarrassed self-consciousness: (1) there is a loss of the normal sense of boundaries between self and other; (2) there is a diminished sense of agency, as the person feels helpless and not in control; (3) there is a loss of the sense of *coherence* in the organisation of self-experience; (4) there is a disturbance in the balance of awareness of self from inside and awareness of self from the other's position (Mead's

I and Me), with a skewing towards the latter; and (5) there is a negatively evaluated image of the self – self-esteem is low. These in fact
correspond to five of the seven categories of self-disturbance which I
outline later.

In order to understand such experiences and in order to help
patients suffering from disturbances in the sense of self, we need to
gather strands of theory and observation that have a bearing on how
the sense of self and structure of the self develop. It is not easy to see
how disturbances of the experience of self can be understood in terms
of traditional psychoanalytic frameworks such as Freud's biologically
based model of instincts and the tripartite mental structure of id, ego
and superego. Nor does Klein's theorising around early object relational phantasy and the paranoid–schizoid and depressive positions seem
of much help; although describing object relational phantasy, Klein's is
not an interpersonal theory and it is rooted in the biologically based
life and death instincts. On the other hand, contributions from more
recent theorists such as Winnicott and Kohut, which place the child in
an *interpersonal* or *intersubjective* context – taking account of the
interplay of two experiencing subjects – are of some help. Both these
authors wrote extensively about the experience of self; Kohut's framework eventually becoming termed 'self-psychology'.

In recent years there has been an explosion of increasingly sophisticated studies observing the interaction between mothers and babies or
young children, providing perspectives which were not available to the
early psychoanalysts. Dan Stern, a psychoanalyst and developmental
researcher, who has summarised a great deal of this work in his book
The Interpersonal World of the Infant, organises much of his theorising
around the sense of self. This emphasis on self within the play of two
experiencing subjects has been taken further in the 'intersubjective'
framework of the post-Kohutian author Stolorow and colleagues. In a
recent discussion of the status of the 'self' in psychoanalysis, Kirshner
(1991) writes: 'Consciousness, contrary to classical and commonsense
views on the matter, is not adequate to explain a human subject, nor
can the experience of the subject be taken for granted as some biological epiphenomenon. A "self", even a sense of self, is not intrinsic, but
we must suppose requires intersubjective experience. It is built up out
of interactions with others.'

The complexities of what the self is and how it develops and how it
can be disturbed are the subject of this book. Are disturbances of self
entirely non-oedipal, as Kohut argues? Is the problem entirely one
between child and mother? Is the relationship to the father important
in the development of the self? How do patients seek the building or
restoration of self in therapy? These are some of the questions I set out
to answer.

This theoretical and clinical exploration is an interweaving of themes of narcissism and themes of the self, with the aim of unveiling the underlying *structure* of narcissistic disturbance.

In Chapter 1 I consider the question of whether a concept of self is actually necessary in psychoanalysis. Having argued that it is, and discovering a variety of different concepts of self prevalent in the literature, I propose a taxonomy of seven categories of self disturbance.

Chapter 2 considers the concept of narcissism – drawing primarily on the myth of Narcissus and Echo and Freud's view of narcissism.

Chapter 3 explores those affects, such as shame and self-consciousness, which inherently concern the sense of self. These I term the 'narcissistic affects'.

Chapter 4 compares nine different theories of narcissistic personality. These are chosen to represent the broad spectrum of views. They are examined for their themes and are seen to relate to different categories of the taxonomy.

In Chapter 5 I propose a more comprehensive model of narcissistic disturbance, resting on a combined base of a failure of mirroring and a failure of oedipal triangulation. The role of the father is crucial to this formulation. This is seen to account for disturbances in all seven categories of the taxonomy.

Chapter 6 is a clinical exploration of this new model, examining the therapy with four patients. The material is presented relatively schematically in order to expose the underlying structure of their psychopathology. These patients demonstrate a variety of 'false selves', all more complex than was implied by Winnicott's (1960) original formulation. I also examine Kohut's clinical illustrations, with particular reference to his well-known case of Mr Z.; I show that all of his examples are consistent with the model I present.

Chapter 7 outlines the model of the healing process arising from the new formulation. I also explore ways of working in analytic psychotherapy which are inspired by self-psychology but go beyond the confines of Kohut's framework. Work with very disturbed patients is described, including a process over several years with a schizophrenic patient. The theme of my concluding argument is that the therapist should aim to grasp what kind of *development-enhancing* response the patient is seeking in the selfobject dimension of the transference and then *articulate this to the patient.*

Phil Mollon
January 1993

Acknowledgements

A writer is a channel for many and diverse influences. A book is always multi-authored; it would indeed be a narcissistic illusion for a writer to claim sole authorship of the text. A list of acknowledgements could therefore be extremely long. Nevertheless, some individuals deserve particular mention for their contributions.

I would like to thank Harold Maxwell for originally suggesting that I write this book and for his encouragement and support throughout.

The following individuals have been very helpful in a variety of ways: Patrick Casement, Peter Hildebrand, Malcolm Pines, Helen Morton, Anthony Storr, Peter Fonagy, Mannie Sher, Ernest Wolf and David Black.

Above all I am grateful to my wife Ros, and daughter Olivia, for their constant love, support and tolerance.

Contents

Chapter 1
The self

The concept of self: is it necessary?

When we speak of 'narcissism', with its meaning either of an emotional investment *in* the self, or the relationship *to* the self (Kinston, 1980) – we are implicitly assuming some concept of self. A theory of narcissism requires a theory of the self and the development of the self. Without this, any idea of narcissism will be very limited. In the following I argue that the 'self' cannot be taken as given, either philosophically or clinically.

The clinical and theoretical need for a concept of self may not be immediately apparent. Freud evidently saw no need for it. He used an ambiguous term 'ego', which in his early writings (e.g. his 1914 Narcissism paper) appeared to refer partly to an idea of self, but which with the introduction in 1923 of the tripartite structural model, moved more towards what Hartmann (1950) termed the 'system ego' – a constellation of ego functions mediating between the two other mental agencies, the id and the superego, and the external world. Whilst Hartmann argued for a clear distinction between the system of ego functions and the internal 'self-representation', others argued for the value of what was a possibly deliberate ambiguity in Freud's usage. For example, Weiss (1960), Laplanche and Pontalis (1980), Spruiell (1981), Kernberg (1982), Bettleheim (1983) and Smith (1985) emphasise that Freud used the term 'ego' to refer to a phenomenological experiential entity as well as a structure or organisation of functions. Smith argues that Hartmann's restriction of the ego to the metapsychological meaning of an organisation of functions has 'impoverished clinical psychoanalytic discourse' and 'has resulted in a profusion of popular terms designed to take up the slack left by the vanquished phenomenological ego'. Thus, analysts such as Federn (1953), Winnicott (1960), Guntrip (1968), Fairbairn (1952), Schafer (1976) and Kohut (1971, 1977) all address the experiencing ego or self, many of them in fact using the term 'self'. Federn, Kohut and Winnicott describe fundamental

1

anxieties that concern neither the instincts nor the objects but essentially focus on threats to the self. (For a fuller discussion see Mollon, 1988a.)

It is easy to take the self for granted, not seeing it as presenting any kind of philosophical or psychological problem. The phenomenological philosopher Wilshire (1984) states the problem bluntly:

> What is an individual self? The response of the man in the street is perhaps to laugh a bit and point to one. There's one – call it number 1 – and there's another – call it number 2. Just as one number cannot be another number, so each self is itself and not the other. Each self is right there in its own place – and that's the end of the matter. With stunning clarity Bishop Butler said 'Each thing is itself and no other thing'. The surest way to beg the question of the identity of a self is simply not to see that it is a serious question at all. But if we beg the question we ought to have a guilty conscience, I think, because if people are just as separate as their bodies, then why is their behaviour so lacking in individuality so often? Why is it that contagions of imitative and mimetic behaviour have swept through human history so regularly?

Wilshire notes that much of earlier philosophy and social theorising considered the problem of how we come to know *other* selves – e.g. Strawson's (1963) idea that we implicitly reason, by analogy, that there are other selves through noting other bodies that appear similar to our own. Impressed by the prevalence of mass movements and mob or herd behaviour, Wilshire suggests that the question should really be reversed into one of how we come to know our own selves, or how one comes to be a self at all.

Wilshire raises the question of how a self can become conscious of itself – and if it is not self-conscious, whether it can really be termed a self at all. He suggests that, rather than being individual selves, we exist *primarily* in a state of 'mimetic engulfment' with each other, a kind of automatic identification involving bodily gestural mimicry – unconsciously influenced by and embedded in one another far more than we realise; in this point can be seen the idea of illusion which seems so central to narcissism. Mahler's model of separation–individuation, the process of the establishment of a sense of self through the differentiation of self from an initially undifferentiated state with mother, also implies this – Mahler and her colleagues (Mahler et al., 1975) speak of *illusory* states of symbiosis. Thus Wilshire, as a phenomenological philosopher, and Mahler, as a psychoanalytic developmental researcher and theorist, both regard the self not as given but as gradually achieved. Mahler's studies grew out of her earlier (1968) study of psychotic children – these are children in whom the existence of a 'self' cannot be taken for granted.

Whilst in many personalities and clinical states the self *can* be taken as given, there are psychotic states and narcissistic pathologies in which the self or sense of self is disturbed. In these states the self, which is normally a background to one's experience, is brought into the foreground of awareness. Such persons may be narcissistically vulnerable, their sense of self fragile (Mollon, 1986), easily disrupted by the responses, or lack of responses of others – they may have a great need for affirming responses from others in order to feel that they have a self, that they exist. For these people a central concern is the sense of self, a concern with establishing it or maintaining it. They may also be prone to the narcissistic affects of shame and self-consciousness, which involve the sense of self. Similarly there are certain periods of life – adolescence, for example – when the sense of self is normally more prominent a concern.

Not all psychoanalysts dealing with psychotic states see a need for a concept of self. For example, M. Klein and most of her followers appeared to assume that a separate self in relation to objects exists from the beginning of life. In this model, disturbances of self are seen in terms of a defensive confusion of self and other by means of the mechanism of projective identification – part of the self is in phantasy placed inside the object (for a variety of motives) – e.g. Rosenfeld (1971). Similarly theorists such as Fairbairn (1952) and Guntrip (1961), who criticised Freud and also Hartmann's ego psychology for their mechanistic models which leave no room for the experiencing person, tended to place emphasis upon the relationship to the *object*, the other, rather than on a relationship to the *self*.

The focus on the self tends to foster a more phenomenological approach, a more elaborate description of self-experience than is usual in psychoanalytic theorising. This is apparent particularly in Kohut's work and, especially, the post-Kohutian writings of Atwood and Stolorow (1984). An early psychoanalytic account of disturbances in self-experience which shows a phenomenological bent is that of Federn (1953), who wrote about *ego feeling* and *ego boundaries*, and described subtle disturbances of these in states of shame and depersonalisation. Moreover, some of what I term here the 'narcissistic affects' such as shame and self-consciousness, inherently direct attention to phenomenology. Thus the concept of self links between phenomenology and psychodynamics.

The development of Kohut's model

Kohut described disturbances in the self that may not be immediately apparent but are manifest through the distinctive transference-like states, which he terms 'selfobject transferences'. In these states the analyst is used as a functional part of the self – the analyst's empathic availability becomes essential to the analysand's sense of well-being.

Disruptions in the analyst's availabilty – through holiday breaks or empathic breaks – leads to disturbances in self-experience.

Kohut's evolution of his framework is worth examining in more detail for its indication of his gradual recognition of the need for a concept of self. His development of what he eventually termed 'self-psychology' took place in roughly three stages. The first stage (1971) began with his awareness of a group of patients who suffer feelings of inner emptiness, low self-esteem, lack of initiative and disruption in their sense of inner cohesion and continuity. He regarded these as disturbances in what he called the 'self-representation', following here essentially Hartmann's (1950) concept – i.e. disturbances in the continuity, cohesion, vigour and value of the self as represented in the mind. These painful states of mind would be lessened if the analyst were accurately empathic and exacerbated if he or she were not. Whilst seeing the self as an important *content* of the mind, Kohut argued against the notion of self as a fourth agency of the mind, analogous to ego, id, superego, as some had proposed (e.g. Lichtenstein, 1964). This was on the grounds that: (1) the self, on the one hand, and the three agencies of Freud's structural model, on the other hand, are not on the same conceptual level; and (2) he saw no need for such a concept, the traditional framework being adequate to accommodate the self in this way as a subordinate concept. At this stage Kohut cast his geography of the pathology of the self in the framework of narcissism. However, he was one of the very few to see narcissism as more than merely a turning away from the object. He was able to postulate that narcissism followed its own line of development from primitive to mature.

Later, Kohut was able to develop from psychoanalytic material a theory of the self as a *supraordinate* organisation – i.e. not a *content* of the ego, and not a fourth agency, but a central organising structure and 'centre of initiative'. From his psychoanalytic practice, Kohut felt he could discern disturbances in a *central* bipolar structure of the mind which he saw as consisting of ambitions at one pole and ideals at the other, and also containing the person's skills and talents. This formulation stemmed from his observations of the bipolar transference states which are, on the one hand, grandiose–exhibitionistic and, on the other hand, idealising. Put very simplistically, the patient would want to be admired and responded to empathically, or would want to admire and idealise the analyst. Thus at this point, Kohut envisaged the experience of self as consisting of the awareness of enduring ambitions and ideals, coupled with the capacity to exercise skills and talents, and further associated with the sense of being an independent 'centre of initiative'.

Kohut emphasised that the bipolar self was conceptually independent of the Freudian mental apparatus and its agencies; he argued (1977) that this framework of the self could exist alongside and be complementary to the traditional framework of drive conflict. Kohut's formulation of a supraordinate self seemed to stem from his growing awareness of oscillation between states of wholeness or cohesion, and states of disintegration – states that could not easily be conceptualised in terms of drive conflict and the tripartite structure because they seemed to be determined so much by the response of the analyst. Kohut also wanted to distinguish his insights from those that could be formulated within an object relations or interpersonal framework. For example (Kohut, 1983), he referred to a clinical example presented by a colleague of a patient who dreamt that a ship at sea was about to disintegrate, its structure to fall apart – this was shortly before a break and the analyst interpreted that the patient was afraid of psychic disintegration in response to the analyst's going away and the loss of the safe shore of the analysis. Kohut argued that this was only partly correct – in his view the patient was indeed anxious about disintegration of his self, and this was indeed in the context of the analytic break, but the patient was not anxious about the analyst's going away per se; the analyst was not experienced as a separate person (an object), but *functionally as a part of the patient's self*, as a selfobject.

Even if we do not follow Kohut's particular conceptual framework, it must be admitted that the human concerns which he has highlighted, to do with ambitions and ideals, with non-sexual wishes to exhibit and to gain recognition and admiration, do not easily find a place within Freud's structural model which rests ultimately on a dual instinct model of aggression and sexuality.

Other views of the necessity for a concept of self within psychoanalysis

Meissner (1986), whilst criticising Kohut's formulation for being exclusively tied to narcissistic concerns of grandiosity and idealisation, also sees a need for a supraordinate notion of self: first because it 'provides a locus in theory for articulation of the experience of a personal self as the active and originative source of personal activity'; secondly because it takes account of the function of introspection and self-observation; thirdly because it 'provides a vehicle for the articulation of certain personal qualities that reflect complex integration of components derived from more than one substructural component of personality organisation', e.g. the concept of autonomy reflects the integration of elements from id, ego, superego.

G. Klein (1976), Gedo (1979), and Atwood and Stolorow (1984) are impressed clinically by the prominence of the human need to establish and protect a self-organisation or self-schema, resting on the experience of autonomy. For example, Gedo, drawing on Kohut, postulates a 'self-organisation' consisting of a hierarchy of goals and values.

Havens (1986), in a well-argued contribution, points to the capacity to introspect and reflect as indicating the presence of a self supraordinate to the tripartite Freudian structures, which combines the sense of self as subject and the observed self as object. For Havens, the self arises in the context of mental conflict, the *acknowledgement of both impulse and prohibition as one's own*; this is a function which goes beyond the role of the ego in the Freudian model, which acts as mediator between id and superego.

On the other hand, the proponents of the concept of a supraordinate self have met with criticism. For example, Ticho (1982) and Richards (1982) argue that these theoretical developments shift attention (1) away from a notion of unconscious division and conflict and towards the patient's subjective sense of unity and disunity, and (2) away from psychic reality and phantasy and towards enviromental influence. Richards further complains of a trend towards 'a unidimensional view of of human nature and psychopathology, in which self-cohesion is the highest aim and loss of self the greatest danger'. It is certainly true that self-psychology brings issues of self experience into the foreground, temporarily eclipsing other areas of mental life, but this is surely not a problem. As always in psychoanalysis, theorising moves partly in the wake of clinical discoveries and partly through sheer fashion, but always finding balance.

A variety of concepts of self

Whilst the concept of self is used in a variety of ways, it is fortunately possible to divide these broadly into just a few categories: self as object and self as subject; self as mental director; background self and foreground self.

Self as object and self as subject

A major distinction can be drawn between the self as object (as in the notion of self-concept, self-representation and self-esteem) and the self as subject (as in the notion of self as agency or as locus of experience and initiative). In different ways, numerous authors draw this distinction. William James (1900), in an extensive discussion, distinguished the 'empirical Me', an objective aspect of self capable of scientific study, and the 'Pure Ego', a subjective experience which he regarded as not amenable to empirical investigation. The various models of self-concept discussed by Wylie (1974) clearly refer to an objective notion of self. In the social psychology tradition, Cooley (1902, 1964) referred to the social self, derived from the images others have of one's self; similarly, Mead (1934) distinguished the 'Me' that is observed by others, the objective self, from the 'I', the subjective experience of self; for Mead the self is the integration of the 'I' and the 'Me'. Buss (1980), again in the context of social psychology, distinguished private self consciousness, one's subjective awareness of oneself, from public self-consciousness, one's awareness of oneself as an object for others. Experimental infant researchers Lewis and Brooks Gunn (1979), in investigating the point at which the infant can recognise itself in a mirror, distinguished between 'existential self' (subjective) and 'categorical self' (objective). An early contribution which drew this distinction was that of Federn (1953) who wrote of the ego as subject and the ego as object. Bach (1980), specifically discussing forms of narcissistic disturbance, distinguished between subjective awareness – a state of mind in which the world is experienced as 'all me' – and objective self-awareness, a state of mind that might involve feelings of depersonalisation and of insignificance.

Analytic theorists in the ego psychology tradition have tended to emphasise an objective view of self through their concept of self-representation – e.g. Hartmann (1950), Jacobson (1964), Sandler and Rosenblatt (1962) – the self-representation is seen as complementary to the internal representation of objects. Whilst this term often refers to something like 'self-concept', it is also sometimes used to denote a more subjective aspect of self. Thus, Stolorow and Lachmann (1980) discuss narcissistic disturbance, which they equate with disturbances in the sense of self, in terms of disruptions in the 'temporal continuity, structural cohesion and positive affective colouring of the self-representation'.

Returning to Kohut's work, it is apparent that although he describes many disturbances in the subjective experience of self – e.g. feelings of emptiness, unreality, fragmentation etc. – he is also regarding the self as a *structure* with a particular organisation, e.g. the bipolar self of ambitions and ideals. Disturbances in this structure can be described (Kohut, 1977). Thus, whilst this is an objective idea of self, it does not denote a *content* of the mind, such as a self-concept or self-representation, but is a supraordinate structure. Both objective and subjective aspects of self are inherent in Kohut's formulation. Disturbances in the *subjective* sense of self are seen as determined by pathology in the *objective* structure of the self.

Adequate psychoanalytic accounts of self must incorporate both subjective and objective aspects. Grossman (1982) notes that 'there is an essential tension in psychoanalytic theory between subjective and objective points of view regarding patients' experience' and that 'any psychology that takes subjective experience as one's starting point and as a communication from the patient will be involved in this tension between subjectivity and objectivity'. He concludes that 'the self appears to be both supremely subjective yet also an objective organisation, an organismic property discernible by others'.

Self as mental director – the capacity to be both subject and object

Subjective and objective aspects of self are intertwined – the self experiences itself as both subject and object. For Mead, the self is the interplay of the subjective I and the objective Me. Havens (1986) argues that 'a central property of the self is its self-reflectiveness, or capacity to be both subject and object'. For Havens, 'the self finds itself in the superego'. His argument is as follows: the superego is the locus of values, ideals, prohibitions and is able to judge behaviour – to 'supervise the ego'. In this sense, the superego is closer to a self-regarding agency than is the ego. However, the concept of 'self' transcends this superego activity insofar as the person is able to reflect upon his or her superego. Havens summarises thus (p. 371):

> Why is the self structure necessary? ... My answer is twofold. First the self is not part of the ego for the same reason the superego is not part of the ego. The self arises as a separate structure out of the relation between ego and superego, just as the superego arises out of the ego's relation to the world. Second, self reflection is not simply an ego function, because the self that does the reflecting, as well as the self reflected upon, includes prohibitions, ideals, defensive style and fantasies. The phenomenon of reflecting derives from the ego, but the self that reflects and is reflected upon partakes of much more.

Lovlie (1982) also sees the capacity to reflect as the basis of self. Similarly, Wilshire (1982) stresses the importance of the capacity to reflect upon one's being for others: 'To be a self is to be for oneself as one's own through an articulation of what one is for others.' Lichtenberg (1983) presents a concept of self-as-a-whole, the capacity to relate to the self in relation to the other – a capacity which he sees as also associated with ownership of impulse and prohibition, the 'self-as-mental-director'. This is a self that transcends and combines both subject and object.

One outcome of successful psychoanalytic therapy, with its prolonged provision of a space for reflection, is the development of an expanded self-as-mental-director – a self that can act with a consciousness of itself that is both widened and deepened.

Foreground self and background self

As we have seen, theorists sometimes speak of self as experience, as agency, as centre of initiative, and as knower – notions of self as experiential core of the personality. An early statement of this idea is provided by Cooley (1902, p. 182):

'I', then is not all of the mind, but a peculiarly central, vigorous, and well-knit portion of it, not separated from the rest but gradually merging into it, and yet having a certain practical distinctiveness, so that a man generally shows clearly enough by his language and behaviour what his 'I' is as distinguished from thoughts he does not appropriate. It may be thought of ... under the analogy of a central coloured area on a lighted wall. It might also, and perhaps more justly, be compared to the nucleus of a living cell, not altogether separate from the surrounding matter, out of which indeed it is formed, but more active and definitely organised.

A further aspect of self is in the notion of there being a kind of background perceptual organisation to this experiential core. Thus Spiegal (1959) thought of the self as an organisation of core images or self-representations, which function as a kind of flywheel maintaining a stable background against which to orient and perceive the world outside. A similar idea is developed by cognitive psychologists who conceptualise self as a system of schemata. For example, Markus (1977) postulates that each schema is a generalisation about the self and contains specific information about past events, situations and characteristics of self. Similarly, Rogers (1981) regards self as an internal cognitive hierarchical category (p. 196):

> ... the elements ... are self-descriptive terms such as traits, values, and possibly even memories of specific behaviours and events. These terms are ordered hierarchically, becoming more concrete, distinctive, specific and less inclusive, with increasing depth into the hierarchy. Making a self-referent decision involves comparing the stimulus item with (this structure) to determine if it 'fits' into the structure.

Thus the self here is seen as a background organisation defining what is and what is not the self. We can link this to Kohut's emphasis on the importance of a stable organisation of ambitions and ideals which defines the bipolar self.

In the present writer's view, in many narcissistically disturbed patients the normal silent functioning of this background organisation is disrupted. For example, in states of shame and self-consciousness, the self is in the foreground of awareness instead of being comfortably in the background. Grossman (1982) makes a similar point in discussing his notion of self as an organisation of fantasies:

> In presenting the elements and dimensions of the self as a fantasised entity, it should be recognised that these are a kind of framework, the categories of experience of the self. Ordinarily they are not within awareness or a matter of concern – like the framework of the analytic setting they are taken for granted unless something happens to focus attention on them. It is precisely those borderline and otherwise narcissistic patients who are in one way or

another preoccupied with defining, characterising and defining themselves who are also extremely attentive to and concerned with the setting, framework and details of the analytic situation.

It seems that when the structure of the self is not coherent and stable, then the stability and responsiveness of the external enviroment acquires exceptional importance. As Kohut described, the self disordered analysand is exquisitely sensitive to the reliability, admirability and empathic responsiveness of the analyst.

Conclusion

The existence of self, an individual identity, cannot be taken for granted, although many analytic theorists have done just this. A self must be developed. Moreover a *concept* of self is necessary within psychoanalysis in order to take account of clinical phenomena where the experience and organisation of the self is disturbed. It is apparent that the term 'self' has been used in a variety of ways. Distinctions can be drawn between self as subject and as object, and also between self as experience and as structure. It is argued that an adequate model of self must combine these dichotomies. The capacity to reflect, to take the self as both subject and object seems a crucial component of self-hood. It would appear that normally there is an experiencing subjective self in the foreground against an objective self in the background of awareness; in narcissistically disturbed individuals this balance is distorted.

A taxonomy of disturbances of self

Drawing on the preceding discussion, it is possible to conceptualise a variety of disturbances of 'self' – most of which in some way relate to issues of subjective and objective self and the relationship between these. The following is a provisional taxonomy.

Differentiation of self

First, drawing on Wilshire's insights, we could consider failures to differentiate self from other – the state of remaining 'mimetically engulfed' in the other, in one's family, class, culture, or in the 'mother country' or in the mother as the primary object. In this state one is unable to have a perspective on oneself, unable to reflect and lacking a *consciousness of self*. A moderate degree of lack of differentiation might be illustrated, for example, by a preadolescent child who expresses political and religious views identical to those of the parents; this is normal for a child, but in an adult would indicate a significant failure of differentiation.

Complete failures of differentiation are extremely rare. Stern (1986) presents evidence that some basic differentiation of self and other is present even in very young babies. The theorist who has written most extensively on the process of differentiation is Mahler (Mahler et al., 1975) in the context of her model of separation–individuation. In an earlier work (Mahler, 1968), she described the failure of this processs of differentiation of self from other in psychotic states. The notion that this failure of differentiation is a core disturbance in psychotic states has been extensively discussed by other theorists, notably Jacobson (1971) and Federn (1953). For example, during a psychotic episode, a patient felt that she and her therapist were of one mind, sharing the same thoughts, and that he talked to her continuously in her mind when she was physically apart from him; confrontation with the fact of his separateness was extremely disturbing and confusing for her.

We might also include here the point that a person may be undifferentiated, from mother say, in one part of his or her mind, whilst differentiated in another. This would be analogous to Freud's (1927b) description of of the splitting of the ego in fetishism, one part of the mind being oriented towards reality, whilst another part maintains the delusion that the woman possesses a penis. For example, Masterson and Rinsley (1980) describe the common syndrome of an adolescent with a borderline disturbance, who has one self-image as 'fused with mother and good' and another as 'separate and bad'. A patient in her mid-twenties, seen by the author, was struggling to free herself from her mother in order to move away and live with her boyfriend. In her adult mind she recognised that this was reasonable and also quoted remarks of her mother indicating that the latter too was accepting of her daughter's need to pursue her own life. However, it became apparent that both shared a delusion in another part of their minds that the patient was an extension of her mother, or at least a possession of her mother – for example, in the assumption that the mother should dictate her daughter's reading material.

Subjective self

Next we might consider disturbances in the subjective sense of self. These would include disturbances or impediments in the sense of agency, or autonomy or efficacy. Some psychoanalysts have given great emphasis to these. Broucek (1979), for example has suggested that the sense of efficacy is the basis of the sense of self. G. Klein (1976) and Gedo (1979) have particularly emphasised the importance of the sense of autonomy and activity. Gedo places this at the top of his hierarchy of a person's values. We can also link these points to Kohut's notion of the self as an 'independent centre of initiative'. One kind of disturbance in the subjective self would be *deficits* in the sense of autonomy, efficacy etc.; however, at the other end of the spectrum we can include disturbances involving an unrealistically enhanced sense of efficacy – e.g. an illusory experience of omnipotence. For example, one person may feel he or she has no direction to his or her life and little capacity to influence people or events; another may grossly overestimate his or her capacities. In adolescence it is common for feelings of great passivity and powerlessness to exist alongside illusions of omnipotence.

Grotstein (1986) suggests that an extreme sense of powerlessness, or lack of efficacy, characterises severely disturbed borderline and psychotic states – in his view fantasies of omnipotence arise to counter this sense of powerlessness. Other analysts working within the Kleinian tradition tend to describe ways in which a patient may attempt, in an attitude of omnipotence, to control the analyst through projective identification (for an excellent discussion of this see Ogden, 1982). Achievement of the 'depressive position', which characterises health, involves a surrender of attitudes of omnipotence.

Kohut emphasised how the child may feel strong when mirrored by empathically responsive parents, but experience rage when this selfobject response is absent – i.e. experience rage when prematurely or 'phase inappropriately' confronted with impotence.

Objective self

Disturbances in the objective aspect of self may form a further category – for example disturbances in the self-image and pathology of self-esteem, including grandiose self-images. It is a matter of how a person regards and evaluates him- or herself. A person may have a single coherent self-image, or multiple contradictory self-images – different one's being evoked under different conditions; a person may be motivated to avoid or ward off negative self-images. For example, a patient strove unconsciously to maintain her self-image as adult and mature, by avoiding intimate relationships with men, in order to avoid experiencing the self-image of a helpless rejected little girl, that was originally evoked by her father's desertion of her and her mother when she was age eight. Another patient with a very negative self-image, characterised by a sense of being defective, ugly and unlovable would often fantasise around a compensatory self-image of being very important, a celebrity loved by millions.

It must be borne in mind that images of the self may be unconscious. This category assumes that self-images have been formed – that the process indicated in category 1 has taken place. However, self-images can be developed partly through identification; a global kind of identification with the object may result in a loss of differentiation between images of self and images of object (as described, for example, by Jacobson (1964) in her account of psychosis). Included in this category are also one's anticipation of the images that the other has of the self – Mead's 'Me'. Sandler and Rosenblatt (1962) provided a detailed discussion of the 'self representation'.

Structure–organisation

Disturbances in the structure and organisation of self seem to occupy a point midway between subjective and objective aspects of self. An objective disturbance in organisation may be accompanied by a disturbance in the *sense* of being structured or organised, of being coherent, and of possessing constancy in the midst of change. Stern (1986) uses the term 'emergent self' to refer to the infant's early sense of growing organisation of his or her experiential world.

An example of a severe breakdown in the sense of structure and organisation – and perhaps a regression to the state of the 'emergent self' – is shown by a psychotic patient in therapy with the author whose perceptions would fragment when under stress; her perception of a person talking to her would be of an incoherent jumble of movements and sounds; at the same time she would experience her own body as undergoing breakdown and metamorphosis. Some degree of coherence would be restored by the calm empathic and explanatory responses of the therapist.

Much of Kohut's work also concerns disturbances in this sense of organisation – in particular the organisation of stable ambitions and ideals. Kohut (1971) sees narcissistic patients as characterised by a proneness to temporary and reversible states of disorganisation of the self, whilst in his view borderline and psychotic patients have a more profound vulnerability in this area which is less easily reversed. Similarly, Ping-Nie Pao (1979) bases his model of schizophrenic disturbance around the notion of a catastrophic breakdown in the sense of cohesion of the self.

This category would include the disorganisation experienced during states of shame and self-consciousness. As described later, these *narcissistic affects* can be understood as disturbances in the relation of self to selfobject and thus can be linked with Kohut's work.

A further area of experience that could be included in this category is the sense of *having* structure and substance; some patients may, for example, complain of feeling insubstantial. A common cause of feeling insubstantial is the defensive projection into others in phantasy of parts of the self, especially aggressive parts, leaving the self depleted. Related to this is the extent to which a person feels real or unreal, located in their body or detached from it. This aspect of experience would be affected by how much the person is in touch with their feelings – acute depersonalisation or derealisation, for example, may result from a defensive effort to dissociate from a strongly feared feeling. Severe dissociation, stemming from extreme childhood trauma, results in the profound breakdown of the coherence of the self known as multiple personality disorder (Putnam, 1989).

A further kind of dissociation may take the form described by Freud (1911b) as withdrawal of cathexis – or, in more ordinary language, withdrawal of emotional investment – from the world and the patient's significant others. For example, a schizophrenic man described a sense of inhabiting his body like a stranger and observing himself going about his life like an actor; he could not feel a sense of recognition when he looked at himself in a mirror. His inner voices would feel more real to him than external people. When his emotional links to others were restored he experienced himself and other people as more real.

Thus some disturbances in the sense of being real, structured, coherent etc., may be due to dynamic defensive activity, but in addition these aspects of the background sense of self may also be a function of selfobject unavailability – the selfobject being those empathic responses of the other that are necessary to sustain the self. Kohut's work indicates that in the absence or failure of the selfobject all these aspects of a person's sense of well-being may become disturbed. For example, when a needed response of interest or enthusiasm from another person is missing, then the individual may feel depleted, lacking energy, disorganised and hypochondriacal.

Thus there appear to be broadly two causes of disturbance in this category:

1. Selfobject failures.
2. Unconscious defensive manoeuvres involving projection of, or dissociation from, threatening feelings.

Balance between subjective and objective self

Disturbances in the *balance* between objective and subjective aspects of self form a further category. The importance of this balance has been pointed to in Mead's (1934) notion of the communication between the 'I' and the 'Me'. For example, some highly self-conscious individuals seem to experience themselves predominantly as all 'Me', wholly preoccupied with the other's image of them, and are quite out of touch with their 'I', their own feelings on a deeper level. For example, an actress in therapy immediately took on the role of 'patient', skilfully adapting to what she sensed was required of her, but then complained that she had no identity of her own and no awareness of her real emotions. This skewing towards the Me can be related to Winnicott's (1960) concept of the 'false self'. On the other hand, Bach (1980) has described certain narcissistic disturbances in which the experience is of the world being all 'I' – with little sense of others as real people. The balance, the awareness of and communication between the 'I' and the 'Me', may also be linked to Lichtenberg's (1983) notion of the 'self-as-a-whole' and the 'mental director', the question of to what extent there is a person who is in charge of the personality. A recent discussion of the interplay between 'self-as-subject' and 'self-as-object' is provided by Wright (1991).

Illusions of self-sufficiency

A further disturbance may be conceptualised as lying in the relationship between self and external reality. This is an area traditionally thought of as narcissistic disturbance. It concerns the extent to which the person maintains an illusion of self-sufficiency as opposed to acknowledging dependence on others; and also to what extent there is the 'totalitarian ego' described by Greenwald (1980) which distorts reality in order to maintain its own illusions – these illusions would include those of grandiosity, omnipotence etc. This might be seen as an exaggerated sense of subjective self, which brooks no opposition and reacts with narcissistic rage (Kohut, 1972) to any thwarting of its intention. It may involve a refusal to allow others to be subjects and an attempt to maintain them in the position of object. A mad dictator such as Hitler, or a 'Hitler' or 'Satanic' part of the mind, which aims to rule the world, to take the place of 'God', is an extreme version of this. A related narcissistic phenomenon described by Modell (1980) is the non-communication of affects, a subtle form of defensive refusal to communicate. Freud (1914) noted that this emotional withdrawal was found in an extreme form in psychotic patients (for a more recent discussion of this point see Giovacchini, 1986).

Sense of lineage

This category emerges from consideration of the clinical material of the four main cases discussed later and from the theoretical discussions of narcissism, rather than from theoretical discussions of the self. The sense of lineage concerns the sense of knowing who one is and where one has come from, of being able to locate oneself in a family line – a sense of being part of a *line* extending in time. This aspect of self can be disturbed if in the child's imagination the father is not allowed his appropriate place as husband to the wife – a parental couple understood to give rise to the child through their intercourse. If this situation is not allowed in the child's imagination, perhaps with the collusion of the mother, the child will be left uncertain of his or her origins; the fantasy may emerge that the child was his or her own omnipotent creation. One patient, whose mother very actively discouraged her curiosity about her father and gave her the explicit messsage that fathers are not important, imagined that she was *found* by the mother, the product of unknown parents; she was deeply troubled by a sense of not knowing who she was or where she came from.

A related disturbance in the sense of lineage may also be experienced by displaced persons who have left their original home, family and culture, who no longer feel a sense of continuity between who and what they are now and their origins – the sense of a familial or cultural line being broken.

The taxonomy and levels of disturbance

The taxonomy does not distinguish levels of disturbance, which may range from mild to very severe and incapacitating. The discussion has alluded to the way in which psychotic patients may be very seriously disturbed in the areas of differentiation of self (category 1), sense of agency/efficacy (category 2), and organisation/coherence (category 4). It is indeed quite conceivable that schizophrenic patients may be disturbed in all seven areas.

In line with Kohut's (1971) formulation, narcissistic patients may be regarded as those for whom disturbances in the self are a predominant feature, yet whose overall level of disturbance is less than that of borderline and psychotic patients. This point is discussed further in section 6 where narcissistic patients are distinguished from other kinds of patients.

The taxonomy and narcissistic affects

Some states of mind cut across several of these categories. For example, in the case of the *narcissistic affects*, shame, self-consciousness, humiliation etc., there is a negative self-image (category 3), an image of self as defective, pathetic etc.; there may be a subjective experience of helplessness (category 2); the awareness of the other's image of the self (Mead's 'Me') may predominate (category 5); there may be a subjective and objective disorganisation and incoherence (category 4).

The taxonomy and theories of narcissistic disturbance

It will be apparent that different theories of narcissistic disturbance stress different categories of this list.

For example, those theories such as Rosenfeld's Kleinian based position, which see narcissism solely as a defensive retreat from relatedness to others address category 6 (but for a further discussion of the Kleinian tradition, see page 98). Kohut's theorising, on the other hand, addresses all the first six categories to some degree, although his

Table 1.1 Summary of taxonomy

Category	Characteristics	Main authors
1. Differentiation	Failure to distinguish self and other Inability to have reflective awareness of self At an extreme, psychotic loss of boundaries	Mahler Jacobson Masterson/Rinsley
2. Subjective self	Impaired sense of agency and autonomy – or illusions of omnipotence	Kohut Broucek G.Klein
3. Objective self	Pathology of self-esteem Negative images and low esteem, or else grandiose self-images	Jacobson Sandler/Rosenblatt
4. Structure–organisation	Breakdown in the sense of cohesion and coherence of the self Disorganisation of the perceptual world and experience of the body Depersonalisation and derealisation	Kohut Stern
5. Balance between subjective and objective self	'False self' – excessive accommodation to the other Embarassed self-consciousness or inability to be aware of other's point of view	Mead Winnicott Bach Wright
6. Illusions of self-sufficiency	Grandiosity, sense of omnipotence, denial of need for others 'Totalitarian ego' Narcissistic rage	Numerous authors, including Freud
7. Sense of lineage	Denial of, or lack of connection to, origins Inability to locate the self in a family and cultural line	Lacan Abelin

particular focus is upon category 2, the sense of having an independent centre of initiative, and category 4, the structure and organisation of the self. Kernberg's theory, which draws considerably on the Kleinian tradition, addresses categories 6 and 3; he regards the essential pathology as consisting of grandiose self-images (category 3) which support illusions of self-sufficiency (category 6).

Stolorow (1975) makes the suggestion of simplifying and unifying concepts of narcissism by conceptualising narcissistic activity as that which is aimed at preserving the 'structural integrity, temporal continuity and positive affective colouring of the self-representation'. This definition clearly refers primarily to categories 1 and 3 and perhaps also 4. One of the conceptual problems in relying solely on this definition is that the notion of a self-representation implies an image that a person has of him- or herself, just as he or she has images of others; thus there must be another self which is observing and evaluating and forming an image of the self (the subjective self). To this extent the concept does not quite capture the immediate experiencing self and its disturbances, and the relationship between subjective and objective aspects of self. The 'self-as-a-whole' is not represented here. Thus categories 2 and 5 do not find a place.

Winnicott's (1960) model of the 'false self', whilst not overtly a theory of narcissistic disturbance, focuses primarily on categories 2, the subjective sense of agency, and 5, the balance between the I and the Me. People with a false self are more aware of how they must present themselves to others than of their own inner feelings. According to the theory, because of their early experiences they suffer a profound sense of helplessness and lack of agency; their 'true self', their early communications were not recognised and responded to.

Later we examine nine specific theories of narcissistic disturbance and see how they relate to different categories of the taxonomy.

Preservation of the self – autonomy and 'despotism' in the subjective self

Much mental activity is in the service of preserving the subjective self, the sense of agency (category 2). This can involve attempts to preserve illusions about the self. At its psychotic extreme, this can become delusional and highly destructive with efforts to sustain fantasies of omnipotence by subjugating others – the mad dictator syndrome. A number of authors have addressed this theme of illusion and delusion of the self.

Becker (1973) considers that the basis of narcissism is people's need to preserve an illusion of self-sufficiency. Bromberg (1983) links this viewpoint with similar ideas of Sullivan and Fromm and suggests there is a trend in theorising towards 'the concept that narcissistic pathology is fundamentally mental activity designed by a grandiose interpersonal self representation to preserve its structural stability and to maintain, protect or restore its experience of wellbeing'. Pyszcynski (Pyszcynski and Greenberg, 1986), a social–cognitive psychology theorist, also draws on Becker's work to develop a 'terror management' theory of self-esteem regulation, focusing on the pervasive human need to avoid experiences of existential helplessness – a need which Freud (1927a) also addressed in his account of the function of religious illusion.

A tendency towards an avoidance of reality and the possibility of development is also implied in discussions by Pritz and Mitterauer (1977), who emphasise the paramount human motive of preserving images and illusions about the self. They propose (1977) a model of narcissism based on 'the fact that the process of maintaining the circular organisation of an organism, i.e. of maintaining its identity, must be treated as an invariable logic of living systems'. They quote Massermann (1955):

> ... any human being ... has at the basis of his metaphysical system, a set of solipsistic formulas to this outstanding effect: once I was absolute, transcendent and inviolate, and what I was once perhaps I have always been and shall continue to be forever more.

They suggest that the 'feeling of being inviolate relates to the innate self-repair potential of living beings' and go on to state:

> We view narcissism as those principles of self reference which guarantee maintenance of the circular organisation (identity) and which are responsible for constructing progressively maturing models of self repair whenever identity is threatened.

and:

> Narcissistic conflicts arise whenever a particular organismic program loses its power to control effectively the process of the maintenance of identity.

Pritz and Mitterauer argue that the accompanying phenomenology of this action of self-reference is the sense of autonomy; autonomy here means that the goals of organismic systems are internally defined. They conclude that: 'Narcissism can be defined as intraorganismic "despotism" ...'.

It could also be said that narcissism, as described by Pritz and Mitterauer, attempts to guarantee not only the continuation of identity, but also of sameness, lack of development, growth and learning. Narcissism here seems to involve a regressive tendency, as if operating according to a principle more suited to lower biological levels.

Greenwald (1980) introduces a similar perspective in talking of the 'totalitarian ego', describing a variety of experimental evidence for the way in which people consistently distort information so as to maintain their own cognitive structure, their own assumptions about the self and the world. Epstein (1987) proposes a similar 'cognitive self theory' in which the need to maintain a particular view of self and the world is seen as a motive on a par with that of seeking pleasure and avoiding pain.

On the other hand, Klein (1976) has also emphasised the overriding motive of preserving the organisation of the self as part of a progressive developmental process:

> The concept of self draws attention to the establishment of identity and its maintenance as a basic biological principle that defines a person's development ... From the first emergence of a self schema, preservation of its identity and continuity is a prominent organismic concern.

One aspect of this organismic concern that Klein has emphasised is the attempt to maintain some degree of autonomy and control over self and the world. He describes how a great deal of development may be understood in terms of the attempt to turn experiences of helplessness or lack of comprehension into actively repeated, self-initiated action in which the self is the active agent rather than the passive victim. (A similar point is made by Broucek (1979) who actually suggests that the sense of control or 'efficacy' is the core of the sense of self.)

Klein states that 'repeated thwarting of self-initiated activity, even in the infant, can be catastrophic'; in such a situation the child is not allowed the experience of self as subject, as active agent. He refers to Bettleheim's studies on autism and concentration camp survivors; the ones who survived were those who had managed to find at least one area in which they could experience the self as controller rather than as controlled. (Similar points are made in Frankl's (1973) account of concentration camp survival and the importance of being able to give *meaning* to an experience, to make sense of an experience; this giving meaning might be seen as another aspect of mastery, of bringing an experience under cognitive control.)

Klein suggests that another means of mastering an experience that is injurious to the self may be to repeat it actively as something pleasurable. This is essentially Stoller's (1976) theory of perversion – which he sees as a means of preserving gender identity; early experiences which are injurious to gender identity – e.g. mother or sisters denigrating a little boy's masculinity, which might even include dressing him in female clothes – may be mastered through transvestite cross-dressing, in which the original trauma is turned into a triumph; the danger of loss of male identity is denied through the achievement of an erection while dressed in female clothes. In these ways, described by Klein and

Stoller, the self, initially deprived of subjectivity and agency, becomes the active one, the initiator and thus able to *own* the experience.

Implicit also in the model of Mahler et al. (1975) is the importance of preservation of a vulnerable sense of control and autonomy (category 2, subjective self), as well as the achievement of the sense of self as separate (category 1). Thus, in the 'practising' subphase of separation– individuation the toddler is exuberantly exercising new motor skills, as well as the recently acquired ability to say 'no'. It is a time of great emotional lability – an excited 'love affair with the world' as well as tears and rage, battles over autonomy and who is in control.

There is a tension between the need to establish and preserve autonomy, emphasised in these contributions, and the need to develop, learn and change, implied in Freud's (1914) original model of the transformation of the infantile illusion of perfection into the ego ideal. If the 'temporal stability, structural integrity and positive affective colouring of the self-representation', to quote Stolorow's (1975) definition of the aims of narcissism, were preserved *too* well, this would not be adaptive. It would mean at least some denial of reality, and at worst would involve a psychotic state of grandiosity. Growth and adaptation to reality mean giving up illusions, allowing change and development and a continual processing of information about self in relation to others. Without this we would have the 'totalitarian ego' described by Greenwald (1980), actively distorting perceptions of reality to fit pre-existing assumptions. Here then a dichotomy between narcissism and object-relatedness (or reality-relatedness) can be discerned.

The other in the self – illusion and captivation by a false image

The idea that the self is in some way derived from others and that these others are taken into the very structure of the self has a long tradition. Cooley (1902), for example, spoke of the 'looking glass self' – his idea that we develop a self on the basis of the appraisals of others, using the reactions of others as a mirror.

This view was elaborated by Mead (1934), who argued that awareness of self derives from the perspective of others:

> He becomes a self insofar as he can take the attitude of another and act towards himself as others act. It is the social process of influencing others in a social act, and then taking the attitude of others aroused by the stimulus, and the reaction to this response, which constitutes a self.

James (1890) distinguished between the 'pure ego' – or conscious I – and the 'empirical me', which is one's integration of the response one gets from others. Mead considered the self to be the integration of both aspects: the 'I' and the 'Me'. The 'I' is the actor, whilst the 'Me' is a simultaneous anticipation of how the actor will be seen. Mead saw the 'I' and the 'Me' within the personality as in constant communication with each other. The 'Me' anticipates the reaction to what the 'I' is about to do; the 'I' then acts upon what the 'Me' has just felt, and so on. In this way, Mead describes a kind of communicative balance between the 'I', the 'Me' and the other – a balance which, as we shall see, is disturbed in persons with narcissistic pathology. Mead also provided here the beginnings of a description of the way in which the views and desires of the other get into one's self, and the way an objective image of oneself – the self-concept – is formed within the mind. The importance of the communicative balance between the subjective and objective self is indicated by category 5 of the taxonomy – disturbances in this balance are particularly apparent in states of shame and self-consciousness.

Work deriving from Lacan provides a deeper understanding of the way in which the other becomes part of the structure of the self. Duruz (1981) emphasises that the mother, the 'auxiliary ego' of the baby, is not only supportive and mirroring, but also *desiring* – and that trauma is inherent in any desiring relationship. According to Duruz, in trying to free itself from dependence on the mother's desire, the infant creates within his or her self, mental structures which represent aspects of the relationship with the mother that the infant is trying to free itself from. Paradoxically, in seeking autonomy, the infant has to use the very modes of frustration and gratification that have shaped its interaction with the mother – the mother's desire is taken into the self. In Duruz's view, this takes place largely through the ideals the child sets up – these ideals derive partly from ideal *states* with the mother, in gratification of mother's desire. Setting up his or her own ideals allows the individual to assert some autonomy, but these also exert a regulatory censoring function:

> The individual tends to misperceive the double function of ideals – he claims to be independent of the desire of the other, whereas he has actually been determined in his very identity by this.

Duruz concludes:

> Deep within himself he bears the mark of an *otherness*, the source of irrevocable tensions.

Wilshire (1982), the phenomenological philosopher already referred to, makes a similar point when, in drawing on Hegel, he argues that 'a human being can become itself, its self, only when it makes its own what others ... have made of it'.

This body becomes myself by taking over ... my mother's stance towards myself as her son, or if I rebel it is not just against her, but against that of her in myself that I rebel.

Wilshire presents his analysis in terms of a theory that people are continually unconsciously *mimetically* responding to one another – a process of unconscious imitation and response to the social cues offered by the other. He argues that we become a conscious self through becoming aware of our self as we are for the other – and that this is facilitated particularly through art, theatre and theatre-like activity:

Art and art-like activity – [is] a condition of the body's realising this; a condition of its being *its* self. To be a self is to be for oneself as one's own through an articulation of what one is for the other.

At this point let us consider Lacan's work in more detail. Lacan emphasises the way in which he sees the ego, the self, as based fundamentally on illusion and alienation. This is represented in his account of the 'mirror phase' (1937) which he sees as taking place somewhere between the eighth and eighteenth months.

Lacan describes the infant's prematurity – in its insufficiency, fragmentation and motor incoordination – as a condition marked by 'gaps'. He equates this with Freud's autoerotic stage of development, prior to the stage of primary narcissism. This condition is in sharp contrast to what the infant experiences as its reflection in the mirror, the human body as a gestalt, seen as possessing wholeness, cohesion and imagined stature. Lacan argues that the infant jubilantly identifies with this image, affirms 'that is I' and thereby makes a profound shift from its actual experience to its idealisation. The idealised form of this I promises a coherence that is in contrast to the experience of felt bodily fragmentation. Lacan sees this as the first 'captivation' by an external image, which forms the basis, and provides the model for all subsequent identifications and alienation.

Thus, at the same time that the specular image makes possible a kind of knowledge of the self, it also introduces an alienation. Merleau-Ponty (1964) describes it as follows:

I am no longer what I felt myself immediately to be. I am that image of myself that is offered by the mirror. I am captured by the spatial image. I leave the reality of the lived me in order to refer constantly to the ideal fictitious or imaginary me, of which the specular image is the first outline.

In identifying with the image the person locates himself externally and distorts his own reality. According to Lacan, this prepares for the still more serious alienation, the alienation by others since others also have only an external image of one's self. As Lacan (1937) sees it, a fundamental misconstrual is structurally ingrained in the self.

G. Klein (1976), whose work was discussed in connection with efforts to establish the subjective self, also describes how the other enters into the self paradoxically in the very process of developing its unity, continuity and autonomy. He suggests that experiences of disunity and discontinuity, as well as experiences felt to be outside of one's control, come to be a source of distress. He describes two basic principles involved in organising the self and maintaining the sense of continuity and integrity: 'reversal of voice' and 'repression'. Both of these 'are rooted in the proposition that the self schema cannot tolerate more than a certain level of imposition and victimisation'.

Both of Klein's principles involve the internalisation of a relationship – but in the case of reversal of voice the self-schema is modified, whereas in the case of repression a schema is split off from the self-structure. The basic point in reversal of voice is the active repetition of a passively endured encounter (Klein, 1976, p. 285):

> There is no greater contribution to controlling an alien experience – and to this extent making it a more tolerable one – than its being self-initiated and experienced as such.

Klein quotes Loevinger (1966) who pointed out that one is controlled simultaneously or in turn by one's impulses and one's parents – one therefore needs to control something, and if not one's parents then ones's impulses. This point may also be compared with Broucek's (1979) suggestion that the sense of *efficacy*, the sense of having some control over the world, forms the basis of the sense of self.

Klein suggests the following sequence of successive reversals of voice (p. 288):

1. He does to me – I suffer what he is doing to me.
2. I put myself in a replica situation – I make the experience happen (through play, substitute objects etc.).
3. What did or could happen to me, I do to my impulse.
4. I control my impulse – part of me – as an ethical principle.

Klein sees reversal of voice as the basis of identification – really Klein seems to mean identification with the 'controlling other' (p. 288):

> Wishing to destroy the restraint, but appreciating the danger of doing so, the child comes to turn his vengeance on that part of the self – the impulse – that provoked the restraint.

Klein argues that the various occasions prompting this kind of identification all share a common dynamic theme – they are all 'passively imposed, self-dystonic experiences ... when the unity and autocracy of the self are threatened'. They fall into the following categories:

- An uncontrolled impulse.
- Inadequacy of self-initiated control.
- Inability to control aggressive intent.
- Depletion produced by failures in love.

These experiences which Klein points to might be thought of as 'narcissistic blows' – injuries particularly to the agency of self in category 2 of the taxonomy – they necessitate repair to the self as an experiencing and structural entity. In reversal of voice, mastery and autonomy is achieved through taking the other into the self and doing actively to oneself or to others what was once suffered passively.

An extreme instance of the drive to turn passive into active is shown by the case of a woman who had been severely abused as a child. Her father had repeatedly held her head under water with his hands around her neck, almost but never quite to the point of her drowning. She bitterly hated herself for not having died at that time. She felt that her life was an obscenity, that she was kept alive only to be abused and controlled. When these issues began to surface in her middle age, from a state of complete repression, she desired above all to kill herself. Her preferred methods, which she attempted on many occasions, were either of drowning or self-strangulation through hanging. She regarded this as the ultimate goal of her life, to triumph in this way over her father by completing the act of dying which he had thwarted. She viewed this as an act of assertion and ownership of her own life.

In the processes described here, there is an attempt to repair the self by taking the other into the self; the self is deformed and misperceived in the image of the other. The person who hates a parent is puzzled to find that he or she behaves like the parent. A degree of alienation from true self seems inherent in the human condition – but perhaps this is a matter of *degree*. A less distorting kind of internalisation is described by Kohut through his concept of 'transmuting internalisation'. By this he means the gradual taking over of *functions* of the other (the parent, the analyst) as a result of repeated non-traumatic failures of the other. In this way the functions and qualities of the other are woven into the fabric of the self, rather than the other being taken in as a foreign body. This mode of internalisation leads to a strengthening of the authentic spontaneous self.

The dialectic of self and other: differentiation, triangulation and the capacity to reflect

How do we become able to reflect upon the self – to take the self as the object of our awareness? Can a person fail to achieve this capacity? Whilst some degree of capacity to distinguish self from not self seems to be present from birth (Stern, 1986), the development of a sense of self as separate has been described by Mahler et al. (1975) as taking place through the stages of separation–individuation – the development of the intrapsychic representation of the self takes place in parallel with the development of physical separation from the mother. The role of the mother in impeding or facilitating this has been described (Masterson and Rinsley, 1980); the role of the father has also been described, particularly by Abelin (1971, 1975).

Lovlie (1982) has drawn a link between separation, differentiation and the capacity to reflect – i.e. the capacity to have a point of view on oneself and one's experience. Lovlie stresses that the emergence from symbiosis and the gradual awareness of self and other occur simultaneously – but that without differentiation, the infant remains 'identical to itself', he or she living without any reflection on his or her mental content; under these circumstances the child *is* its content. Kegan (1982) makes a similar point that, in the beginning, the infant does not *have* an impulse, he or she *is* the impulse; each stage in development involves the achievement of a perspective, a metaview on the previous organisation. Without differentiation, argues Lovlie, the infant cannot relate to him- or herself, cannot reflect upon him- or herself.

Lovlie sees the ability to have a relationship to 'the self in relation to the other' as the foundation of the capacity to reflect and hence of freedom. However, the 'other' may attempt to interfere with this capacity (Lovlie, 1982, p. 102):

> If I can reflect on my action and other people's actions, I can relate to that action: change it, choose it, like it, whatever. In that sense I am free. It is tempting to postulate that in man's quest to forcefully dominate and conquor his fellow men, it has served a purpose to maintain men in the imprisonment of inability to reflect. The problem is that both the master and slave are 'stuck' and imprisoned – and life is impeded – master and slave are both 'dead'.

A person who is unable to reflect is prevented from having a sense of self, self-awareness – from experiencing the self as an 'independent centre of initiative' (Kohut, 1977); in short, she is prevented from experiencing herself as *subject*. Such people must experience themselves as object in relation to an other as subject. *Intersubjectivity* is not

achieved. It is then the other who appears to possess subjectivity and
to be a centre of initiative. As Glynn (1984) states:

> Now objects do not mirror other objects, therefore the fact that I do see
> myself reflected or mirrored as an object in the look of the other, necessari-
> ly implies that I see the other not as an object but as a subject.

We might add here, by contrast, that what is clearly implied by
Kohut's (1971, 1977) discussions of the 'mirroring' which he sees as
necessary for the child's dvelopment of self is a situation of subject in
relation to subject – an active agent (parent) recognises the child as an
active agent. This is the mutuality of the I–Thou relationship described
by Buber (1937) – as opposed to the objectifying I–It relationship. The
contrast between these two positions is extensively and excellently discussed by Wright (1991).

Glynn is describing here a situation in which intersubjectivity – a relationship between two 'centres of initiative' is not possible: 'The other ...
cannot be an object ... unless by that same stroke myself ceases to be an
object-for-the-other'. What is illustrated here is Hegel's master–slave
dialectic, wherein 'it seems that the only alternative to being an object
(slave) for the other is to become a subject (master) for whom the other is
an object (slave)' (Glynn, 1984). Such a relationship is essentially a sado-
masochistic one, involving a struggle for control, for who is going to be
master and who is going to be slave. As Sartre states:

> While I attempt to free myself from the hold of the other ... the other is try-
> ing to free himself from mine; while I seek to enslave the other, the other
> seeks to enslave me.
>
> (Sartre, 1956, p. 364)

One point that is crucial to this kind of description is that it assumes
the presence of only two parties in relationship to each other; one is
subject, or master, and the other is object, or slave. Normally, however,
relationships are not purely dyadic. The child normally has a relationship to two parents who are in relation to each other – as well as a relationship to siblings. The child in relation to the parents is in an
essentially triadic relation. Moreover, even if we consider an apparently
dyadic relationship, e.g. the child in relation to the mother, providing
there is some capacity to reflect, there is an observing self in relation to
the self-in-relation-to-the-mother. It seems that for a relationship to be
a sado-masochistic subject–object dyad, there must be an active exclusion of a third party.

For the child with mother, the original third party is of course the
father. The father's role in facilitating separation–individuation

(differentiation) has been noted (Abelin, 1975; Mahler et al., 1975) and also his function as a representative of the 'law', the boundary (Lacan, 1957). Under certain circumstances, the father and his paternal function may be excluded, leaving the child incompletely differentiated from mother. Thus it can be seen that differentiation, the capacity to reflect, to experience the self as subject, and the role of the father as third party are all intertwined. These points are taken up later when I present a model of narcissistic disturbance.

A further dichotomous relation addressed by several theorists is that between the 'I' and the 'Me'. James (1890) divided the self into the I, the Material Me, the Social Me and the Spiritual Me. The Social Me is the integration of the response one gets from others – the 'Me' that is in terms of other people's definitions. This notion is close to the 'Me' of Mead (1934). However, Mead considered the self to be the integration of both aspects – the experiencing 'I' and the social 'Me' - and the relationship between the 'I' and the 'Me'. Thus the 'I' is the actor whilst the 'Me' is the simultaneous anticipation of the response of others to the action ; the 'I' in turn responds to the 'Me'. Mead emphasised the reversibility between gesturers – that one person's 'I' communicates with another person's 'Me'. In addition the 'I' and the 'Me' within the self are in constant communication. As Lovlie argues, it is the capacity to reflect that results in the ability to see the self as both subject and object. She emphasises that the 'I' and the 'Me' aspects of the self are in a dialectic relation, they presuppose each other – 'The Me becomes thesis, the I antithesis – and the self is the synthesis in an ongoing process of change'.

Lichtenberg (1983) implies a similar notion of the dialectic of 'I' and 'Me' and its association with the capacity to reflect. He postulates that it is the *imaging capacity* that is decisive in establishing the sense of discreteness and objectivity of self and other in the second year of life. Lichtenberg links the imaging capacity to a shift to a sign–signal level of information exchange with the awareness of a distinction between signifier and what is signified; prior to this, the infant is embedded in the exchange between self and other without awareness of separate entities. The implication is that there emerges a capacity to relate to self in relation to other, a three party structure. Lichtenberg refers to this as the emergence of the 'self-as-a-whole'. He quotes Stechler and Kaplan (1980) (Lichtenberg, 1983, p. 99):

> If a child is behaving and monitoring her own behaviour in the context of an interpersonal relationship is observing and recording how the other person reacts to what she is doing, and is then influenced by her perceptions, so that she proceeds to integrate her own acts with social cues, we conclude that there is self-awareness.

Lichtenberg regards this as the emergent 'self-as-a-whole'. Clearly this concept refers to the dialectic between the 'I' and the 'Me'. Another aspect of the emergent self-as-a-whole, according to Lichtenberg, is the sense of ownership of self – and the self-as-a-whole as 'mental director'. Lichtenberg implies how this may be influenced by the mother's attitude (Lichtenberg, 1983, p. 118):

> The achievements the growing infant makes during open-space intervals, when mother exists only as a supportive background, are the basic intervals around which the toddler's emergent self-as-a-whole builds a sense of ownership of one's images and responses, as well as a sense of privacy of one's mental space.

Lichtenberg reasons that the 'I' consists of experiences – sometimes feelings, impulses – from within, in contrast with the 'Me', the awareness of the other's view, the *outside* perspective. The self-as-a-whole must encompass both these, must have a perspective which relates to both points of view. Noy (1979) discusses this balance between inside and outside points of view, in terms of primary and secondary process modes of thought. In the following quote from Noy, the terms 'I' and 'Me' have been inserted in brackets to indicate the link with the preceding argument (Lichtenberg, 1983, p. 118):

> A mature normal self image is based on a combination of primary and secondary modes. According to the primary process mode, a person perceives himself as from *within*, as a collage of sensations, wishes, needs and experiences ['I']. According to the secondary process mode, a person perceives himself as from *without*, as a group of objective phenomena, an object among other objects, a collection of physical substances and forces. ['Me'] ... This double perception and representation pertains to any part of the body, with body self as an overall image and to the subordinate self in all dimensions. The all-inclusive self-image is an inner representation made up of the two aspects, which I would call the *experiential self* ['I'] and the *conceptual self* ['Me']. A healthy sense of self results from a sound balance and optimal fit between these aspects.

The balance between the 'I' and the 'Me' (category 5 of the taxonomy) seems crucial, but clearly it can be skewed in either direction. Painfully self-conscious persons, for example, seem at times to experience themselves as all 'Me' with very little 'I', constantly taking an outside judgemental position on themselves. Other patients seem deficient in their 'Me', their ability to anticipate the social consequences of their behaviour.

Some related ideas worth mentioning here are provided by the excellent discussion by Emde (1988) of the significance of infant social referencing in facilitating self-development. Emde draws on a variety of authors and researchers to suggest three interacting pathways of self-experience – the sense of I, the experience of the Other, and the experience of Self with Other. He sees the emerging concern with the intersubjective self, explored by Stern and others, as drawing on the legacy of Mead and as constituting a 'we psychology' complementary to 'self-psychology'

To summarise so far, we have linked the differentiation of self and other with the capacity to reflect and use symbols. We have seen how the other is represented in the self by the 'Me'. We have also seen how a third point of view is required in order to take a perspective on the self and other, the 'I' and the 'Me', so that there can be a self-as-a-whole. Without this third perspective, there can be no capacity to reflect and no ownership of self. The person may be locked in a dyad of self and other, a master–slave dialectic. Disturbances in the balance between the 'I' and the 'Me' may be associated with painful self-consciousness.

The following clinical example from a psychotherapy session illustrates some of these themes: incomplete differentiation; difficulties with thinking and reflecting; sado-masochism; the missing third party. The patient is an unmarried man in his early thirties. His father had died when he was five, leaving him with a highly dominant mother. Recently he had separated from his girlfriend with whom he had felt trapped and unable to be himself – this girl had originally been his lodger and they had somehow slid into a relationship. In one particular session he described his wish for a stern father, and talked approvingly of a schoolteacher who was firm but encouraging. He then went on to talk of his anxieties that he might become involved with another girl in the same block of flats. From his account it appeared that he was afraid that having a coffee with this girl would automatically lead to going to bed with her and a total kind of involvement with her. He then talked of difficulties in trusting his own judgements and perceptions. In the way he talked, he conveyed a confusion and a difficulty in disentangling his own perceptions from those of his girlfriend – in recent sessions there had been similar material about the problem of disentangling his perceptions from those of his mother. As he talked about this, he conveyed that he was having great difficulty in thinking and judging for himself – indeed at times he manifested a curious kind of stupidity. He remarked that it seemed to be a situation in which either his view or his girlfriend's view prevailed – this had also been the case with his mother; there could never be any reconciliation between the two opposing views. Eventually he remarked: 'Something seems to be missing.' The therapist commented that what seemed to be missing was the father, as a third party, who could give a third point of view, could provide a perspective and a separate view of both these positions. This seemed to make sense to him and he went on to describe having observed a little girl with her mother and father. Apparently it had seemed very clear that she was trying to get between her parents. The father had been friendly but firm – he responded to the little girl but did not give way. The patient remarked that this seemed to be a 'good triangle'. This prompted the therapist to comment that, when there is a triangle, there are three points of view instead of just two, there is room to move, perspective to see, and a space in which to think.

One of the implications of the formulations of Mead, Lovlie and others is that the self arises in the context of a relationship with others. The consciousness of self and other arises simultaneously. Kaye (1982) suggests that the moment when the infant is first self-conscious is the moment when he or she looks round to see if anyone is watching – at that moment attributing thought to others and regarding him- or herself as an object of their observation. Kaye further suggests that there emerges a complex consciousness of the self in a context:

> The consciousness that emerges is at one and the same time the consciousness that makes human behaviour *rule governed*, the shared consciousness that makes people behave as *social systems*, and the consciousness that forms the essence of self.

This suggests that aspects of the sense of self involve becoming aware of one's place in relation to others, one's position in the social system at a given time. As I describe in more detail later in the model of narcissistic disturbance, if the father as the third party is ineffectual or is denigrated by the mother, the child in an oedipal situation may be left feeling confused about where he or she is in the family system – resulting in a variety of disturbances of self, especially in the sense of lineage.

Conclusions

- The existence of a 'self' cannot simply be assumed. The concept requires philosophical and empirical examination.
- A concept of self and an account of the development of the self is required in psychoanalysis because many patients manifest disturbances in many aspects of the experience of self which cannot easily be addressed through those theories of object relations (personal relationships) which do not also involve some account of the relationship to the self.
- The concept of self is used in a variety of ways, each addressing different aspects. Out of this review a taxonomy of disturbances of self is developed.
- A number of authors argue that there is a basic tendency for people

to attempt to maintain their identity, to establish a sense of autonomy, to preserve an illusion of personal continuity and immortality.
Some authors appear to view this as a positive developmental
thrust, while others see in this a much more negatively valued turning away from reality.

- Illusion appears to be inherent in the very structure of the developing self. The individual may believe he or she is independent, but in
the very act of achieving autonomy the 'other' is taken into the self.
As a person develops in childhood they are prone to become captivated by images that others have of them.

- One aspect of human self-hood is the capacity to reflect upon oneself – i.e. to know that there is an I who thinks and feels certain
things, perhaps in relation to an other. It is the capacity to assume a
third point of view that allows a perspective on self and other.
Perhaps the presence of the father is of crucial importance in facilitating the differentiation of child from mother and in providing this
third perspective. Without this triangular relationship, the person
may be restricted in their capacity to reflect on who they are and
what they feel and think.

Chapter 2
Narcissism

The story of Echo and Narcisssus

The themes and structure of the myth

Many aspects of narcissistic disturbance can be found represented in the themes of the myth of Narcissus and Echo as told by Ovid (e.g. Vinge, 1967).

The origins of Narcissus are violent – a violent 'primal scene' as the nymph Liriope is raped by the river god Cephisus. There is no continuing parental couple and no father available to Narcissus.

Narcissus's origins are preceded by the pronouncement that he should not know himself, that he should remain in ignorance of who he is and where he comes from. This foreshadows the tragic events to follow as Narcissus becomes trapped in his incapacity to recognise himself. Tiresias's pronouncement also foretells that Narcissus' search for his self will lead to his death at the pool.

A 'narcissistic' quality is apparent in the character of Narcissus: his aloofness, his spurning of all his admirers' attentions – his 'pride so cold that no youth, no maiden touched his heart'. Behind this, his underlying fear of being exploited or possessed is apparent. In response to Echo's approaches he shouts 'Hands off! Embrace me not! May I die before I give you power over me!' Some commentators (e.g. Vinge, 1967; Schwartz-Salant, 1982) have suggested that a narcissistic quality is implied in descriptions of his mother Liriope. Drawing on a thirteenth-century story of Liriope – Robert de Bois' *Floris et Liriope* – Vinge describes Narcissus as 'proud and unapproachable as his mother was'. Schwartz-Salant (1982) speculates that it may have been the aloof unresponsive nature of Liriope that provoked her rape by Cephisus. Liriope is described as 'beauteous' just as Narcissus is beautiful – 'a child whom a nymph might love even as a child'. This may imply that the love of a nymph such as Liriope cannot be taken for granted but is

33

perhaps dependent upon a beauty which mirrors her beauty.

The evocation of envy is a prominent theme. Narcissus's admirers experience envy because Narcissus is desired yet is completely unobtainable and unreachable – as if he wishes to retain all his desirable qualities for himself. The curse uttered by a spurned lover and granted by the god Nemesis – 'so may he himself love and not gain the thing he loves' – is that Narcissus should experience the same envy. This dreaded emotion of envy seems to become a kind of currency which is passed backwards and forwards.

Violence, envy, sadism and masochism pervade the story, which is one of repeated victimisations. Narcissus treats Echo and his other admirers sadistically – particular sadism is represented in the reference to Narcissus sending one suitor a sword with which to kill himself (Graves, 1955). On the other hand, masochism is represented in Echo's enslavement to Narcissus, her inability to take any initiative in the 'dialogue', her entrapment in a position of passive response to Narcissus. Like sadist and masochist, Narcissus and Echo are enslaved to each other. Hamilton (1982) sees Echo and Narcissus as fitting together perfectly and as mutually trapped in a 'mirroring or doting symbiosis which resists change'.

A motif of central importance is that of reflection and the associated theme of illusion. This is repeated twice: first in the auditory mode in the Echo episosde; and secondly in the visual mode in the final drama at the pool. There are two significant components to this theme of reflection. First, Echo is enslaved and restricted to echoing and mirroring Narcissus's own words. She is forced, as a result of her own victimisation to appear no more than a mirror and cannot initiate any dialogue herself; her own separateness and individuality cannot become apparent. The second component is Narcissus's *captivation* by the image at the pool. He does not know himself and is in love with, is fascinated by, an illusion – a state of affairs remarkably close to Lacan's (1937) description of the 'mirror stage' wherein the young child is captivated by the illusion of the image in the mirror, the image 'out there' becoming thus alienated from the lived experience of self.

We might wonder whether the prolongation of Narcissus's fixation to the pool and his inability to move away points to the intensity of his need for a mirroring response of a more human kind. Trapped in his illusion, Narcissus seems to be struggling to grasp something elusive, indeed his own self – again suggesting that he is alienated from himself. Frazer, in his *Golden Bough* (1963) provides evidence that the shadow or reflection has often been taken as a representation of the soul. Thus Narcissus could be understood as gazing at, and trying to grasp, his own soul, his own deeper self. His recognition that it is his self that he is trying to reach, and that it is unreachable – he can never be united with himself – leads to despair and the whole episode ends in death.

Death and deadliness is indeed foreshadowed in the description of the lifelessness around the water:

> There was a clear pool with silvery bright water, to which no shepherd ever came, or she goats feeding on the mountainside, or other cattle; whose smooth surface neither bird nor beast nor falling bough ever ruffled. Grass grew all around its edge, fed by the water near, and a coppice that would never suffer the sun to warm the spot.

This deadliness might be understood as reflecting the cessation of growth as Narcissus becomes trapped in a developmental cul de sac.

Stein (1976) sees the myth as containing several developmental warnings. First there is a warning against vanity. Stein points out that the story parallels that of Oedipus, in that the moments of tragic realisation centres on the moments of discovery who the beloved really is. He argues: 'Whereas the tragedy of Oedipus is based on the horror of mother son incest and evokes the archetypal incest taboo, the tragedy of Narcissus is based on the horror of solipsism and evokes the vanity taboo'. Stein also sees the myth as a warning against 'violating the other-directed impulses of loving' and of becoming 'a self-absorbed, soul-absorbed, navel gazer'. He adds that 'The myth of Narcissus seems to function as a lightning rod for the fear of getting locked into a solipsistic system, a libidinal oeuroborus'.

Themes of the Narcissus myth

- Illusion and the captivation by a deceptive image.
- A lack of self-knowledge and knowledge of origins.
- Reflection and mirroring – both auditory and visual.
- Sado-masochism: Echo's 'masoschistic' fidelity to sadistic Narcissus.
- The fear of being possessed and taken over.
- Vanity and pride – and a turning away from object-relatedness.
- Envy.
- The dangers of self-absorption and illusion: a developmental cul de sac and death.
- Origins in a violent primal scene and the absence of a continuing parental couple.

Freud's views on narcissism

Freud's concept of narcissism draws together a number of features of mental life and emotional development. In his elaboration of the concept over several years, he referred to: (1) a stage of development; (2) an attitude and relationship towards the object (i.e. towards other people); (3) an attitude toward the self; (4) the sense of unity or disunity of the self; (5) a mode of thought; and (6) a state of illusion.

Freud's first references to narcissism were in 1910, in a footnote to the *Three Essays on Sexuality* (originally 1905) and in his *Leonardo* paper. In the former, he suggested that narcissism was a developmental stage between an original state of *autoerotism* and a later state of *object love*. In the *Leonardo* paper he described a syndrome in which a man, having been adored as a child by his mother, identifies with the mother and loves a boy as he himself would desire to be loved.

In 1911 Freud explored further his idea of narcissism as a developmental stage, at this point suggesting a normal homosexual stage between autoerotism and object love (1911a). This was in the context of a discussion of paranoia, in which he proposed that in this psychosis there is a detachment of the libido from objects and a regression through homosexuality to narcissism, followed by delusional reconstitution of the lost object world. Freud regarded the autoerotic stage as being characterised by an absence of an ego, an unintegration of the drives, a lack of object relations, and a seeking of instinctual satisfaction in the body. The narcissistic stage was seen as involving a unification of the drives and the formation of an ego. In this stage the infant finds its first object, the self or ego.

Freud's major paper on the subject – *On Narcissism* – appeared in 1914. Here he elaborated on his previous ideas and used the concept also to explain several additional phenomena including hypochondriasis, self-esteem, the development of an internal ego ideal, and a special type of narcissistic object choice in which the other is loved as a representative of oneself as one is, as one used to be or as one would like to be. The paper addresses essentially two intertwined themes: (1) the development of object libido out of ego libido; and (2) the transformation of infantile grandiosity, leading to the setting up of the ego ideal. Much of the description is framed in terms of an economic model, to do with the quantity and distribution of libido. Thus, self-esteem is seen as varying according to the amount of libido remaining invested in the self, megalomania occurring if there is massive withdrawal of libido from objects into the self, and low self-esteem occurring in states of unrequited love when an unusual amount of libido is invested in the object; hypochondriasis is considered to result from excessive libidinal investment in the body. As Smith (1985) comments, the implication is that the transformation to object love occurs through economic pressure – the experience of hypochondriacal anxiety as a result of dammed up libido drives the infant to seek out external objects. However, in addition to economic considerations, Freud is also concerned with the relationship to reality and the inevitable blows to infantile narcissistic *illusions* of perfection. In order to preserve this illusion to some degree, the child locates perfection in an object, usually a parent; this projected ideal is gradually reinternalised to form the *ego ideal*.

One significant implication in Freud's model of the transformation of narcissism into ideals, in terms of the thesis to be developed here, concerns the notion of time and the necessity of development. So long as the illusion of 'perfection now' prevails, there is no sense of the necessity of development, the passing of time and the need to strive towards future goals. The setting-up of an ego ideal marks the crucial step from an insistence on 'perfection now' to an acceptance of present limitations, coupled with a striving to develop.

Freud describes a further feature, associated with the grandiosity of the primary narcissistic state of libidinal investment in the self, as magical thinking or omnipotence of thought. However, an anomaly arises because in 1913 (*Totem and Taboo*), Freud proposed another stage of development, the anal sadistic stage, which he described as pregenital but *postnarcissistic*. Smith (1985) suggests that it was partly because of this inconsistency that in 1915 (*Instincts and their Vicissitudes*) Freud began to talk in terms of a *gradual* shift from narcissism to object love. At the same time the idea of an original stage of autoerotism was abandoned and the ego was seen as present from the beginning of life. Smith suggests that at this point there was a 'subtle but pervasive terminological shift' in Freud's writings as he began to consider narcissism in more cognitive terms. Thus the essential feature of narcissism was seen in terms of the infant's primitive conception of the origin and sources of pleasurable experiences. Freud argued that the infant does not need to recognise its true dependence on external caretakers and instead perceives the body as the source of pleasure. By implication, Freud is describing here a *misperception* and an *illusion* as the basis of the narcissistic state. It is the gradual breakdown of this illusion that initiates the move away from narcissism. This is quite different from the framing of narcissism in terms of the distribution of libido.

Freud's concept of narcissism was again recast when he developed his structural model in 1923 (*The Ego and the Id*). Here, having differentiated conceptually the ego from the id, he described the state of primary narcissism as being when all libido is contained in the id. However, by 1940 (*Outline*) he wrote of the 'undifferentiated ego–id' – a model which again implies a process of gradually giving up the narcissistic state in favour of relating to reality and to others.

The relationship to reality and its association with illusion was a recurrent theme in Freud's writings. For example, in *The Two Principles of Mental Functioning* (1911b) he wrote:

We have long observed that every neurosis has as its result, and probably therefore as its purpose, a forcing of the patient out of real life, an alienating of him from reality ... Neurotics turn away from reality because they find it unbearable – either the whole or parts of it.

Indeed it was in this paper that he stated most clearly his idea that the recognition of reality follows an earlier state of illusion which is in opposition to this:

> ... I suggest that the primary state of psychical rest was originally disturbed by the peremptory demands of internal needs ... The setting up of the reality principle proved to be a momentous step.

The necessity of relating to reality in order to satisfy inner demands was later described as one of the major functions of the ego in the structural model of *The Ego and the Id* (1923). However, the recognition of reality was always seen as somewhat tenuous and partial and the seductions of illusions ever present. Religion, for example, was seen as an illusion protecting against man's sense of helplessness. In his paper on *Fetishism* (1927), Freud described how part of the mind may recognise reality whilst another part disavows this reality. The aspects of reality that are repudiated in these instances are the threat of castration by the father and the associated recognition of the difference between the sexes in terms of presence or absence of a penis – the fetish symbolically representing the penis and thereby functioning to deny that the woman does not have one. In a much later contribution, *An Outline of Psychoanalysis* (1940), Freud broadened his idea of the splitting of the ego to suggest that this partial repudiation of reality is a characteristic not only of psychosis and fetishism, but of neurosis in general and of the infantile ego:

> It must not be thought that fetishism constitutes an exceptional case in exhibiting a split in the ego; it is merely a particularly favourable subject for study. We must return to our statement that the infantile ego, under the domination of the external world, disposes of undesirable instinctual impulses by means of what are called repressions. We can now supplement this by a further assertion that, during the same period of life, the ego often enough finds itself in the position of warding off some claim from the *external world* which it feels as painful, and that this is effected by *denying* the perceptions that bring to knowledge such a demand on the part of reality. Denials of this kind often occur, and not only with fetishists; and whenever we are in a position to study them, they turn out to be half-measures, incomplete attempts at detachment from reality. The rejection is always supplemented by an acceptance; two contrary and independent attitudes always arise and this produces the fact of a split in the ego. The issue once more depends upon which of the two can command the greater intensity.

However, it may be significant that the splitting of the ego in its relationship to reality was first brought to Freud's attention through a clinical syndrome in which it is a threat from the *father* that is feared. A further interesting allusion to the relationship to the father is apparent in Freud's discussion of his disturbance of memory on the Acropolis

(1936). He describes here a disruption of his sense of reality, as if a part of his mind did not believe he was there; he related this to guilt about being more successful than his father who could (1) not have afforded to travel, and (2) lacked the education to appreciate the historical significance of Athens.

One significant implication in Freud's model of the transformation of narcissism into ideals, in terms of the thesis to be developed here, is the notion of time and the necessity of development. So long as the illusion of 'perfection now' exists, there is no sense of the necessity of development, the passing of time and the need to strive towards a future goal. The setting up of an ego ideal marks the crucial step from an insistence on perfection now, to an acceptance of present limitations and a striving to develop.

The theme of narcissism, the relationship to reality and the relationship to the father, are taken up later.

Freud on femininity, illusion and narcissism

A further relevant aspect of Freud's views is his association between narcissism and femininity. For example, in *On Narcissism* Freud wrote:

> ... strictly speaking it is only themselves that ... women love with an intensity comparable to that of the man's love for them. Nor does their need lie in the direction of loving, but of being loved ...

It is the difference in boys' and girls' oedipal situations that Freud sees as the basis of women's greater narcissism and lessened superego. Through Freud's papers on femininity and the oedipus complex can be seen a juxtaposition between narcissism and oedipal development (a juxtaposition later particularly emphasised by Grunberger, 1971). In Freud's view, both little boys and little girls start in an active masculine position, desiring the mother as a love object. The difference is that the little boy fears castration whereas the little girl has to accept that she does not have a penis and so cannot satisfy mother. In optimum masculine development, according to Freud, the little boy's oedipal desires are given up, the oedipal complex is destroyed, 'literally smashed to pieces' (1925), as the boy abandons his rivalry with the father to form the superego. By contrast the little girl does not give up her oedipal desires for her father, but rather *arrives at her oedipal complex*:

> Whereas in boys the oedipus complex is destroyed by the castration complex, in girls it is made possible and led up to by the castration complex.

Whereas boys are impelled by their castration anxiety to give up infantile desires, the little girl can preserve them towards the father.

Thus, as Van Herik (1985) points out, for Freud, masculinity involves renunciation through the relationship to the father, whereas femininity involves fulfilment through receiving love from the father. Van Herik shows how Freud's negative view of femininity is linked to his negative view of religion. Freud (1927) in *The Future of an Illusion* argues that the idea of God is an expression of the desire for protection by the father against the sense of helplessness aroused by perception of nature which is indifferent to our well-being. His account of the passive relationship to the powerful external authority of God is similar to his account of the little girl's relationship to the father – in both cases the moral prohibitions are external rather than internal as the superego; in each case the desire is to be loved by an external authority.

That Freud saw religion as providing *narcissistic* illusions – of being favoured by an idealised object – is indicated by the following passage from *The Future of an Illusion* (1927) describing the religious attitude (p. 18):

> ... Everything that happens in this world is an expression of an intelligence superior to us, which in the end, though its ways and byways are difficult to follow, orders everything *for the best – that is to make it enjoyable for us.* Over each one of us there watches a *benevolent Providence which is only seemingly stern* and which will not suffer us to become a plaything of the overmighty and pitilesss forces of nature. Death itself is not extinction ... but the beginning of a new kind of existence which lies on the path of development to something higher. And, looking in the other direction, this view announces the same moral laws which our civilisations have set up govern the whole universe as well, except that they are maintained by a supreme court of justice with incomparably more power and consistency. In the end all good is rewarded and all evil punished ... . In this way *all the terrors, all the sufferings and the hardships of life are destined to be obliterated ....* And the *superior wisdom* which directs this course of things, the *infinite goodness* that expresses itself in it, the *justice* that achieves its aim in it – these are the attributes of the divine beings who created us and the world as a whole ...

This religious attitude of basking in illusions is contrasted by Freud with the 'scientific' attitude which aims to accept reality as it is. Thus the religious attitude, and femininity, are for Freud more narcissistic and less oriented towards reality than is masculinity.

Themes from Freud's account of narcissism

In Freud's various discusions of narcissism we find the following ideas:

- The turning towards the self, retreating from or avoiding object relations.

- The loss of a sense of unity of the self, associated with hypochondriacal anxiety.
- Illusions of perfection and self-sufficiency, associated with grandiosity and fantasies of omnipotence and a general avoidance of reality – and implicitly the denial of time.
- States of mind in which the separateness of the object is not recognised.
- The idealisation of the object in order to preserve the illusion of perfection somewhere – the related notion of the development of the ego ideal as an internal structure established through the transformation of the original narcissistic illusion – a step which implies the acceptance of time, of current limitations and the necessity of development.
- A link between femininity, narcissism and illusion.

Chapter 3
The narcissistic affects

Shame and the self*

In the following, some characteristics of shame are outlined, distinguishing it from guilt. A clinical illustration is described and from this several points are developed – the importance of the visual modality, the link with sexuality and the body, the early precursors of shame and its association with the unexpected, and shame in relation to depression. My thesis is that shame functions to enhance and preserve the sense of self, and that shame arises particularly in people whose early environment has impeded the emergence of various aspects of the sense of self. It is proposed that shame is an affect central to disturbances in the sense of self, whilst guilt is a central affect in disturbances of object relations and that, although these are related, they can to some extent be distinguished. The clinical implications of this formulation are discussed and it is argued that failure to take account of the ramifications of shame may seriously impede successful psychotherapy.

In spite of its importance, shame is relatively neglected in the psychoanalytic literature. For example, there are no references at all to shame in any of the writings of Melanie Klein. Some of the major sources on shame are: Piers and Singer (1981); Pines (1987) has provided an excellent recent review; much of Kohut's work (1971, 1977) also concerns shame, although not always directly. Somewhat outside the psychoanalytic tradition, Bradshaw (1988) writes of 'toxic shame' and argues persuasively that this is the core affective problem behind addictions, compulsions and an excessive drive to achieve.

In disentangling shame and guilt it can be seen that whilst both are *about* something, only shame an object, in the sense that one can say 'I am ashamed of ...'. To say 'I am guilty of...' does not have the same kind of experiential referent. Sartre states: 'Consider shame. Its

*Reproduced, with the permission of the British Psychological Society, from the *British Journal of Medical Psychology* (1984) 57, 207–214.

structure is intentional. It is a shameful apprehension of something and that something is me.' Whereas in guilt we feel remorse in relation to something we have done in actuality or fantasy to another, shame concerns identity and the sense of self. As Thrane (1979) puts it, in guilt we say 'How can I have done *that*!'; in shame we say 'How *can* I have done that!'. Sartre (1956) again states: 'I am ashamed of what I am. Shame therefore realises an intimate relation of myself to myself. Through shame I have discovered an aspect of my being.' Here shame relates to the image and evaluation of the self (objective self; category 3 of the taxonomy).

G. Klein (1976) and Gedo (1981) have emphasised that a major aspect of the developing organisation of the self is the transformation of passive experience into a more active mode, to do actively what was once suffered passively and thereby move from helplessness to activity and thus to guilt. Lewis (1971), in discussing the passivity in relation to the other in shame, points out that this may lead to the wish to turn the table and to triumph over the other, a 'righting tendency' which may then give rise to guilt. Here we are concerned with the subjective self and the sense of agency (category 2 of the taxonomy).

Lewis, along with Lynd (1958), emphasises that shame, unlike guilt, is about the *whole* self, involves a global condemnation of the self and a heightened awareness of the self. Guilt, on the other hand, may have a more discrete reference to particular actions. The heightened awareness of the self in states of shame, whereby that which is normally quietly in the background is suddenly in the foreground, may cause a marked disruption of functioning, often involving feelings of confusion and a flooding of autonomic stimulation. This tends to release rage. Levin (1971), for example, writes of 'defusion of the instincts' in shame, so that unbound aggression is let loose. Kohut (1977) similarly writes of 'narcissistic rage' as a 'disintegration product' of the break-up of the self. In terms of the taxonomy, this concerns the structure–organisation of the self (category 4).

Shame heightens the awareness of the self. Lewis (1971) has suggested that this is precisely the function of shame. She sees guilt and shame as complementary superego modes and quotes research suggesting that shame-prone personalities are more 'field dependent' than those who are guilt-prone, i.e. they are less able to differentiate themselves and maintain their orientation in space (category 1 of the taxonomy). Such people may more easily lose themselves in identification with the other; shame brings back the awareness of self. It may be that people are most prone to experience shame at those times when they are in the process of emerging from identification with the other, for example, in adolescence and certain periods of infancy.

There are certain obvious defences against shame. One is to inhibit all exposure so that no shame is risked. Another might be termed 'countershame', a kind of manic denial of shame in which the person behaves as if he or she has no experience of shame. Lewis (1971) has also described the phenomenon of 'bypassed shame'. The following example illustrates this:

A 30-year-old man whose father died when he was 5 was still very tangled with his mother, feeling obliged to phone her every day and visit her very regularly. He appeared to feel quite passive and helpless about this. One day his mother took him shopping to buy him a coat. In describing this he mentioned that the shop girl seemed scornful in the way that she looked at him. He felt angry with her and decided that he would not buy the coat for this reason. When the therapist suggested that he had felt the girl to be scornful of his relationship with his mother, he seemed initially puzzled, but then recalled that he used to experience shopping with his mother as excruciatingly embarrassing, whereas now he would just blank out (i.e. bypass) the experience and saw himself as a 'clothes horse being dressed'. He was not conscious of the shame but aware only of his anger with the girl who he felt was scornful.

There are some typical components of the shame constellation here – the sense of helplessness, the feeling like an object, the sense of being looked at, the entanglement with the other (his mother). Bypassed shame often seems to be associated with paranoid ideation, constructed to rationalise the inner state, the unacknowledged shame.

In distinguishing the different superego modes of shame and guilt, Lewis, Piers and Kohut, to some extent, all employ the following paradigm: that guilt reflects *transgressions* against the prohibitive, object-related aspects of the superego; shame, on the other hand, reflects *shortcomings* in efforts to live up to the ego ideal, which is part of the narcissistic economy, the inheritor of primary narcissism in Freud's model. Whilst there may be some value in this formulation, I believe it is too narrow and that shame is more pervasive and fundamental than this model implies.

Clinical illustration

The following case illustrates many aspects of the shame syndrome, particularly the central conflict between the attempt to *suppress* the self and the wish to *express* the self.

Mrs L. sought psychotherapy complaining of depression and of a difficulty in maintaining her sense of self when in a relationship. Her profession involved performing and her manner was consistent with this, one of her most striking features being how initially accommodating and compliant she was. In the first session she assumed her place on the couch and proceeded to talk, with no comment about the unfamiliar nature of the analytic set-up. She was never late, although it became clear that the practicalities of getting to the clinic involved considerable effort.

Very soon the themes of shame, embarrassment and self-consciousness became prominent. Her feeling of shame was consciously linked in her mind with an overwhelming sense of having to fit in with what she termed the other person's 'atmosphere' – particularly what she perceived to be the therapist's atmosphere of control and restraint. She complained of experiencing a paralysing self-consciousness the moment she walked in the door, and described the walk of a couple of yards from the door to chair where she put her coat, and from chair to couch, as agonisingly embarrassing. This was to do, she said, with being an object of someone else's observation. At the end of each session she would usually hurry out in an obviously embarrassed state. Thus, although she behaved in many ways in an extremely accommodating manner, as if she had no *separate* self, she actually experienced her self as embarrassingly apparent. At the same time her appearance was far from subdued: her clothes were always colourful and striking, drawing attention to her body and her sexuality, even though she was extremely anxious about the whole area of sexuality. Similarly, although she often complained of feeling inhibited and constrained in the therapy, she would describe fantasies of what she called 'anarchic behaviour': of not lying on the couch, of walking around the room, of moving the therapist's possessions, of asking questions and demanding answers.

She hated the sense of being observed and evaluated, and found any experience of rejection quite devastating. Yet her work of performing publicly involved her in these dangers all the time, especially the endless auditions which she found dreadfully humiliating. The impression was of someone having to face again and again the situations of greatest danger to her. On the other hand, when her performances went well and the audience was admiring, she felt wonderful, drunk with success, feeling strong and certain of herself, epitomising then Kohut's grandiose self mirrored by the 'gleam in the mother's eye'.

As might be expected, she had experienced her mother as highly controlling and intrusive. She perceived her as an extremely anxious, hypochondriacal and dissatisfied woman who had always looked to her daughter for support. The patient spoke at certain times of feeling dragged down into a void, or into a sea in which she feared she would drown. She clearly felt very much entangled in her mother's concerns, represented by a dream of tentacles pulling her down a tunnel. She was very fond of her father, but he was a distant figure. At a certain point in the therapy there emerged longings for an idealised strong figure who could lift her out of the void. These longings were associated with intense shame and an enormous sense of vulnerability in relation to men. In terms of Kohut's work, the patient could be seen as presenting the two principal narcissistic positions of the grandiose self and the idealised other respectively.

At certain times Mrs L. experienced a profound feeling of being unloved and this she found unbearable. It was associated with a sense that she might have spent much of her life in an underlying state of emptiness and an intense craving which could not be met. She would scream that she could not stand the therapist seeing her and knowing how she felt. She imagined that the therapist must pity her, or else feel scornful of her; then she would feel trapped in the other's image of her, frozen in a helpless needy state in a cold and unempathic world.

Another prominent theme concerned Mrs L.'s relationship to her body and her sexuality. In many ways she seemed to be out of touch with her body and it came to be understood that this reflected her feeling that her body did not belong to her but rather was an object for others, primarily her mother who, according to the patient, was always anxiously-preoccupied with illness, food and routine. Mrs L. herself would constantly rush around, denying her need for food and rest, and then feel enraged when she found herself exhausted. Lying on the couch took on the meaning of the therapist controlling her body. However, the gradual discovery of bodily pleasures and her sexuality and acceptance of herself as a sexual woman was particularly pleasing to her. These phases when she felt filled with sexual strength could, however, easily give way to shame and anger when the man left her. Then she would feel like a discarded object, feeling that she had been used, and she would be filled with rage. The ending of each therapy session seemed to have a similarly humiliating meaning for her.

In summary, it could be said that one of the central concerns of Mrs L. in her therapy was to liberate herself from her sense of engulfment within her mother and to establish her own self. This involved a move away from the compulsive accommodating to the other which was initially so characteristic of her. Thus the therapy involved a shift in the balance between the I and the Me (category 5 of the taxonomy).

Shame and the look

One of the main points about this material is that the patient's shame has a great deal to do with looking and being looked at.

Mrs L. indicated that for her there were different kinds of looking and being looked at. There was the admiring look of loving interest when she felt in harmony, at one with her mirroring audience or her mirroring therapist. But there was another kind of look which she experienced as objectifying and dehumanising, causing her intense shame. The first is reminiscent of Kohut's (1971) description of the 'gleam in the mother's eye' which supports the child's self. The second had a quality more akin to what Sartre termed an 'internal haemorrhage'.

The section of Sartre's *Being and Nothingness* which deals with shame is, interestingly, entitled 'Being-for-Others', and one of the major subsections of this is entitled 'The Look'. His well-known keyhole passage illustrates the point:

> Moved by jealousy, curiosity or vice, I have just glued my ear to the door and looked through the keyhole. I am alone ... but all of a sudden I hear footsteps in the hall. Someone is looking at me!
>
> (Sartre, 1956)

For Sartre this unexpected intrusion is profoundly disorienting: 'an internal haemorrhage – a regrouping of all the objects which people my world.' All Sartre's examples of shame involve this look of the other, of being frozen in the grip of the other, e.g. his description of walking in the park:

> What I apprehend immediately when I hear the branches cracking behind me is that I occupy a place and that I cannot in any case escape from the space in which I am without defence – in short that *I am seen.*
>
> (Sartre, 1956)

Shame results in the wish not to be seen. Darwin noted that the response of the shamed person is always to look away, downward to avoid eye contact. Similarly, Wurmser (1981) states that the basic aim of shame anxiety is to hide. Erickson (1959) writes: 'shame supposes that one is completely exposed and conscious of being looked at – in a word self-conscious. One is visible and not ready to be visible.'

Why is the look so important? Wurmser (1981) writes:

> Love resides in the face – in its beauty, in the music of the voice, in the warmth of the eye. Love is proved by the face, and so is unlovability proved by seeing and hearing, by being seen and heard. A child can be loved without being given the nipple, but love cannot exist without face and music.

Perhaps the significance of the look may also be related to the child's realisation at some point that it is possible to see, yet not be seen, to be seen, yet not see. Associated with this is the internal eye of conscience, the superego which cannot be seen, and the notion of the all-seeing God. Nietzsche and Sartre both railed against the shame-inducing notion of a God that is all-seeing and all-knowing – the God that violates. Sartre writes of 'the recognition of my being an object before a subject that can never be an object'. He adds that 'God here is only the concept of the Other pushed to the limit'. Similarly Merleau-Ponty (1964) discusses the child's self-conscious reaction to the mirror image in terms of the child's ability to take an attitude of self-observation; this is the change from a sense of self as experienced, to a new awareness of the self as a perceived object – a sudden alienation from the experiential living self. Wright (1991) has also recently discussed shame in relation to the look; this material can be understood in terms of his description of the shift from 'self-as-subject' to 'self-as-object'.

Shame and sexuality

Shame and sexuality were clearly linked for Mrs L. Certain German terms illustrate the association in language. For example, the genital region is called *die Scham*, the pubic mound *Schamberg* and pubic hair *Schambaare*. Moreover, in the biblical myth of Genesis, Adam and Eve became self-conscious, conscious of their sexuality and were ashamed.

Amsterdam and Levitt (1980) suggest that a major source of painful self-consciousness is the negative reaction of the parent who looks upon the infant anxiously when the child is engaged in genital exploration or play. They argue that the mother's disapproval of genital play may be one of the first narcissistic injuries. Whilst Kohut (1971) has emphasised a child's derivation of a sense of self from the admiring gleam in the mother's eye, Amsterdam and Levitt point out that mothers in our culture do not normally beam whilst their infants play with themselves. Thus 'the child's dream of his own perfection is destroyed and that which has been pleasurable, his own bodily sensations, now produce shame'. As in the Genesis myth, sexuality leads one out of the Garden of Eden.

Mrs L.'s sense of self seemed to be intimately tied up with her sexuality, a source of narcissistic well-being as well as shame. Lichtenstein (1961) has argued that sexuality is indeed a major contributor to identity, that the libidinal pleasure in the different bodily zones at each stage of development functions to affirm and strengthen the sense of self.

Shame in relation to the body and the omnipotent other

Mrs L. appeared to regard her body at times as something to be transcended because it essentially did not belong to her. Green (1982) has described how the body can come to be experienced as an omnipotent other, insofar as the body and the instincts cannot be controlled. He refers to patients who, like Mrs L., attempt to transcend the body and make a virtue out of self-deprivation; for this he coins the term 'moral narcissism'.

> In the case of the moral narcissist, hell is not other people – narcissism has eliminated them – but rather the body. The body is the Other, resurrected in spite of attempts to wipe out its traces. The body is a limitation, a servitude, a termination ... their body is their absolute master – their shame.

> (Green, 1982)

This attitude seems to be very close to the 'profound ascetism of adolescence' described by Anna Freud (1966), adolescence being a time of particular shame-proneness.

Green relates this kind of moral narcissism to circumstances similar to those which Winnicott (1960) sees leading to a 'false self' development. Rather than meeting the omnipotence of the infant and making sense of it, the mother substitutes her own gesture which is to be given sense by the compliance of the infant. Mrs L. clearly experienced her mother as intrusive and engulfing. Green suggests that the omnipotence attributed to the mother may often be reinforced when it corresponds to the mother's desire to bear a child without the contribution of the father. In my experience, many patients who are particularly shame-prone seem to have had controlling mothers who devalued the father.

The following passage from Sartre (1956) is very relevant to this theme:

> 'To feel oneself blushing', 'to feel oneself sweating' etc., are inaccurate expressions which the shy person uses to describe his state; what he really means is that he is physically and constantly conscious of his body, not as it is for him but as it is *for the other*. This constant uneasiness which is the apprehension of my body's alienation as irremediable can determine ... a pathological fear of blushing; these are nothing but a horrified metaphysical apprehension of the existence of my body for the Other. We often say that the shy man is 'embarrassed by his own body'. Actually this is incorrect; I cannot be embarrassed by my own body as I exist it. It is my body as it is for the Other which may embarrass me.

Shame and depression

Depression is a state of mind in which problems of guilt rather than shame have been more frequently emphasised. However, my own impression is that if one enquires sympathetically into the preoccupations of depressed patients, one may often find repetitive ruminations over shameful and narcissistically injurious events. The characteristics of the 'depressive personality' as described by such authors as Rado (1928), Fenichel (1946), and Arieti and Bemporad (1980) – i.e. narcissistic vulnerability, sensitivity to slights, insults, criticisms and disappointments – may be seen in terms of proneness to shame. Depression itself may be viewed partly as a narcissistic disturbance, the disruption in the sense of self and self-esteem being quite central (Mollon and Parry, 1984).

It is often argued that depression is a response to loss. However, Mrs L. emphasised how *humiliating* separation was when it was experienced as rejection. Much appears to depend upon the meaning of the loss. It is possible to distinguish the shame component, the humiliating and narcissistically wounding aspects of loss, from the pain of separation per se. For example, to feel that the loved person is lost through one's own destructiveness is not narcissistically wounding, but to feel that one is left because one is unworthy or unlovable is mortifying.

Some depressive patients seem to avoid the experience of helplessness in the face of rejection and consequent shame through a resort to active destructiveness. This point is similar to Guntrip's (1969) argument that sado-masochistic internal object relations function as an escape from intolerable weakness and helplessness. In this way depression can be seen sometimes as an attempt to protect the sense of self. One depressed patient, who may be typical of a certain group, had never separated from her mother, with whom she had maintained a hostile masochistic dependence. She described how all her life she had felt she had to *be* something for other people, whether they be mother, friends or the therapist in the transference; she felt that she always had to slot into the 'vision' that her mother had for her. During her therapy she became quite explicit regarding her fear of dependence because this meant to her being taken over by the other and becoming an object for the other. During her therapy she made several serious plans for suicide, which she seemed to see as one way in which she could escape from the grip of the other and affirm her self, asserting that it was *her* life, it belonged to her and was therefore hers to end. Each time she made these plans she threw out all her personal possessions and letters and anything that had any emotional meaning for her. Eventually she was able to say why she did this; it was, she said, in order to prevent others prying into her personal belongings after she was dead. In all this can clearly be seen her lifelong struggle to emerge from the position of being an object for the other, and her wish to protect the integrity and autonomy of her self even after her death. In terms of the taxonomy, this concerns the sense of agency (category 2) and her efforts to shift the balance from the Me to the I (category 5).

The early precursors of shame

Lynd (1958) observed that shame tends to be a response to the unexpected. Izard (1977) has reported on infants' reactions to strangers and argued that shame arises from disturbances in recognition. Broucek (1982) described 'an acute distress state associated with the inability to influence, predict or comprehend an event which the infant expected on the basis of previous experience, to be able to control or understand'. He suggests that so-called 'stranger anxiety' may be better understood as shame-shyness.

These authors are describing a basic shame reaction when the environment does not respond as expected, when it does not respond as an extension of self. Thus shame seems to be associated with a sudden disruptive awareness of separateness, of self *and other*. Sartre (1956), in an allusion to Genesis, remarked: 'my original fall is the existence of the Other.' This could be seen as referring to the premature birth of the psychological self. Another way of putting this might be to say that the other intrudes too early. This may throw further light on Winnicott's (1960) concept of the 'false self'. Winnicott suggests that if the early environment does not sufficiently adapt to the infant, so that it impinges unempathically with its 'otherness', the self may split into an adaptive false self and a protected true self. It seems very likely that the catastrophe that this manoeuvre is protecting against is actually a very basic experience of shame, when the self reaches out and is met with an unresponsive or uncomprehending maternal environment.

The experience of shame leads to protective manoeuvres, defending the boundaries and integrity of the self. It gives rise to the wish for privacy, for protection against violation from outside; but also the fact that we experience shame when we act against our own ideals indicates its function of signalling violation of self *internally*.

Clinical implications

There are certain features of shame which tend to make it difficult to detect. Because it evokes the wish to hide and to protect the self, shame by its very nature tends to be hidden; often it may be concealed behind rage or guilt. A therapeutic stance that is oblivious to the pervasive role of shame in narcissistically disturbed patients may tend to provoke a sado-masochistic relationship and a therapeutic stalemate in which the patient is constantly struggling to master narcissistic injuries unknowingly inflicted by the therapist.

An exclusive focus on guilt to the neglect of shame may seriously skew the therapy and constitute a major impediment to working through. On the other hand, if the patient is helped to articulate and understand feelings of shame, these become increasingly tolerable, less overwhelming in intensity and primitive in quality. Less energy than has to be invested in protecting a fragile sense of self and considerable movement may occur in patients who might otherwise appear intractable.

Pines (1987), drawing on Thrane (1979), offers the following table of comparisons between shame and guilt.

	Shame	*Guilt*
Feeling	Always implied, e.g. to be (feel) ashamed	Feeling is not intrinsic, e.g. to be guilty may not be to feel guilty and vice versa
	Self-referential. I am ashamed of something I have done	
As a verb	I can 'shame' another make the other feel ashamed	I cannot 'guilt' another
To be without	Shame-less reveals the inner self. Not a virtue	Guilt-less is a virtue. Does not relate to inner self
Sense of identity	Bound to	Not bound to
Relation to society	Not rule bound; linked more to inner self	Transgression of moral rules
Relation to peers	Peer pressure high	Peer pressure not as salient
	Peers as mirrors	
Relation to body	The principal object	
Physiology	Highly reactive. Almost impossible to control or conceal	Less reactive. Can be controlled and concealed to considerable extent
Facial involvement	Very high	May not be revealed facially
Relation of response to size of offence	Very variable. A small offence may produce a very marked shame response	Response may well be proportional to offence
Discharge from affect	Through repair to self-image	Through payment of debt – penance, punishment, confession
Openness	Flight into silence and concealment	Sought in confession
Response to humour	Protective, reparative	Not susceptible

Self-awareness, self-consciousness and preoccupation with self*

Although in the last few years there has been a growlng psychoanalytic literature on shame, there has been very little focus on self-consciousness as a specific aspect of this experience. In the following, I describe the phenomenology of self-consciousness and link it with psychodynamic and developmental aspects. Whilst the clinical examples are of pathologically intensified disturbances of self-experience, I believe that they demonstrate vividly the processes involved in more everyday states of self-consciousness.

First it is important to distinguish three varieties of self-consciousness:

1. Self-awareness, the ability to introspect and be conscious of one's self.
2. Embarrassed self-consciousness, a painful and shameful awareness of the self as an object of other's unempathic attention.
3. A compulsive, and hypochondriacal preoccupation with the self: a compelling need to look in mirrors and to evoke mirroring responses from others.

Writing from a phenomenological base, Wilshire (1982) describes the normal state of mimetic engulfment one with another, in which we all exist to some extent much of the time. He discusses the way in which theatre and other arts can give us the means to reflect upon our position and thus become self-aware and more individuated. Speaking developmentally, the achievement of normal self-awareness may be described from various points of view. There is considerable evidence (summarised by Stern, 1983) that the infant can distinguish the self from other at birth and has a good deal of innate perceptual organisation. Mahler's stages of separation and individuation describe the gradual development of a sense of self in parallel with the increasing ability to be physically separate from mother (Mahler et al., 1975). However, the ability to take the self as an object, the emergence of a self that observes the self, must also depend on the beginnings of the representational thinking that is described by Piaget (e.g. 1951). There are a variety of indications that this development takes place in the second half of the second year (Kagan, 1981). Children at this time begin to show signs of concern over behaviour that violates adult standards. Kagan quotes observations which reveal major changes in children's reactions to the distress of others; at this stage they act as if they can

*Reproduced, with the permission of John Wiley & Sons Ltd, from *Self and Identity: Psychological Perspectives* (1987), edited by K. Yardley and J. Honess, pp. 273–284.

infer a psychological state of the other, presumably based on their own experience, and give appropriate responses, such as a hug, a kiss or a request for help from an adult. The most striking evidence is provided by Lewis and Brooks-Gunn (1979) using an experimental method in which a spot of rouge is placed on the child's nose and he or she is then held in front of a mirror; they report that between the ages of 18 and 21 months there occurs a large increase in the number of infants demonstrating self-recognition abilities.

So the development of self-awareness, and the emergence of an observing self, appears to take place according to a largely innately determined timetable interacting with social conditions. However, we might imagine that the appearance of an observing self might be enhanced by the following kind of incident. A child runs indoors, joyfully anticipating telling his mother what he has been up to, but the mother's response is to remark 'Look what a mess you are!'. Here we enter my second category, that of embarrassed self-consciousness. This is much more determined by social conditions, the responses of the caretakers.

The phenomenology here is interesting. The normal situation of an experiencing self against an orienting background self (Spiegal, 1959) is disrupted. The background self is suddenly in the foreground of awareness. The distance between the object of awareness and the subject of awareness collapses, the self becomes as if two-dimensional, and a spiralling feedback ensues, resulting in a panicky disorganisation. An analogy can be drawn with the collapse of the distinction between signifier and signified in psychotic states, as described by Lacan (1957/1977): the normal tripartite structure of symbol, object symbolised, and user of the symbol break down, so that the word, the symbol, is confused with the object or action. Similarly, in states of embarrassed self-consciousness, the distinction between the background and the foreground of awareness collapses, and indeed the experience does seem to have a rather psychotic quality to it. The coinciding of experiencing self and observed self creates a cybernetic problem. In order to function, the experiencing self has to focus on something which is not immediately itself (even if this be a memory or an anticipation of the self), it requires feedback from outside. Interestingly Yardley (1979) explains the efficacy of social skills therapy in relation to social anxiety in terms of the facilitating of other-awareness in place of self-preoccupation.

It is my impression that this kind of self-consciousness often arises when there is an experience or fantasy of an unempathic other observing the self; the more total this identification with the observing other, the more intense the self-consciousness. The presence of the other may be felt to be overwhelming, pushing the subjective self to the margin. Self-consciousness then emerges as a response to the threat to the self.

Like the return of the repressed, the self refuses to be suppressed. One aspect of this experience is the sense of having to be something for the other – initially of having to play a role for the mother. Self-consciousness arises in the threat to this role, in the jarring between the collusive fitting in with the desire of the other and the actual separateness of the self.

A patient spoke of his surprise, pleasure and relief whenever I seemed to be remembering details about him and his history correctly. He described his considerable anxiety that I might make a mistake and confuse him with another patient. The embarrassment he feared was actually my embarrassment: that he might turn out to be other than I expected, that his real self might embarrassingly emerge.

I have consistently found in patients who are prone to self-consciousness a background of a mother who required a child to function as an extension of herself, in such a way that there was no place for the child's separate self. Aspects of the child that were not consistent with the mother's expectations were not recognised. The mother reinforced separation only and ultimately in relation to herself, applauding only those achievements that confirmed *her*. To a significant extent, the child colluded with this need of the mother, often because the pay-off was the maintenance of the special or privileged position in relation to the mother. In these circumstances, the child's real rival for the mother's love is then the false image the mother has of the child. This is the dilemma portrayed in Oscar Wilde's novel, *The Picture of Dorian Gray* (Green, 1979). Here it is the picture, the image, that is loved and with whom Dorian wishes to swap places; the unseen and unmirrored self becomes increasingly degenerate and filled with envy, represented by the hideously deteriorating picture locked away in Dorian's attic. Often with these patients the father, denigrated by the mother, did not function effectively as an oedipal rival, or as a third person who could help separate mother and child. Thus, the child did not receive recognition of his or her own self. In each case, this resulted in strong needs for recognition and affirmation and a consequent vulnerability to the responses and opinions of others. Invariably I have found patients who are prone to self-consciousness to be compulsive accommodators, sensing what is required of them and presenting themselves accordingly.

Although embarrassed self-conscious reactions have been observed even during the first year of life, these become much more pronounced in the latter half of the second year. In terms of traditional psychoanalytic stages of development, the anal stage seems particularly important, with its attendant conflicts over autonomy and control of the body and its contents (Heimann, 1962; Oliner, 1982). The child's experience of sitting on the potty and being observed by the demanding mother may well be a prototype of self-consciousness in the presence of the

overwhelming other. Sander (1983) has described how the child normally adopts a contrary position in the second 18 months. Similarly,
Spitz (1957) has pointed to the significance of the toddler's head shaking gesture and the use of the word 'no'. Winnicott (1963) has emphasised the significance of the toddler's option to 'not communicate', to
protect an inviolate inner core. The child becomes aware that it has a
self to protect. Thus it seems that these struggles for autonomy, the taking of a contrary position and so on, coincide with the emergence of
increased self-consciousness.

Recognition by the parents that the child has a self which unfolds
according to its own blueprint seems crucial. Alice Miller (1979), drawing on the work of Mahler, Kohut and Winnicott, states, 'the child has a
primary need to be seen, noticed and taken seriously as being that
which it is at any given time, and as the hub of its own activity. In con-
tradistinction to drive wishes, we are here dealing with a need which is
narcissistic, but nevertheless equally legitimate, and whose fulfillment
is essential for the development of a healthy self-esteem'.

The selfobject matrix

Kohut has described how a coherent sense of self is dependent, particularly in childhood, upon the presence of empathic responsive figures.
As children we need these others to be there not as separate and
autonomous beings, but to be there reliably, predictably, and responsively. We need them there as a background for our own self. Hence
Kohut termed such figures selfobjects, to indicate that their presence is
experienced as part of the self. Kohut has postulated two separate,
albeit intertwining, lines of development: first, the relationship of self
to object and, second, the relation of self to selfobject. The prime roles
of selfobjects are in terms of their mirroring (empathically responsive)
functions, and their availability for idealisation. Toplin (1983) describes
it thus: 'by merger of self and selfobject we mean psychological con-
nectedness – for instance, between delighted child and mirroring audience, between cranky tired child and idealised, uplifting pillars of
strength and support; between the child who wants company and the
lively partners who lend their presence'. The notion of the selfobject
matrix may be compared to similar concepts, such as Sandler's (1960)
'background of safety', Winnicott's (1963) 'environment mother',
Grotstein's (1981) 'background object of primary identification', and
Bion's (1962) 'container and contained' and maternal reverie. Kohut
emphasises that we never outgrow the need for selfobjects, although
their form changes. Similarly, Kegan (1982), a neo-Piagetian, has
described a model of a helix of development, a succession of holding
environments that support us while we individuate and differentiate.
One implication of these formulations is that the background including

the empathic caretaker is experienced as part of the self so that an abrupt disruption of the relationship to the background, especially any failure of the caretaker's empathy, is felt to be a wrenching away from the orienting framework, resulting in disorientation.

Earlier I referred to Spiegel's notion of an experiencing self against a background self. Here I would postulate that normally the experiencing self is held between a background inside mirrored by a background outside. A similar point is made by Schwartz-Salant (1982, p. 46), who writes 'The need for mirroring from another is lifelong, and represents the inevitable incompleteness that accompanies growth. For mirroring is an externalization of an internal psychic reality. It is based upon the fact that consciousness and the unconscious exist in a relationship of mirror symmetry ... The ego's stability is dependent upon an inner sense of being mirrored by the Self'.

Clinical illustrations

In the following I describe three clinical examples, illustrating disturbances in the relation of self to selfobject.

During one of her sessions, Mrs L. was describing how she was increasingly able to be with her small daughter, Lucy, in a much more relaxed kind of way. She talked of how the two of them might play together, or be busy with some activity together, such as re-potting a plant, and how Lucy might play quietly and privately, secure but alone in the presence of her mother in the background (Winnicott, 1958). She contrasted this with her own experience as a child, of activities with her mother always being focused on *achieving*, and her sense of her mother as an intrusive presence. As she went on to relate this new way of being to her experience in therapy, she suddenly complained of feeling acutely self-conscious and of a sense of being observed. This reminded her of her mother's behaviour with Lucy, how she would tend to talk *about* her grand-daughter rather than simply being with her; she would make comments such as 'Isn't she wonderful! Look what she's doing now!' and so on, in a way which Mrs L. felt turned Lucy into an object. It seemed that in talking *about* her experience in therapy, as opposed to simply living it, she felt she had colluded with an intrusive mother version of me (in the transference), who objectified her. Mrs L. would often describe feeling self-conscious in her sessions at moments when she felt treated as an object to be made sense of rather than a person to be empathically understood. She drew a distinction between being understood from inside, from her subjective position, and being made sense of from a more outside position, which she felt was like being slotted into an interpretation. She found the latter experience to be fragmenting, like being a piece on a chess board; she indicated her wish to be grasped in her totality or, as she put it, to be 'understood as the whole chessboard'. On the other hand, she was very prone to fit in with my interpretations in such a way that we created something false together. She displayed a tension between acting as if she had no separate self – assuming whatever role a situation seemed to require of her – and, on the other hand, an acute and painful awareness of her self as an object for the other.

Much of the time Mrs L. appeared to feel that she had either to be there solely as a selfobject for the other, an echo with no self of her own, or else the other had to be there just as a selfobject for her. She sometimes indicated that she felt compelled to accommodate to my 'atmosphere', but on other occasions she would so fill the room with her words and her atmosphere that I would feel that there was hardly any room for me. She described how she tended to feel either in the centre of *her* world, into which others could be invited, or else she felt pushed to the margin of someone else's world. In this way she described the tension, discussed by Bach (1980), between what he termed 'subjective awareness', the feeling that the world is 'all me', and 'objective self-awareness', the sense of being there for someone else. One of the gains of Mrs L.'s therapy was that she became more capable of sharing, a meeting of worlds, without either party needing to be diminished or taken over.

Mrs L. experienced her mother as an extremely needy and demanding woman, unsatisfied by the father, and exploiting her daughter emotionally; it was as if Mrs L. was required to fill the void left in her mother by the missing paternal function. From seeing her mother's manner with her own daughter, Mrs L. observed how she was affectionate and caring, but at the same time intrusive and controlling. We gradually came to understand a very pervasive pattern in which any aspect of Mrs L. of which her mother disapproved was simply not recognised by her mother; sometimes this would amount to quite gross distortions of reality. During her life Mrs L. had colluded with this to deny aspects of herself. As a result she experienced a deep sense of shame at the surrender of her integrity. However, her acute self-consciousness insured that she was not successful in this denial of herself; at times of greatest dishonesty she would feel the greatest self-consciousness. As I have emphasised in a previous study (Mollon, 1984), shame and self-consciousness are the preservers of the sense of self. Persons whose sense of self is fragile or under threat are particularly prone to self-consciousness. Optimally of course, a secure sense of self, which can be taken for granted, removes the need for painful self-consciousness.

Mrs L. was brought up in accord with stern ideals of always putting the other first. She considered, accurately I think, that she tended to be over-empathic with others, unable to assert her own point of view because she always felt so aware of the other person's position. She was so afraid of seeming selfish that she would end up selfless. In this way she felt compelled to diminish herself, to get rid of aggressive or assertive parts of herself and present herself as small, passively accommodating and sweetly smiling. Periodically she would rebel against this position and engage in violent rows in which the important thing for her was to stand her ground. Mrs L seemed to exist in two distinct states of mind, partially split from each other. On the one hand, there was a state of happy merger in which her needs matched those of the other, a marvellous feeling of being 'in the same atmosphere'; on the other, there was the state of enraged suffocation. Her dilemma was how to have the background selfobject support without the engulfment.

Although tending to be so accommodating, Mrs L. was far from subdued. Her clothes were always colourful and striking, and recognition and admiration were very important to her. From one point of view, she might have been described as an exhibitionist. However, I think that it is quite typical that the more the self is suppressed, paradoxically, the greater the wish to display the self and have it recognised. Essentially this is the point made by Kohut (1971) in his discussion of the natural grandiose self and its need for a mirroring response. A related common phenomenon is the fear, sometimes experienced by children in school assemblies or in church, of doing or shouting something shocking. I think this reflects the mobilisation of intense exhibitionist wishes at times of enforced anonymity. Sometimes this expression of the suppressed self may take on a sadistic quality, and then the associated fantasies are of doing something highly disturbing, aggressive or violent, reflecting again the anal stage (Heimann, 1962; Oliner, 1982). For example, Mrs L. often imagined wrecking my room and creating a big mess.

I have worked with a number of patients who experience self-consciousness when feeling their communications are not immediately understood. This seems analogous to the baby's disturbance when the mother's face appears mask-like and unresponsive, as described in studies by Brazelton et al. (1974) and Tronick et al. (1978). Another clinical observation is that a number of patients who seem particularly prone to self-consciousness have suffered the loss of a parent in early life, or some similar experience of an early arbitrary catastrophe. Such early losses cannot easily be mourned by the young child, especially if the remaining caretakers are less than optimally responsive. The experience then seems to be one of a sudden tearing from the empathic matrix, leaving a frightened self at the centre of a cold and hostile world. These people seem to have internalised the absence of an empathic response in the form of the *presence* of an unempathic internal object.

Another patient, Miss B., of much more severe disturbance, would complain of feeling disturbed and self-conscious if I did not immediately respond to her and indicate a correct understanding of what she was trying to communicate. There was some evidence that Miss B.'s mother may not have been able easily to receive and comprehend her daughter's emotional communications. For example, Miss B. recalled that once as a little girl she had a tantrum, which in retrospect she viewed as an attempt to get her mother's attention. Her mother's response was to take her to the casualty department of a local hospital, assuming that she must be ill!

Often Miss B. would attempt to communicate in a very flat, intellectual, and unemotional way, as if fearing to convey her fears. Although hoping that I could understand and make sense of her anxiety, she seemed convinced that I would regard her in a completely non-comprehending way and judge her mad. In terms of Bion's (1962) model of primitive communication between baby and mother, whereby the baby evokes an anxiety in the mother who can then make sense of this and respond in an appropriate manner which restores order to the baby, my impression was that Miss B. had internalised a maternal imago (an internal object) felt to be hostile to empathic communication. As we explored this issue, she actually stated that she did not believe she could be understood other than in terms of 'a psychiatrist's textbook', i.e. a psychiatric diagnosis. She went on to say that she worked very hard to try to express herself clearly in words because she was sure that if she really were to convey her feelings, there would come a point when I would stop trying to understand her and would dismiss her as mad. The alternative seemed equally horrifying, that I might become completely overwhelmed and as confused and anxious as she felt herself to be. She explained that because of her fear of the impact on the other person she was always acutely conscious of herself, constantly observing and monitoring herself. I think that in this continual monitoring of herself she was attempting to take the place of the other, to exclude the other, with the basic motive of warding off the danger of an unempathic and uncontaining response. (The typical counter-transference reaction in the therapist to this warding off is a feeling of sleepiness and boredom.) In this instance of a young woman who felt herself to be constantly on the edge of a breakdown can be seen the link between the absence of an empathic selfobject in early life, and false self-development in which the person compulsively attempts to accommodate to the other, in such a way as to ward off the other and the danger of further unempathic responses.

A related pattern has been described by Lewis (1963) where she describes the role of watching in a 4-year-old psychotic child. The child showed a peculiar, precocious embarrassed self-conciousness whilst her mother demonstrated a kind of total involvement with the child, constantly present and anxiously watching. Lewis suggested that the child seemed to have identified with the mother's watching, and in this way maintained a link to the mother, while at the same time she affirmed her own sense of self and warded off the terror of engulfment. Issues of self-consciousness are often intimately bound up with looking. Merleau-Ponty (1964) has described an abrupt change in the small child's reactions to the look of the other. Prior to a certain point, the other's look is encouraging, but after this it becomes an embarrassment – 'everything happens as though when he is looked at, his attention is displaced from the task he is carrying out to a representation of himself in the process of carrying it through'.

I have described how embarrassed self-consciousness arises in the gap, in the sudden break-up of a selfobject relationship – in a jarring in the fitting between self and other. This may arise either because the other fails to respond as expected, or because the self no longer fits the other's expectations. Just as self-awareness emerges through the gradual process of separation and individuation, embarrassed self-consciousness seems to arise in the sudden jarring awareness of separateness, in the shuddering loss of the sustaining matrix. The small child may experience this, for example, on his or her first day at school, or when confronted with a stranger whose manner and speech is unfamiliar. A new environment is experienced as unknown, unknowing and unempathic. The child is deprived of the familiar matrix which mirrors, precisely because of its familiarity. In the presence of the stranger, whether this be another person or a newly emerging part ot the self, the child feels awkward and disjointed. A previous harmony is disrupted and the self emerges precipitously from its embeddedness. Similarly, the adolescent may feel gauche and disoriented in response to the rapid and sometimes disconcerting changes in his or her bodily and mental self.

A final example also illustrates my third category: hypochondriacal preoccupation with the self. Miss J., an art photographer, sought therapy some months after the break-up of a relationship. At this time she complained of feeling that her appearance had changed, she felt old and ugly and found herself compulsively looking in mirrors and seeking her reflection in shop windows. She was afraid that she might not be seen, that she might become invisible. Constantly preoccupied with her appearance, she told me she felt continually compelled to take photos of herself. She was particularly concerned with what she felt to be changes in the appearance of her eyes (I's), since she had always regarded these as a constant feature against her ever-changing inner state. All these sensations reminded her of similar feelings at the age of five, when she and her family had moved from Italy, where she was born. She quickly settled into a selfobject transference in which I was required to be responsive as a reflective mirroring presence, and to be constantly so as a background for her changing and contradictory states of mind. Any evidence of inattention or boredom on my part was extremely disturbing to her. At one point she went on holiday on her own, feeling very alone. She described looking out of her small room and seeing happy and beautiful people, and then looking in her mirror and seeing an old lady; she felt that she did not fit with her surroundings, she did not belong. She experienced a similar panic and depersonalisation when she had to leave the studio in which she had worked for many years, and which she clearly experienced as part of her. The importance of her studio, she explained, was that wherever she went within it, it reflected her. In both instances, and also in the early experience of leaving Italy, she felt wrenched from an environment or person in which she had felt embedded. She then found herself lost and alone in an alien context which did not mirror her in a familiar way. Her sense of self was then considerably disturbed.

Like Mrs L., Miss J. tended to sense automatically what the other required of her, subtly responding to cues so efficiently that it was not usually at all apparent that she was doing this. She was acutely sensitive to my response to her and would become panicky if she felt I was not interested. She would constantly look at me during the session, and indeed seemed to be always seeking the right kind of look from others. She recalled how when she was young her mother would look at her, and be preoccupied with her appearance; at one time she had felt this to be flattering, but now it seemed to her to have been more controlling. The picture that emerged was that her mother had unrealistically praised her, maintaining an idealised image of her. Although gratifying, this had left her trapped, locked into the look of her mother as Narcissus at the pool, dreading to move away from her mother's orbit. In the world at large she appeared to experience a kind of chronic embarrassed self-consciousness.

What she had not received from her mother, it seemed, was recognition of herself as a separate autonomous being. In the transference she was continually afraid that I would withdraw my support and enviously undermine her attempts to express herself. She described a sense of always having had to be merely an echo, a stooge, for her mother, who indeed may well have been undermining her daughter's attempts to separate and individuate. The corresponding internal object almost certainly consisted of aspects of her mother's actual personality, combined with projections of Miss J.'s own envy and jealousy of her parents' relationship with each other. It appeared that she had longed for, but never felt she got, an admiring and affirming look from her father. Her conscious attitude towards him was one of defensive scorn, but behind this we found a deeper love for him as an idealised figure. It became clear that what she had sought was the look from her father that would release her from the grip of the look of her mother, and allow her to be herself. Her father was the oedipal third term whom she longed for to free her from her prison of narcissism.

A brief consideration of the nature of mirroring is appropriate here. Pines (1982) has explored the concept in a wide-ranging discussion of clinical and historical aspects. The term has been popularised by Kohut (1971), whose concept of mirroring is based on the model of the 'gleam in the mother's eye' in response to the child's natural exhibitionism. However, it is clear throughout his writings that really what he is referring to is the caretaker's general empathic availability (Mollon, 1985). Zinkin (1983), in discussing benevolent and malignant aspects of mirroring, points to the way in which it is through the empathic responsiveness of the other that one comes to know who one is – the original mirror being the mother's face (Winnicott, 1971) – and that Lichtenstein (1977) talks of mirroring in terms of the mother's selective responsiveness to the infant, whereby she picks out only certain aspects of the infant's potential to recognise and encourage, and thereby imparts an 'identity theme'. This is a view that also emphasises the mother's role in facilitating or impeding the development of the sense of self. In the present study I have argued that a familiar environment, including the non-human environment, can have a mirroring function, affirming the sense of self: the environment is experienced as a selfobject. I have also postulated that mirroring is an internal function, the experiencing self against a background self, a relationship which like any other relationship can be disrupted. Another type of internal mirroring is described by Pyszcynski and Greenberg (1987). He reports that certain depressives may selectively focus upon their failings and inadequacies, protecting themselves from disappointment. (A similar view is proposed by Mollon and Parry, 1984.)

In the case of Miss J., the loss of her previous relationship, functioning as a selfobject background, had led to the emergence of a grandiose self, shoring up a disintegrating self-representation, and combined with an imperious demand for mirroring. In the absence of a human mirroring partner, she had turned to actual mirrors and to photographing herself. The use of mirrors to restore the sense of self in lieu of a human mirroring response seems very common. Mrs L., for example, spoke of a compelling need to look attractive. She explained that when she felt chaotic internally she would look in a mirror and feel both amazed and reassured that her outer appearance was still organised. Her body image was actually rather unstable and she often described a feeling that her body was changing shape in some way. She was able to talk to me about this only after she had reached the point of feeling more confident that she could be recognised by others – that she could come to her therapy in different moods and states of mind and still be recognised as the same person. I am aware of the link here with Lacan's (1937/1977) mirror stage, wherein the fragmented body image is jubilantly replaced by the new coherence of the image of the self in the mirror – a process that Lacan sees as involving a fundamental alienation; the lived self is confused with the image out there. However, the glass mirror is a poor substitute for the kind of mirroring that is really needed – which is a more active responsive one, the human empathic response that sees and understands in depth, and goes beyond the surface images to the living, experiencing, and communicating, self.

Summary

A distinction can be made between self-awareness, self-consciousness and preoccupation with the self. *Self-awareness* seems to unfold according to an innately determined timetable in interaction with the early social environment. In the case of patients prone to embarrassed *self-consciousness*, a frequent background is one in which the normal situation is reversed so that the child becomes a selfobject to the mother. The child is not recognised for who she really is, but is captured by a projected image from the mother's psyche. The father does not effectively intervene in such a way as to break this spell and allow the child her own identity. As a result of this, the child becomes prone to embarrassed self-consciousness in the discrepancy between who she is experienced to be, and will develop an abnormally intense need for a mirroring selfobject to sustain the sense of self. In the absence of appropriate mirroring responsiveness, the person falls into the state I have called *hypochondriacal preoccupation with the self.*

Narcissistic vulnerability and the fragile self: a failure of mirroring*

The phenomenon of narcissistic vulnerability

The phenomenon can be classed under the three categories of vulnerability, injury and rage. The term ' narcissistic vulnerability' is used here to refer to a fragility and uncertainty in the sense of self. A narcissistically vulnerable person is prone to show strong reactions to the narcissistic injuries of feeling slighted, ignored or treated without respect or empathy. The most prominent reaction is of narcissistic rage (Kohut, 1972) – with secondary reactions of depressive withdrawal or of a retreat to an arrogant, grandiose and somewhat paranoid state of mind. These overt reactions seem to be protective responses to a more fundamental injury of break-up of the sense of self. For example, in a previ-

*Reproduced, with the permission of the British Psychological Society, from the *British Journal of Medical Psychology* (1986) 59, 317–324.

ous paper (Mollon and Parry, 1984), it was suggested that certain states of depressive withdrawal may function as a protective 'closing off' response in the face of narcissistic injury; often this may take the form of a ruminatory retreat to a mental state of sado-masochistic self-flagellation, or to an equally ruminatory preoccupation with feelings of grudge and fantasies of revenge and triumph.

These manoeuvres seem designed to restore the sense of self. Broucek (1979) has suggested that one important component of the sense of self is the sense of efficacy. Here it is argued that a particularly crucial aspect of this sense of efficacy is the awareness of a capacity to evoke an appropriate and meaningful emotional response in the other person, originally the parents.

History of the concept

The concept of narcissistic vulnerability does not appear in Laplanche and Pontalis' (1973) scholarly dictionary of psychoanalytic terms. It is, however, implicit and sometimes explicit in the writings of a number of theorists, including Freud. Indeed, it seems possible that Freud might have given more prominence to this notion had not Adler made the wish to overcome the feelings of inferiority and narcissistic injury the basis of his rival theory of 'individual psychology' (e.g. 1917, 1929). Indeed, Adler may be credited as the first to write extensively on narcissistic injury and vulnerability, although he did not use these terms. A contemporary view, which, although more sophisticated, is close to Adler's, is that of Rothstein (1980), who speaks of narcissistic injury as an insult to the 'narcissistic image of perfection' which, he argues, we all to some extent try to maintain, some people being more vulnerable in this respect than others. Another notable early contribution was that of Rado (1928) who wrote about certain melancholic patients who showed a marked 'narcissistic intolerance', a tendency to react strongly and depressively to relatively minor disappointments and insults, and also an inordinate need for 'narcissistic supplies' of love and approval.

A number of authors have discussed aggression and rage in the context of narcissistic vulnerability. Rochlin (1973) argued persuasively that much of human aggression is a response to narcissistic injuries, taking as one of his models the rage and hatred of change shown by some autistic children. He did not, however, discuss the possible origins of such vulnerability in early relationships with parents. However, Lichtenstein (1971), in a paper on the 'malignant No', described individuals who had felt negated in their very existence by parental responses and who consequently experienced a great need to impose their will on others. This theme was also addressed in Kohut's (1972) discussion of narcissistic rage. The need to make others obey one's will was seen as an expression of the frustrated normal narcissistic needs to feel that others are available and responsive.

Kohut's psychology of the self (1971, 1977, 1984) provides a broader understanding of normal narcissistic needs as well as narcissistic disturbance. Kohut emphasised the importance of an early empathic milieu in the development of a coherent and cohesive self. The following clinical illustrations are chosen to highlight a particular aspect of this needed empathy, which when absent can lead to narcissistic vulnerability.

Clinical illustration from individual psychotherapy

Mrs W. functioned well in many areas of her life, but suffered from a profound although subtle disturbance in her sense of self. For example, if she felt unfocused upon by another person she would feel overwhelmed with an uncertainty over who she really was, or even with doubts about her existence. She described the experience as like 'being pushed out of the picture'. The worst thing for her was to be in the presence of someone, such as her lover, whom she might expect to focus upon her and to feel that this person was distracted or preoccupied. At such times she would often fly into a rage. During her sessions, by the very nature of the therapy, she more easily felt focused upon and derived a sense of well-being from this. However, she would react with rage or withdrawal if the therapist's comments or interpretations were not quite in line with her own concerns. At these moments she seemed to experience the therapist as a preoccupied mother, not seeing her but with some other picture in his mind, perceiving him as wishing to impose his own order on her. Often she would describe violent, 'anarchic' fantasies of wrecking the room. Eventually it was understood that what she was really rebelling against was the order that she felt kept her at an emotional distance. Her mother did indeed seem to have been a chronically anxious and busy woman, preoccupied with order and routine.

The nature of her difficulty is illustrated in the following more detailed material from a session. First, Mrs W. talked of how her face had been bruised by a dentist's injection the previous day. She said she had phoned the dentist but he had seemed rather casual, suggesting that if it were still bad the next day she could 'pop in some time'. Mrs W. had felt angry afterwards because the dentist obviously did not appreciate that she could not just 'pop in' because his surgery was miles away. Then Mrs W., who is a journalist, talked of how she had recently sent an article to a magazine. Not having received any reply, she had kept phoning them but could not get through to anyone who knew about it. She had then called into the office and spoken to the editor, but he seemed very busy and preoccupied, and said that he had given the article to someone else to read. She was unable to locate this other person. Next Mrs W. spoke of how her lover was very frantic and busy and preoccupied with his work. Then she complained of what a long journey it was to get to her therapy sessions – with the implication that the therapist did not appreciate how difficult it was for her. Then she emphasised her awful state of feeling 'nothing', feeling disintegrated when she was not focused upon, and of having 'no sense of self' (the phrase she used).

The therapist said to her at this point that she seemed to be describing a very fundamental experience of helplessness, a sense of not existing, perhaps like a small child or baby might feel when she does not evoke a thoughtful meaningful response from mother, when she feels she just cannot 'get through', and that, on the other hand, it appeared that she felt real and alive when finding that she could evoke a thoughtful emotional response. Mrs W. seemed calmed by this interpretation and spoke then of her sense of well-being when she was attended to, and particularly when with cheerful people who were in tune with her. She contrasted this with her feeling like 'nothing' if she looked at her lover and found that he was preoccupied and did not look at her, or if he looked at her with an eye that did not really see her. The therapist commented that this must be like looking in a mirror and seeing no reflection. Agreeing, she then spoke of her mother's anxious and depressed state of mind in a way which led to an understanding of her experience of trying to look in the mirror of mother's face but not seeing a lively response that reflected her mother seeing her; instead what she saw reflected the mother's preoccupation which pushed her out of the picture.

Theoretical discussion 1

Winnicott (1967), whose theorising was in many ways close to that of Kohut, described the mirroring function of the responsive mother's face in giving the child a sense of self. He wrote: 'What does the baby see when he or she looks in the mother's face? I am suggesting that, ordinarily, what the baby sees is himself or herself. In other words, the mother is looking at the baby and what she looks like is related to what she sees there' (p. 131) and he gave the formula 'I look, I am seen, so I exist'. Mrs W. illustrates the consequences of not feeling seen – when looking in the mother's face and seeing a reflection that does not mirror.

The mirroring that is required is, however, more than the expression in the mother's face. Mrs W. sought an attentive look, but clearly this was only as surface evidence of the underlying thoughtful engagement with her. The term 'mirroring' and Winnicott's concept of the reflecting mother's face and Kohut's model of the 'gleam in the mother's eye' do suggest a surface reflection – whereas what is needed is a response that sees the child in depth (Mollon, 1985). This point is, however, implicit in the writing of both Winnicott and Kohut. For example, Winnicott sees the analyst's activity, which is clearly not in a visual mode, as 'a complex derivative of the face that reflects what there is to be seen' (p. 137).

Broucek (1979) suggested that the basis of the sense of self is the experience of efficacy. He reviewed experimental and observational studies of infants which point to the importance of the young child's experience of having some influence over the world, the capacity pre-dictably to bring about some event and, conversely, the baby's distress when the mother reacts in ways which are unresponsive to the baby, e.g. the mother with the blank face when the baby expects a smiling face. If this view is combined with Winnicott's observations about the mother's mirror function, it seems reasonable to suggest that the fun-damental efficacy that is important is the child's ability to evoke an appropriate response from the mother or father – to evoke interest and thought. This can be linked to Bion's (1962) notion that the basis of communication between infant and mother is the infant's capacity to evacuate its tension and distress – which initially for the baby has no meaning – and to evoke an anxiety in the mother; the mother then, through responding thoughtfully and appropriately, gives back the baby's proto-communication in a modified and more meaningful form. Thus it may be that it is the successful evoking of a thoughtful and emotionally meaningful response that gives the basic affirmation of the sense of self. Conversely, the fundamental helplessness and rage experi-enced by narcissistically vulnerable individuals may be the response to the inability to evoke a meaningful emotional response.

This suggestion can also be compared to Basch's (1975) model of the mother's function of providing a predictable response which sup-ports the brain's need for ordering of patterns of input; failure of this may result in lowered self-esteem, hopelessness and depression. Similarly Broussard and Cornes (1981) describe the 'mother–infant sys-tem in distress' when the infant's messages are not heard, received and appropriately responded to.

Shame seems to be a further component of narcissistic vulnerability. Discussing the early precursors of shame, Broucek (1982) described primitive shame responses in infants when the world does not respond as expected. One aspect of that shame is the experience of embarrass-ment. As a generalisation, we might say that embarrassment occurs in response to misunderstanding, mismatch or miscommunication – a jar-ring in the expectations one has of another. Broucek's observation is certainly consistent with this. Clinical observations suggest that, if a child grows up with a mother who does not see him or her as they actually are, but who has some other picture in her mind, they will become prone to the experience of shame and embarrassment.

Embarrassment seems to be the response to the jarring disruption of the collusive accommodation to the other's expectations. The related affect of humiliation occurs when one feels rendered powerless, or one's efficacy is removed, by a powerful other. Then, like de Sade, one may experience a compulsion to humiliate and render the other powerless (Lichtenstein, 1971).

Clinical illustration from group psychotherapy

The group is long term, weekly and analytically oriented, and the illustrations are taken from a period of 4 weeks. During this period these issues became highlighted and stimulated for various members of the group by the arrival of a new member, Joan, who sat in silence for most of her initial sessions, her occasional comments when she was spoken to being most remarkable for their cruelty and their apparent lack of empathy. The others complained of how she avoided eye contact with them, and how generally she was a disconcertingly unresponsive presence. Her arrival seemed to function as a contextual stimulus or adaptive context (Langs, 1978) for these concerns, creating a group theme which resonated with the early experiences of several members.

One member, Bill, would at certain times tend to flood the group with endless talk, which effectively destroyed the possibility of any meaningful or creative discourse taking place. Gradually, over a period of time, it had become clear that this was not simply a response to anxiety, but more specifically a reaction when he felt something was going on between other people which he did not understand and could not participate in. His behaviour would give the impression of envious attacks on any potentially creative coupling in the group – a hypothesis later modified. On one occasion when the group was preoccupied with Joan's unresponsive behaviour, he remarked that sometimes he had felt 'psychologically obliterated' when the therapist had turned away from him and not looked at him. It was possible to link this usefully to his experience of his parents as largely uninterested in him. A little later, his relationship with his wife deteriorated and he left home temporarily (although at that point he was not sure whether it was temporary). He mentioned that his wife had told him that the children did not seem to notice that he was not there – ostensibly a reassuring comment, but obviously really a rather hostile one, which was clearly very disturbing to him. This led to an exploration of what he called his 'dread of evaporation', of not mattering, or of not being noticed. It became clear then that this dread of not mattering and of not being noticed was what had led at times to his insistent and demanding chatter in the group.

A further example from the same period concerns Toby, a very narcissistically sensitive man, rather aloof, but very aware of other people's reactions to him, and prone to the experience of shame and embarrassed self-consciousness. His presenting symptom was a fear of sweating in public. A relevant feature of his background was that his father was almost entirely absent during his childhood, visiting only occasionally for sex with the patient's mother; the latter was a rather possessive woman who, for example, tried to hide Toby's shoes when he first began dating girls. During one group meeting Toby asserted his belief that the therapist had certain favourites in the group but that he was not one of them. Since this perception was not shared by others in the group, he was led to consider its origins. He went on to say that, although he tried not to think of his father, he had recently found himself thinking about the fact that his father did not give a damn about him – that his father had visited only in order to have sex with his mother. Describing how when he was 18 he had tried to contact his father, who had not responded, he said, 'He just didn't care at all – it seems unreal – I'm just amazed'. He then became tearful. Some time was then spent understanding his intense wish for closeness to men, and specifically his wish to be close and special to the therapist as a paternal figure in the group. Following this he returned to talking about his amazement at his father's indifference, emphasising how he could not believe it, and how it seemed unreal. At this point the therapist said to him, 'The thought of your father's indifference makes you *feel* unreal – like looking in a mirror and seeing no reflection'. Toby accepted this and went on to describe how he would see others in the group looking at the therapist as they talked to him but he was aware that he could not look – he could not talk and carry on looking. He explained that it is 'because when you are looking at someone you are seeing the empathy'. It then became obvious to him that his dread was of seeing *no* empathic response.

Another member, Jill, who would often complain angrily if she felt the therapist was not paying enough attention to her, remarked that she would look at the therapist to check that he was attending to her, and that this looking was reassuring. Toby commented that whereas Jill would anxiously look at the therapist for reassurance, he was *afraid* to look. He then moved on to talk of what his father's attitude had meant to him – how it felt to him now like a bit of him was missing, adding 'I don't know what I've got to base my sense of self on'. The therapist interpreted that he felt something to be missing from his sense of self that would be based on the presence of a responsive and interested father who cared about him, and that he was experiencing an intense longing for that bit of him that was missing. This seemed to make sense to Toby. A couple of weeks later he returned to a similar theme, this time saying he thought the therapist merely tolerated his presence in the group, and that really he felt he had no place and no role. He thought that the therapist was more responsive to another group member, Jill, because she was sexually attractive. This led him eventually to again associate to his father and the fact that his father had only visited his mother for sex. Toby began to wonder whether he had felt that he had nothing to attract or interest his father, and that in the group he was re-experiencing this in feeling that he did not have this woman's sexual power to interest the therapist. This insight, which he arrived at quite spontaneously on his own, turned out to be crucial to him in helping him to understand a very profound feeling of inadequacy and helplessness.

Theoretical discussion 2

These examples from the normal group illustrate different reactions to the absence of a normally expected response of some degree of interest and empathy. Joan's behaviour in the group would probably have been disturbing to anyone for, as Kohut (1983) has argued, we all need throughout life a measure of empathy from others, as necessary for psychological life as oxygen is for physical survival. For some patients her behaviour was particularly evocative because it resonated with earlier experiences with parents who could not be thoughtfully emotionally engaged. Jill would anxiously scrutinise the therapist to check that he was aware of her, responding to her and thinking about her – rather like Winnicott's (1967) description of the baby studying the maternal visage in an attempt to predict mother's mood and ascertain when mother might be attending. Toby, on the other hand, was afraid to look, as if he might look in a mirror and see no image of himself, an experience that would be profoundly de-realising. Bill, through his non-stop chatter, found a way of insisting that he was listened to, thereby avoiding his own fear of psychological 'obliteration', but at the same time effectively obliterating others.

Why is this lack of response so disrupting of one's sense of self? A plausible generalisation might be that, if one cannot evoke a thoughtful emotional response in the other, one begins to feel unreal and to doubt one's existence. Without the normally expected response, something is felt to be missing and, as Kohut (1971, 1977) has convincingly argued, what is missing is felt to be part of the self. The sense of self seems to be based in part on the awareness of a capacity to be of significance to others.

This may have a bearing on the roots of certain quasi-envious behaviour. The material of the last example led very clearly back to the primal scene (Freud, 1918), the sexual relationship between the parents, which is often thought in psychoanalytic work to pose such a problem for the child of intense envy and jealousy. In the earlier example, Bill's behaviour in the group gave the impression at one point of an envious attack on coupling – on the primal scene – an attempt to prevent meaningful intercourse between members. However, in view of what was eventually understood, Bill's reactions suggest that the apparent envy evoked by the fantasy of the primal scene may stem to some extent from a dread of no longer existing in the minds of the parents so engrossed with each other – a primal impotence, a helpless sense of having no place and no capacity to engage the parents.

Toby's deprivation was particularly in relation to his father, and it may be that the father has a particular significance in facilitating the development of the sense of self. This derives from the fact that the child has not emerged from the father's body. The father is more 'other', the 'knight in shining armour' (Mahler and Gosliner, 1955), beckoning the child towards a more individuated state. This role of the father in fostering separation–individuation, in releasing the child from the dyad with mother, has been emphasised particularly by analysts in France (Lacan, 1957; Grunberger, 1979; McDougall, 1980; Chiland, 1982) and also earlier by Loewald (1951). Moreover, through being empathically responsive to the child's wish to be admired, the little boy for being male and being *like* father, and the little girl for being female and able to *flirt playfully* with father, the father helps to affirm the child's gender identity (Stoller, 1975, 1977).

Implications for clinical practice

If the therapist understands the possible origins in narcissistic injury of a variety of states of mind (rage; arrogant, scornful, grandiose and mildly paranoid states; depressive states), he or she can more easily restore the patient's equilibrium through interpretive comments that communicate empathic understanding. Through the repeated experience of this the patient gradually becomes more aware of narcissistic tensions and vulnerability; this in itself helps him or her achieve greater mastery of narcissistic injuries. This process is discussed from a Kohutian point of view by Goldberg (1973).

The clinical examples also show the patient's effort at recovery through mastery of the original injury. Giving up his characteristically aloof stance, Toby attempted again to evoke an interested response, now in the transference to the therapist. He declared that the therapist disliked him and preferred others; less consciously his hope was that this time he would receive an affirming, empathic and understanding response, and his fear was that he would receive further injury. The therapist's interpretations provided this understanding, thereby demonstrating to him that he could evoke thought and encouraging him to continue seeking the narcissistic sustenance necessary to strengthen his fragile sense of self.

There are, however, certain aspects of the analytic situation which may be very disturbing to narcissistically vulnerable individuals. The analytic stance of neutral listening involves giving minimal facial and verbal responses for much of the time. Thus, even if the analyst can be seen, he or she typically has a non-mirroring face. When the analyst speaks and interprets, this can be an enormous relief to the narcissistically vulnerable patient because it is an indication that, in spite of the absence of facial mirroring, the therapist has been listening and thinking. It may be that the tension between the absence of immediate visual mirroring and the eventual hearing of the interpretation is important; the anxiety of not successfully communicating, and therefore not being empathically understood, is repeatedly relieved via the appropriate interpretation. Brenman-Pick (1985), in a discussion of the role of counter-transference, has emphasised the importance of the analyst's being affected by a patient's communications, suggesting that what really determines whether an interpretation is deep, as opposed to shallow, is the extent to which the patient's communication has been worked through and thought about in the analyst's mind. A superficial empathy is not sufficient. Thus, it may be the repeated experience of being understood in depth that builds up the sense of self, based upon the capacity to evoke feeling and thought in the other.

Summary of the narcissistic affects

Shame concerns the sense of self and the image of the self. Whereas in guilt, a more object-related affect, the pain is over an action or an impulse to action, in shame the pain concerns the image of the self. In states of shame, images of the self as weak, defective, pathetic, exposed and violated come to the fore. Shame may also arise when an *illusion* of grandiosity is exposed. As described by Kohut, deficiences in the availability of responsive mirroring selfobjects in childhood may lead to an intensification and fixation of infantile grandiosity which leave the adult prone to shame. In practice, shame and guilt often occur simultaneously.

Related to shame is the experience of humiliation which is associated with the experience of an other imposing their will and rendering one helpless or impotent.

Also intimately associated with shame is the painful and disturbing state of embarrassed self-consciousness. Embarrassment occurs when a person violates the other's expectation. Embarrassed self-consciousness occurs when a person emerges from a mental state of embeddedness in the other – the self that had been hidden is now painfully in focus. Individuals prone to self-consciousness have felt they must play a role for the mother – must 'be-for-the-other'. Self-consciousness arises in the jarring between the collusive fitting in with the desire of the other and the actual separateness of the self. The person in this state feels him- or herself to be in an unempathic milieu; he or she is identified with an unempathic observer looking on at the self. The 'short circuit' effect of focusing on one's self can be extremely disorganising.

Interestingly, this experience is also one of painful awareness of separateness, of difference, of 'standing out', and thus may function to rescue the sense of self which may otherwise be surrendered.

Embarassed self-consciousness may be distinguished from two other varieties of self-consciousness. First, normal self-awareness which is not pathology but a developmental achievement. Secondly, what might be called hypochondriacal preoccupation with the self – an anxious awareness of a sense of the bodily or mental self breaking up or altering its shape. This seems to relate to the absence or breaking of a stabilising relationship with an empathic selfobject.

Narcissistic vulnerability may be regarded as a sensitivity to slights, insults, experiences of feeling ignored or overlooked or treated without respect or thought. This fragility in the sense of self may make the person prone to reactions of rage or depression as well as shame. This appears to stem from early experiences of failure to evoke a thoughtful empathic emotional response in the parents.

All the narcissistic affects may be understood in terms of Kohut's paradigm as varieties of disturbance in the relationship between self and empathic selfobject.

Narcissistic affects and the taxonomy of self-disturbance

Category 1: differentiation

Lewis (1971) describes shame-prone personalities as having poorly differentiated self-boundaries.

Category 2: agency

Shame is associated with feelings of helplessness, inadequacy and powerlessness – a lack of agency. Humiliation is associated with experiences of the imposition of someone else's power. Narcissistic vulnerability involves a sense of inability to to evoke an empathic emotional response in others.

Category 3: objective self

Shame is associated with self-images as weak, defective, inadequate etc. – perhaps involving the collapse of a grandiose image.

Category 4: structure–organisation

Shame and self-consciousness often involve disorganisation – the person may become incoherent. Hypochondriacal preoccupation with the self involves a sense of personal disintegration or instability of the bodily and mental self.

Category 5: balance between subjective and objective self

In shame and self-consciousness a preoccupation with the other's view of the self, the 'Me', is predominant, overruling the experience from within (the 'I'). A disorganising experience of self-consciousness may give rise to further feelings of shame. In Wright's terms, the self-as-object predominates.

Category 6: illusions of self-sufficiency

The narcissistic injuries giving rise to feelings of shame and humiliation often prompt a defensive narcissistic retreat into protective illusions of self-sufficiency. In Mollon and Parry (1984), this is described in relation to states of depression. When these illusions collapse there may be catastrophic experiences of shame and humiliation.

Category 7: sense of lineage

People sometimes feel shame in relation to their sense of lineage. There may, for example, be shame about parents or ancestry. This shame may motivate attempts at disavowal of lineage.

Chapter 4
Narcissistic personality

Introduction and outline of discussion

Narcissistic phenomena may be found in every personality insofar as these concern processes of maintenance of the various aspects of the experience and structure of self. However, as Kernberg (1974) points out, there are 'a group of patients in whom the main problem appears to be a disturbance of their self regard in connection with a specific disturbance in their object relations ... ' – an observation that can be further elaborated by reference to the more differentiated categories of self-disturbance in the taxonomy. Much of the current debate over the nature of narcissistic personality polarises around the views of Kernberg and Kohut.

In addition to these two, seven other theorists (and in one case a group of theorists) are discussed here to provide a representative spectrum of views.

From these I have extracted prominent themes, which are then compared across the theories. These are also compared with the themes of the myth of Narcissus and Echo. The theories are also examined for the categories of self-disturbance which they address.

Kernberg

Kernberg (1974) sees the main characteristics of these patients as grandiosity, extreme self-centredness and a remarkable absence of interest in and empathy for others. In elaborating these points he describes the following:

- They display an unusual degree of self reference in interactions with others.
- They display a great need to be loved and admired.
- They show an apparent contradiction between a very inflated idea of

themselves and their superiority, and an inordinate need for tribute from others, for 'narcissistic supplies'.

• Feelings of superiority and omnipotence alternate with feelings of inferiority.

• Their emotional life is shallow and they experience little empathy for the feelings of others.

• They idealise some people from whom they expect narcissistic supplies and treat with contempt those from whom they do not expect anything.

• Their relationships tend to be exploitative and sometimes parasitic – they feel they have a right to control and possess others and to exploit without guilt; behind a superficial charm they may be quite ruthless.

• In spite of needing so much tribute from others they are unable to really depend on anyone because of their deep distrust and depreciation of others.

• They are unable to experience depressive feelings of sadness and mourning in relation to others.

In Kernberg's view the narcissistic patient shows some similarity to borderline patients in underlying defensive structure, but the narcissistic patient is more stable, may have relatively good social functioning and may be highly successful or creative.

The pathological grandiose self

Kernberg considers the relative stability of the narcissistic personality may be due to the pathological fusion of the internal images of ideal self, ideal object and actual self – a structure he terms the 'grandiose self'. He suggests that it is as if these patients were saying:

> I do not need to fear I will be rejected for not living up to the ideal of myself which alone makes it possible for one to be loved by the ideal person I imagine would love me. That ideal person and my ideal image of that person and my real self are all one, and better than the ideal person whom I wanted to love me, so that I do not need anybody else anymore.

Thus, in this way the normal tension between actual self on the one hand and ideal object, on the other, is eliminated. The left over unacceptable self-images are repressed and projected onto others who are then devalued and treated with contempt.

Kernberg argues that the devaluation is not only of external figures but also of internalised object images. As a result the internal images are lifeless and shadowy, and this leads to the experience of other people as lifeless shadows or marionettes. Certain others are idealised but these turn out to be carrying projections of the person's own aggrandised self-images: 'All that seems to exist in the inner world of these patients are idealised representations of the self, the "shadows" of others and dreaded enemies.'

What is defended against?

Kernberg suggests that all of these interpersonal and intrapsychic manoeuvres are defending against the experience of 'a hungry, enraged, empty self, full of impotent anger at being frustrated and fearful of a world which seems as hateful and revengeful as the patient himself'. The avoidance of this state of mind is the basic motive for the creation of the crucial pathological fusion of ideal self, ideal object and actual self.

In the development of this feared state, Kernberg places great emphasis upon the 'pathologically augmented development of oral aggression'. Regarding the origins of this augmented oral aggression he suggests it is due to: (1) a constitutionally strong aggressive drive; (2) a constitutional lack of anxiety tolerance; or (3) severe frustration in the first years.

Kernberg does suggest that certain patterns of early relationships with parents may be relevant, but these are not his main emphasis. He comments, for example, that 'chronically cold parental figures with intense but covert aggression are a frequent feature of the background'. He adds that often the patient possessed some inherent quality or talent which could have aroused the envy or admiration of others. This special talent became a refuge against basic feelings of being unloved. In addition, often the patient occupied a pivotal position in the family structure – e.g. an only child, or the only 'brilliant child'.

Limitations of Kernberg's model

Whilst Kernberg presents a convincing account of the personality structure and dynamics of the narcissistic character, his view of the early enviroment seems crude and simplistic. For example, his reference to early 'frustration' is simply not elaborate enough at a psychological level. The concept has an almost biological quality, giving no real indication of what goes on between parent and child. Kernberg does not discuss the way in which the early enviroment may impede normal development and facilitate narcissistic development. He emphasises the patient's exploitativeness but does not examine how the patient may have *been* exploited as a child. The theme of exploitation pervades the myth of Narcissus. Moreover, Kernberg does not discuss narcissistic *needs* in childhood and the consequences of their thwarting.

Prominent themes in Kernberg's model

- Grandiosity – idealisation of self.
- Illusion of self-sufficiency – retreat from object-relatedness and avoidance of dependence.
- Self-centredness and limited capacity for empathy.
- Exploitation of others.

Self-disorder categories

1. [Differentiation] No.
2. [Subjective self] Yes – the grandiose self-image.
3. [Objective self] Yes – the grandiose self-image.
4. [Structure–organisation] No.
5. [Balance between subjective and objective self] No.
6. [Illusion of self-sufficiency] Yes.
7. [Sense of lineage] No.

Kohut

Kohut (1971, 1977) casts his model of narcissistic disturbance in the framework of a particular theory of development. In particular he sees narcissism as having its own line of development rather than simply being given up, surrendered to reality or transformed into object-love, as implied in Freud's (1914) original formulation. According to Kohut, as reality impinges on the original state of narcissistic perfection (perhaps this perfection can be understood as a hypothetical state of the infant, only approximated at times), the child's narcissism develops in two directiions. First to form a grandiose exhibitionistic component, requiring a responsive 'mirroring' from the caregivers; secondly to form an idealising component, which seeks a powerful and good figure whom the child can admire and in whose glory and perfection the child can bask. In the first position, it is as if the child says 'I am perfect'; in the second position the child says 'You are perfect and I am part of you'. The availability of these figures who can either be responsively mirroring of the child's greatness or can carry the child's idealisation is crucial to the child's sense of well-being – insofar as they function in this way for the child they are termed 'selfobjects', the fusion of words 'self' and 'other' indicating that they are *functionally* part of the child's self. If these narcissistic needs are thwarted too much, or if the child is traumatically failed by a parent in his or her selfobject functioning, the normal narcissistic development, whereby those components of the personality are gradually modified, through repeated non-traumatic contact with reality, and transformed into mature ambitions and ideals, cannot take place. The infantile grandiosity and needs to idealise remain repressed and unintegrated.

Selfobject functions and selfobject fusion

Kohut's notion of the selfobject refers to our dependence on psychological *functions* provided by others. For example, a child's sense of liveliness and well-being may depend on the availability of lively responsive caregivers; similarly the analysand may be dependent upon the empathic mirroring responsiveness of the analyst. This dependence on the *functions* provided by others – which Kohut argues we never fully outgrow – does *not* mean a failure to differentiate self and other; it does not indicate a fusion of the representations of self and other, nor, to use Kleinian terminology, does it mean a state of projective identification with the object. However, a reading of Kohut's clinical illustrations reveals that, in many cases, he describes a state of pathological fusion between patient and mother. What he seems to mean here is that if the normal selfobject availability of mother to child is reversed, so that the child is required to be selfobject for mother, required to ensure mother's well-being and mirroring mother's grandiosity, then the child's spontaneous self-development is derailed in favour of the mother's agenda. The child develops a false self (to use Winnicott's term), based on adaptation to the mother.

The bipolar self and the nuclear self

In his 1977 work, Kohut describes a model of a self-structure based on this theory of development through selfobjects. Using an electrical analogy, he postulates a 'bipolar self' – one pole being the grandiose–exhibitionistic component, forming ambitions, the other being the idealising component, forming ideals and values – linked by a 'tension arc' of the person's talents and skills. According to this model, disturbances might lie in either pole or in both – damage in one may be compensated by strength in the other; similarly, in the child's development, failure of the admiring selfobject may be compensated by the child successfully being able to turn to an idealised selfobject, often the father.

Kohut also refers at times to the 'nuclear self', a deep and central structure established early in childhood. He seems to use this term to denote the idea that, although a person may have a variety of ideals and ambitions, there are certain core ambitions and ideals/values which have a direct descendence from those established early in life. He suggests that although there may be many peripheral selves, there is only one nuclear self. This central nuclear self struggles to achieve its goals, to realise its blueprint. Kohut refers to the 'guiltless despair' of those who in late middle age look back and realise that their nuclear goals and ideals have not been achieved. He writes (Kohut, 1985, p. 218):

> There is something very frightening as an adult ... when there is a sense of not fulfilling one's basic program. We realise there is a nuclear program in an individual – a tension arc between early ambitions and early ideals via a matrix of particular skills – that points into the future and points to a particular fulfillment. Once the program is in place, then something clicks and we have a degree of autonomy; this degree of autonomy we call the self. It becomes a centre of independent initiative that points to a future and has a destiny. It also has its own natural, unfeared decline and end.

In one contribution, Kohut's concepts seem very close to Winnicott's notion of the true self. He writes that 'the peripheral and surface selves are those of easy adaptation and comfortable consistency', a description of a false self. Kohut notes that the aspirations of the nuclear self may be in conflict with those of the rest of the personality. The ambitions of the nuclear self are not to be confused with the more superficial arrogant grandiosity apparent in narcissistic personalities. Kohut and Kernberg *both* view this as defensive. Confusion does arise because Kohut refers to the grandiose self as an unconscious repressed structure, whilst Kernberg uses the same term to mean a pathological defensive structure involving overt grandiosity, a fusion of self, ideal self and ideal object; interestingly Kohut (1976) actually described the same structure as a feature of 'messianic personalities'. One implication here, which Kohut does not draw out, is that narcissistic personalities are grandiose and attempt to maintain an illusion of independence because they are afraid both of dependence on others *and* of surrender to their deeper nuclear self; perhaps this is what gives them an air of superficiality and lack of depth.

Kohut's diagnostic criteria

Kohut's primary diagnostic criteria are not in terms of patients' manifest character traits, as with Kernberg, but rather in terms of the patient's spontaneously developing transference. One of his most original contributions is to have delineated the narcissistic transferences in which the analyst is required to function as an extension of the patient's self – the patient's sense of coherence and well-being is dependent on the responsiveness of the analyst who is therefore regarded not as a fully separate being but as functionally part of the patient. The analyst is required to be a selfobject, as the parents originally were.

The two broad transference configurations described by Kohut are: (1) the mirror transference (including 'twinship') – wherein the analyst is required to be reliably responsive to the patient's exhibitionism of his or her 'grandiose self'; and (2) the idealising transference where the analyst is perceived as a container of perfection. Through the establishment of these narcissistic transferences, the patient is attempting to mobilise and ultimately integrate the repressed narcissistic sectors of the personality: the exhibitionistic and idealising sectors.

A second major diagnostic criterion for Kohut is the patient's reaction to narcissistic injury, particularly those that occur within the therapy. He describes how a temporary regressive swing may be precipitated by, for example, a rebuff by the analyst. On the other hand, many symptoms may be relieved by external praise or interest – i.e. by receiving narcissistic supplies; hypochondriacal anxiety, for example, may suddenly disappear in this way. This may be particularly apparent within the therapy (Kohut, 1971, p. 70):

> One of the almost unmistakable and frequent features in the initial and subsequent analytic situation is the patient's obvious need for responses, cues and reactions from the analyst ... we can observe when we speak or respond a distinct pleasure or 'lifting of spirits', a response that becomes more and more noticeable as the analytic relationship gets under way.

Kohut also emphasised that narcissistic patients' symptomatology tends to be ill-defined – there may, for example, be subtly experienced but pervasive feelings of emptiness and depression. Kohut suggests that the vagueness of the patient's initial complaints may be related to the nearness of the pathologically disturbed structure (the self) to the actual seat of self-observation – Kohut quotes Freud's comment that the eye cannot observe itself.

Other secondary narcissistic features described by Kohut are:

- Perverse sexual fantasies.
- Work inhibitions.
- Inability to form significant relationships.
- Delinquent activities.
- A lack of humour, lack of a sense of proportion and lack of empathy for others.
- A tendency to uncontrolled rage (narcissistic rage).
- Pathological lying.
- Hypochondriacal preoccupations with physical and mental health.

The prominent anxieties of these patients are characteristic, according to Kohut. He states (Kohut, 1971):

> The anxiety stems largely from separation, shame, fears of fragmentation or dissolution, and fears of excessive excitement from archaic, grandiose and

exhibitionistic drives. The regression is a structural one – to a less cohesive self – a temporarily fragmented archaic self ...

Forman (1976) has summarised the diagnostic features of Kohut's category. The following is an abbreviated list of these:

* low self-esteem
* periodic hypochondriasis
* feelings of emptiness alternating with hyperactivity
* shyness and fears of rejection
* childhood feelings of lonelines
* strong reactions to separation in childhood
* perverse sexual fantasies
* disturbances in the capacity for empathy
* lack of empathy in the parents, especially the mother
* fantasies of greatness
* strivings for perfection
* search for idealised objects
* intense need for affirmation
* a lifting of spirits when the analyst responds
* complaints of falling apart
* dreams and associations representing fragmentation of the self
* conflicts over a wish to merge with the analyst.

This is a subtle and sensitive model of development with many ramifications. A detailed discussion and critique of Kohut's work and its implications is given in Mollon (1986, 1988b). Other books which explore and extend Kohut's ideas in useful ways are: Detrick and Detrick (1989); Jackson (1991); Lee and Martin (1991); White and Weiner (1986); Wolf (1988).

Prominent themes in Kohut's model

* Grandiosity and idealisation of others.
* Narcissistic vulnerability – regression in the face of narcissistic injury and the prominence of narcissistic rage.
* The need for selfobject responses.
* Disturbance in object relations – the tendency to retreat to a cold, paranoid or grandiose state in the face of narcissistic injury.
* Fears of fragmentation and loss of coherence – hypochondriacal anxiety.
* Shame.
* States of lethargy and depletion – empty depression.
* The idea of the self as a *structure*, as well as experiential core – a structure which may be weakened or defective.

Self-disorder categories

1. [Differentiation] No – not explicitly. Problems of pathological fusion are apparent in many of Kohut's clinical illustrations, but this is not prominent in his theorising.
2. [Subjective self – sense of efficacy] Yes – the 'independent centre of initiative'.
3. [Objective self] Yes – the repressed archaic grandiose self.
4. [Structure–organisation] Yes.
5. [Balance between subjective and objective self] No – not explicitly, but this is implied in some of Kohut's clinical discussions.
6. [Illusion of self-sufficiency] Yes.
7. [Sense of lineage] No.

Robbins

Robbins (1982) argues that the child who is to become a narcissistic personality fails to form 'a viable unconditional symbiotic bonding' with the mother. In many ways, this account is similar to Winnicott's (1960) description of false self development. The mother is 'neither responsive to, nor encouraging of, the infant's need signals and initiatives, but instead imposes an agenda consisting of her own fantasy attributions'. The infant adapts to this by formation of a 'possessed' imago in relation to the mother as 'possessor'.

Robbins sees some similarity to the early environment of borderline patients, but he argues that 'The mother of the narcissistic personality is more realistically responsive to infantile need signals and autonomous gestures than the mother of the borderline, but her goal is positively not encouragement of the infant's autonomy'.

The mother responds to the infant's own need signals with devaluation and disapproval. This leads to an active internalisation of the maternal devaluation – the appropriated maternal 'no' is directed towards the nascent representation of initiatives and needs. Robbins makes an important distinction between this situation and the more normal internalisation of parental prohibitions – instead of an internalisation of a maternal 'no' towards selected impulses, this 'no' is much more global. As a result, 'The infant is left without a reliable, autonomous perceptual apparatus, without the rudiments of instinctual development, without dependable instincts. He has only a shared illusion to cling to'.

Robbins argues that the narcissistic personality has established a *conditional* symbiotic relationship – which at least gives some greater stability than in the case of the borderline personality who has not experienced any kind of early symbiotic relationship. However, this relationship with mother depends on the child's disavowal of his or her own autonomous perceptions, needs and initiatives. The resulting narcissistic personality is then both compliantly passive and subtly self-destructive and self-devaluing. In this way the child was able to retain mother's love and develop unrealistic attitudes of grandeur and complacency. He strives to fulfil the grandiose aspirations of his object (originally mother) but his accomplishments feel unauthentic to him.

Robbins describes a configuration of 'possessor' and 'possessed' – these representing the dyadic relationship between narcissistic personality and object. The possessor (originally mother) functions *projectively* to disavow and attribute, whilst the possessed functions *introjectively* to overinclude what the possessor projects. The dyad functions as discrete parts of a single entity, and disavowed parts of the self are recognised in the other. The narcissistic personality attempts to be the possession of another person with dissociated narcissistic problems: 'As one thus possessed the narcissistic personality lacks self-esteem and devalues his own needs, interests and autonomous aims, whilst paradoxically clinging to grandiose fantasies of his own and vigorously supporting the narcissistic agenda of the object.' At the same time the narcissistic personality takes the role of *possessor* to other devalued figures who becomes the carriers of disavowed states of neediness, dependency and imperfection. Through this disavowal and projection, the narcissistic personality fosters an illusion of perfection, self-sufficiency and omnipotence. Here the link to Kernberg's formulation is clear in the idea of warded off states of enraged helplessness.

Prominent themes in Robbin's model

- The mother's failure to recognise and facilitate the child's autonomy.
- A consequent lack of awareness of self.
- The child's attempts to fulfil the ambitions of the mother.
- The focus on the dyad of possessor and possessed.
- Illusion of perfection, self-sufficiency and omnipotence.

Self-disorder categories

1. [Differentiation] Yes – the notion of symbiosis with impaired development towards separateness and autonomy; a lack of awareness of self.
2. [Subjective self – sense of efficacy] Yes – impaired autonomy is described.
3. [Objective self] Yes – low self-esteem, coupled with grandiose images.
4. [Structure–organisation] No.
5. [Balance between subjective and objective self] No.

6. [Illusion of self-sufficiency] Yes – illusions of self-sufficiency with projection of neediness onto the other.
7. [Sense of lineage] No.

Gear, Hill and Liendo

The formulations of Gear, Hill and Liendo (1981) are in some ways similar to those of Robbins, but they develop a novel framework postulating a basic bipolar structure of the psychic apparatus. They emphasise what they describe as a sado-masochistic function of the narcissistic mirror, and a distortion in the way one person normally confirms another's identity or sense of self. They argue that the narcissistic personality has not been given the basis for knowing who he or she is (p. 7):

> In narcissism as in any form of personality structure, it is only through the other that one can have one's identity confirmed. What obscures this in the case of a narcissistic partnership is that the other does not confirm one's identity through himself, but rather by holding up a mirror to the other, as Echo does for Narcissisus ... We can argue that 'identity' can be defined and acquire meaning only through opposition and difference. With alterity our image depends not only on the image that we have of ourselves, but also on the image that others have of themselves and of us. Identity and alterity always form a bipolar structure.

The formation of narcissistic disturbance is described thus (p. 14):

> The survival and pleasure of the infant depend entirely on the aid that it receives from the mother and father. It is in this bipolar relationship, where the initiative rests primarily with the parent (since the infant is dependent), that the narcissistic structure may originate, if the mother and father fail to recognise the desire of the infant, but instead induce in it the complement to their own unconscious and repressed desire. Thus the child is educated to be a mirror and to find others who will in turn mirror its own repressed unconscious desire.

It can be seen that this is close to Robbin's description of the selectively distorting responses of the mother.

Gear, Hill and Liendo describe two fundamental modes of excercising authority in relation to the child. In the normal situation authority defines rules and then rewards a child for compliance or punishes for rebellion – but, beyond insisting on these rules, authority recognises the child's separate identity. Within these rules, the child can develop an autonomous sphere and gradually through learning, develop a relationship of equality with the other. However, the alternative mode prevents this normal resolution and perpetuates an asymmetrical relationship of dominance and submission:

The significant other who is responsible for exercising authority on behalf of the culture, either uses this position to assert omnipotent control over the child, or else surrenders it to the child ... authority remains unmediated by the values of the culture it is supposed to transmit and is simply excercised for its own sake.

Gear, Hill and Liendo argue that in such circumstances the child can adopt either a masochistic or a sadistic position, but no other – the psychic possibilities are grossly restricted. They describe this restriction as a 'mutilation of psychic space':

Just as it is impossible for someone to recognise the unconscious mutilation of himself on which the structure of his ego and alter rests, so it is impossible for him to recognise the extent to which his repetitive interactions with others rest upon an unconscious failure to take other possibilities in reality into account ... The narcissistic paradigm is set between two reflecting mirrors that define the range of cognition and affect by constantly inverting and reflecting it in a self-enclosed system impenetrable from the point of view of the person located in it.

Thus the narcissistic character is restricted in his or her capacity to think and feel and is aware only of the sado-masochistic mode of obtaining pleasure or security. Moreover, the very same mutilation prevents him or her being aware of the mutilation.

Prominent themes in Gear, Hill and Liendo's model

- Sado-masochism.
- Mirroring as a distortion and restriction of identity.
- Parental failure to recognise the child's own desire, needs and autonomy.
- A consequent lack of self-awareness and self-knowledge.
- A perversion of authority – lack of mediation of the wider culture.

Self-disorder categories

1. [Differentiation] Yes – the child's separateness is not recognised and he or she consequently lacks self-knowledge.
2. [Subjective self-efficacy] Yes – lack of awareness of own desire and of autonomy.
3. [Objective self] No.
4. [Structure–organisation] No.
5. [Balance between subjective and objective aspects] No.
6. [Illusion of self-sufficiency] No.
7. [Sense of lineage] No.

Schwartz-Salant

Schwartz-Salant (1982) writes from a Jungian perspective, but his conclusions are in part similar to those of Robbins and Gear et al.

First he places a Jungian view of 'self' at the centre of his formulation, seeing the narcissistic character as out of touch with this core or source. He regards the self as both a content of the ego and at the same time a structure which expands beyond this into the archetypal realm; he emphasises its 'numinous' quality. The narcissistic character he suggests is terrified of the self.

He states (Schwartz-Salant, 1982, p. 12):

> The self manifests as both a seemingly well-ordered continuous process and one which can burst in upon the ego with unknown energies and shake the very core of the conscious personality.

And referring to its numinous quality:

> The numinous strikes a person with awe, wonder and joy, but may also evoke terror and total disorientation. Being confronted with the power of the self arouses just such emotions, which always and everywhere have been associated with religious experience.

This account of the numinous is very close to Kohut's description of the awesome experience of the encounter with archaic narcissism. Also similar is the reference to the 'joy' associated with the unfolding self – unfolding according to its blueprint. Schwartz-Salant quotes Jung's view that the self wants to 'live its experiment in life'. He states the essence of narcissistic pathology thus (p. 23):

> In terms of Jung's approach to the psyche ... it would be the rejection of the self, the failure to live one's true pattern that leads to what are now called narcissistic character disorders.

Jung's own view is most clearly stated in his seminars on Nietzsche's *Thus Spake Zarathustra* (unpublished lecture, quoted in Schwartz-Salant, 1982):

> If you fulfil the pattern that is peculiar to yourself you have loved yourself, you have accumulated, you have abundance; you borrow virtue then because you have lustre, you radiate, from your abundance something overflows. But if you hate yourself, if you have not accepted your pattern, then there are hungry animals, prowling cats and other beasts in your constitution which get at your neighbours like flies in order to satisfy the appetites which you have failed to satisfy. Therefore Nietsche says to those people who have not fulfilled their individual pattern that the bestowing soul is

lacking. There is no radiation, no real warmth; there is hunger and secret stealing. [Quoting Nietzsche: 'Upward goeth our course from genera to supergenera. But a horror to us is the degenerating sense, which saith: "All for myself".']

You see that degenerating sense which says 'all for myself' is unfulfilled destiny, that is somebody who did not live himself, who did not give himself what he needed, who did not toil for the fulfillment of that pattern which had been given him when he was born. Because that thing is one's *genus* it ought to be fulfilled and in as much as it is not, there is that hunger which says 'all for myself'.

So why is this 'self' rejected in the narcissistic character? Schwartz-Salant describes three major fears of the self which are experienced by the narcissistic character:

1. The fear of being flooded by archetypal energies and being overtaken by a will greater than that of one's ego, one's conscious mind. (This seems close to Kohut's description of the fear of encountering archaic boundless grandiosity, or of becoming merged with an awesome archaic idealised object.)
2. The fear of abandonment, as if the narcissistic character thinks: 'If I contact all that strength and effectiveness, no one will be able to be with me. I'll be too powerful and everyone will send me away.' In Kohut's terms this seems like a fear of encountering archaic grandiosity which receives no mirroring confirmation.
3. The fear of envy. Schwartz-Salant argues that the narcissistic character has generally been subject to massive envious attack in childhood. In an effort to avoid a repeat of that he or she 'hides his prize from others *and* from himself'.

Like Kohut, Schwartz-Salant emphasises the need for mirroring responsiveness – indeed seeing the external mirroring between parent and child as paralleling an internal mirroring between ego and self. For the narcissistic character the early mirroring has been distorted (p. 48):

Narcissistic characters have generally experienced a chronic lack of mirroring, often stemming from parental envy. When parents lack a sense of their own identity they become sensitive to how their children like *them*, or how it adds or detracts from *their* sense of esteem. Not only will they be unable to mirror the child's emerging personality, but they will want to be mirrored by the child who feels this keenly. Often the child feels it has something special the parents want, yet this specialness must be subverted to mirroring the parents, to giving back the responses that make the parents feel secure. Otherwise there will be an uncomfortable feeling in the enviroment, a disquiet due to the parents' discomfort with their child's uniqueness. This undertone is the working of envy, the spoiling effect stemming from the parents insecurity and jealousy of their own children who may create an identity they themselves lack. The end result of this process is that rather than feel its self loved and accepted, the child feels hated.

Schwartz-Salant argues that it is against this feeling of being envied and hated that the narcissistic character erects defences. Like Gear, Hill and Liendo, Schwartz-Salant notes the masochistic development that may ensue from the distorted parental response to the child's self (p. 159):

> ... the early experiences of the narcissistic character – and this is true to some degree for everyone – is that the self was psychically attacked. As a consequence the child's self withdrew and instead a more compliant and masochistic attitude developed.

The child retreats to a masochistic position because this is felt to be safer. The self is suppressed and in identification with parental attitudes is hated. In the course of psychoanalytic therapy, this 'masochistic child' position is given up and there emerges the long suppressed and feared 'joyful child'.

Prominent themes in Schwartz-Salant's model

- The 'self' as a broader and deeper entity than the conscious ego.
- Fears of this deeper self – its numinous quality.
- An inner pattern, fulfilment of which leads to joy and suppression of which leads to hatred and a superficial narcissistic position of 'all for myself'.
- Fears of precipitating abandonment, or evoking envy, if the pattern of the deeper self is fulfilled.
- Hatred of the self in identification with the parents – adoption of a masochistic position.

Self-disorder categories

1. [Differentiation] No.
2. [Subjective self-efficacy] Yes – the subject's true initiatives are not encouraged.
3. [Objective self] No.
4. [Structure–organisation] No.
5. [Balance between subjective and objective aspects] No.
6. [Illusion of self-sufficiency] No.
7. [Sense of lineage] No.

Rothstein

Most theories of narcissistic disturbance have emphasised parental undervaluing or selective ignoring of the child's spontaneously unfolding self. Rothstein (1980), in contrast, addresses what is perhaps the other side of this situation – the way in which the child may be overvalued in certain areas. He argues that the narcissistic personality defensively clings to the feeling of being special and valued in order to avoid the feared state of abandonment and experience of helpless rage or depression. An exaggerated overt grandiosity and sense of 'entitlement' is continually fuelled for defensive purposes – in this way Rothstein's formulation is close to Kernberg's.

Rothstein suggests that narcissistic personalities have experienced their mothers as confusing and contradictory – at one moment hostile, cold and rejecting, and at other moments overvaluing of the child when the latter is gratifying to her. The child clings to the memories of gratifying moments to form an attitude of 'entitlement' in order to ward off frightening memories of mother's hostility or coldness. Rothstein describes this mother–infant situation thus:

> Mothers who engender an ego attitude of entitlement use the child to fill an inner void ... Appropriate behaviour by the child fills the mother with positive feelings. She smiles at him and infuses him with correspondingly gratifying affects. This contributes to a feeling of prolonged fusion between mother and child. At times the toddler feels excessively gratified – at others when the mother is unempathic or self-involved, he feels a disorganising anxiety. When the child cannot narcissistically gratify his mother, she will be disinterested and/or depressed – the child will feel enraged and alone, humiliated and mortified at his lack of power to stimulate her interest.

The child who becomes a narcissistic personality develops an attitude of entitlement which facilitates a denial of the unrelated and frustrating aspects of mother – essentially this protects the child from the 'realisation that mother cannot love him for himself but loves him primarily as a reflection of herself'. Rothstein argues that, in spite of this defence, many narcissistic patients experience their selves as somehow defective without being able adequately to explain why. He suggests that this self-image 'is derived in part from internalising the mother's narcissistically deflated or depressed, disinterested or innappropriately angry facial representation into the germinal self-as-agent'.

Unlike many other theorists who stress what they see as 'pre-oedipal' issues, Rothstein also emphasises oedipal contributions. He suggests that the narcissistic personality has experienced 'confusing and contradictory oedipal situations that were simultaneously and/or alternatively gratifying, frightening and disappointing'. At times the little boy (several authors write as if narcissistic personality was exclusively male) experienced what felt like an oedipal victory over father – he would be mother's little lover, preferred to father. Yet somehow he sensed the exploitation and also greatly feared father's revenge:

> He is intoxicated by that aspect of his oedipal situation experienced as an implicit victory and this further interferes with his mourning his grandiose self. He is frightened and enraged at his mother for treating him extractively. He is terrified she will denigrate and destroy him if he does not perform adequately. In addition he fears father's retaliation for his symbolic oedipal victory. Both factors contribute to his intensive castration anxiety.

In addition, Rothstein argues that the partial oedipal victory makes the little boy's perception of his real position of being a child, with a child's body, and that mother sleeps with father, an even more intense narcissistic injury than otherwise – further contributing to underlying feelings of inadequacy.

Rothstein's view of narcissistic personality is embedded in his more general model of narcissism. He suggests that a definition of the term 'narcissism' should refer to 'a felt quality of perfection' which he sees as being built upon the core of 'the original experience of the preindividuated era'. Rothstein here seems to be referring to what Freud termed the state of primary narcissism, or the oceanic feeling of oneness – or Andreas Salomé's (1962) 'deep identification with the totality'. The content of narcissistic perfection he sees as having affective, physical and cognitive components. The cognitive component is a conception of perfection expressed in ideas of omniscience or omnipotence, and associated with the superlative designations – 'most','number one', the wish to be the 'one and only'. The sense of narcissistic perfection is associated affectively with high self-esteem and is often linked to a more physical sense that one's body is functioning well. Rothstein sees narcissistic perfection as a ubiquitous defence:

> Narcissistic perfection is a defensive distortion of reality – an affectively laden fantasy based on the original perfection of the selfobject bliss of the symbiotic phase. Its loss is a ubiquitous developmental insult from which few if any human beings ever recover.

Within Rothstein's framework, narcissistic injury is defined as the disruption of the sense of perfection. The narcissistic personality is defined in terms of a predominant investment of narcissism in the self-representation (self-image). Those patients whose predominant narcissistic investment is in the object representation he sees as masochistic – and suggests the term 'suppliant personality disorder'.

Prominent themes in Rothstein's model

- Selective overvaluation of the child by the mother insofar as he or she gratifies her narcissistic needs.
- Defensive clinging to these experiences in order to ward off experiences of helpless rage when mother was uninterested or self-absorbed – vague sense of being defective.
- Sense of entitlement.
- Mother's narcissistic use of the child fosters prolonged fusion between them.
- Illusion of oedipal victory fostered by the mother – the child's underlying sense of being exploited.
- Fear of father's revenge.
- Narcissistic injury of recognising the true position of being a little boy rather than mother's lover.
- Illusion of perfection

Self-disorder categories

1. [Differentiation] Yes – the prolonged fusion with mother.
2. [Subjective self-efficacy] No – except by implication.
3. [Objective self] Yes – the self image as 'defective', and the compensatory images of perfection.
4. [Structure–organisation] No.
5. [Balance between subjective and objective aspects] No.
6. [Illusion of self-sufficiency] No – except by implication in the illusion of perfection.
7. [Sense of lineage] No.

Grunberger

Whilst not making use of a concept of narcissistic personality, Grunberger (1971) has developed an elaborate theory of narcissism. He does not emphasise 'pre-oedipal' factors, but rather juxtaposes narcissism and the oedipus complex. He sees a fundamental antagonism between narcissism and the instincts (including the instincts of object relating). He further argues that the fetal state of equilibrium is the source of all forms of narcissism – and that the narcissistic components of the psyche seek a return to this source. (It can be seen that this is very similar to Rothstein's view of the narcissistic pursuit of perfection.)

Grunberger notes Ferenczi's (1913) observation that the child experiences the absolute sovereignity of physiological need as a humiliating constraint. The narcissistic wish is to live without need, to exist free from both desire and the body. At every stage of development, the narcissistic wish is to achieve or recover a state of harmony or integrity, represented unconsciously, Grunberger believes, by the image of the phallus. This relatively non-specific 'wish' is largely silent, apparent only when a state of equilibrium is disrupted. Grunberger sees the infant as an outcast of both worlds, the instinctual and the narcissistic – he or she has sexual wishes but is *inherently impotent*. Grunberger makes the interesting and novel suggestion that the incest barrier protects the child against narcissistic injury – the little boy experiences sexual desire for his mother, but if there were no taboo on expressing this he would be faced with the humiliating fact of his impotence, his possession of a child's body. However, through the incest barrier, the *inner* inadequacy is transformed into the threat of castration from outside – castration in Grunberger's model taking on a broader meaning of loss of the harmony or integrity represented by the phallus.

Grunberger suggests that, as well as experiencing oedipal desire, the child wishes to avoid the oedipal struggle altogether – indeed to reject sexual life as a whole and to replace it with an asexual narcissistic universe. As an expression of this wish there arises the fantasy of the 'narcissistic triad' or 'Divine Child', the two parents together in adoration of their infant. This is the counterpart to the fantasy of the primal scene, where the parents are united in a sexual relationship from which the child is excluded.

The narcissist within the child wishes to avoid an oedipal struggle, to avoid identification with the rival parent and to deny the origin from two sexual parents. Grunberger cites the instance of the child's 'treasure hoard', a collection of, literally, rubbish that has not been given but simply found. The importance of the treasure is first that it comes from no-one, thereby ruling out an oedipal origin; it has not come from the parents. Secondly, it is rubbish – unconsciously anal matter, the base matter of alchemy, intended to triumph magically over the genitality of the parents, especially the father. This represents an attempt to skip over the whole lengthy and painful process of maturation. The more perverse forms of narcissism represent the wish to remove the father, or sodomise him, so as to avoid an encounter with him at the genital level – the perverse narcissist will denigrate adult genitality and break the whole system of filiation, seeking a place outside of it.

Grunberger makes a novel interpretation of the Sphinx of the oedipus myth. He suggests that this creature represents a hodge podge of projections, like the child's treasure trove put together from odds and ends – 'the sphinx has no real body but masks a void bearing symbols'. The Sphinx offers the magical and seductive possibility of avoiding the slow process of development through growth and identification. Grunberger sees the Sphinx as analogous to the teenage idol:

...the sphinx represents the anal sadistic mother, whose deep and obscure entrails seem to conceal the paternal attribute ... the tacit promise of the

sphinx ... [or the idol] hints at the possibility of aquiring the phallus magically through avoidance, leaping over maturation.

Like the idol, the seductive sphinx is dangerous. Mythology told that
the sphinx destroyed young people. Grunberger sees the dual between
the sphinx (narcissism) and Oedipus as central:

> ... Oedipus, conqueror of the sphinx, is a hero not because he solved the
> riddle, but because in doing so he swept away in a single stroke, a whole
> pseudo-civilisation concocted of sorcery, magic formulas and fear of mystery
> ... he proved that projection alone was what gave the sphinx life and
> omnipotent authority.

Prominent themes in Grunberger's model

- The narcissistic wish to maintain a state of harmony and integrity,
  based ultimately on the fetal state.
- The fantasy of the 'Divine Child'.
- The juxtaposition of narcissism and instinctual–oedipal development.
- The narcissistic wish to avoid the painful process of development –
  to avoid the oedipal struggle and to magically acquire the 'phallus'.

Self-disorder categories

1. [Differentiation] No.
2. [Subjective self-efficacy] No.
3. [Objective self] No.
4. [Structure–organisation] No.
5. [Balance between subjective and objective aspects] No.
6. [Illusion of self-sufficiency] Yes.
7. [Sense of lineage] Yes.

Rosenfeld

Writing from an essentially Kleinian point of view, Rosenfeld (1971)
bases his formulation of narcissism on the concept of the death
instinct. He regards it as:

> ...a destructive process directed against objects and the self. These proces-
> ses seem to operate in their most virulent form in severe narcissistic condi-
> tions.

He quotes Freud's views concerning a basic hatred of the object and
the external world (Freud, 1915, *Instincts and Their Vicissitudes*):

Hate, as a relationship to the object is older than love. It derives from the narcissistic ego's primordial repudiation of the external world with its outpouring stimuli.

Rosenfeld emphasises how the narcissistic patient is enviously depreciative and devaluing of the analyst, attempting to demonstrate his or her own superiority. He draws on Klein's concept of envy, describing it as 'a hostile life destroying force in the relationship of infant to its mother and is particularly directed against the good feeding mother because she is not only needed by the infant, but envied for containing everything the infant wants to possess himself'.

Rosenfeld argues that the narcissistic patient attempts to deny the separateness between self and object, because the awareness of separateness leads to feelings of dependence and envy:

In terms of the infantile situation, the narcissistic patient wants to believe that he has given life to himself and is able to feed and look after himself. When he is faced with the realisation of being dependent on the analyst, standing for the parents, particularly the mother, he would prefer to die, to be non-existent, to deny the fact of his birth, and also to destroy his own progress and insight representing the child in himself which he feels the analyst, representing the parents, has created.

For Rosenfeld, the narcissistic patient wishes to maintain a state of omnipotent superiority and prevent the experience of dependence. Rosenfeld's formulation is noteworthy for its description of the internal 'mafia' or 'gang' which attempts to maintain control of the personality:

The destructive narcissism of these patients appears often highly organised, as if one were dealing with a powerful gang dominated by a leader, who controls all the members of the gang to see that they support one another in making the criminal work more effective and powerful. However the narcissistic organisation not only increases the strength of the destructive narcissism, but it has a defensive purpose to keep itself in power and so maintain the status quo. The main aim seems to be to prevent the wrecking of the organisation and to control the members of the gang so that they will not desert the destructive organisation, or betray the secrets of the gang to the police, the protecting superego, standing for the helpful analyst who might be able to save the patient. Frequently when a patient of this kind makes progress in the analysis and wants to change he dreams of being attacked by members of the mafia or adolescent delinquents, and a negative therapeutic reaction sets in.

It is apparent that Rosenfeld's formulation is essentially the same as Kernberg's – with an even greater emphasis on destructive features of the narcissistic personality. He gives no consideration to the possible origins of narcissistic disturbance in interactions with the parents – he appears to envisage a closed psychic system.

Interestingly, in a later work (1987), Rosenfeld discusses what he sees as corrections to his earlier approach, now giving much greater emphasis to early damaging interactions with parents. He also distinguishes between 'thick-skinned' and 'thin-skinned' narcissists, emphasising the underlying vulnerability and sensitivity of the latter and seeming to recommend a more Kohutian technical approach for this group. However, his more recent suggestions, published posthumously, are insufficiently elaborated to merit further discussion here.

Prominent themes in Rosenfeld's formulation

- The destructive *organisation* of narcissism.
- Its association with the 'death instinct'.
- The hatred of dependence.
- Attempts to avoid awareness of separateness from the object.
- Devaluing of the object and the attempt to maintain an illusion of omnipotent superiority and self-sufficiency.

Self-disorder categories

1. [Differentiation] Yes – the defensive denial of separateness.
2. [Subjective self-efficacy] No.
3. [Objective self] Yes – grandiose self-image.
4. [Structure–organisation] No.
5. [Balance between subjective and objective aspects] No.
6. [Illusion of self-sufficiency] Yes.
7. [Sense of lineage] This is implied in Rosenfeld's view that the narcissist wishes to believe he has given life to himself and to deny the facts of his birth.

A note on the Kleinian school in general

Although Melanie Klein's writings do not provide an elaborated theory of narcissism, nor of the self or sense of self, much of Kleinian theory can be understood as implicitly referring to themes of narcissism. The earliest state of mind is described as the paranoid–schizoid position, in which the infant's relation to both internal and external reality is pervaded by defences of splitting and projection. These defences are mediated by a complex geography of phantasy, which Melanie Klein described and illustrated in considerable detail. These defences and accompanying phantasies are characterised by the infantile attitude of omnipotence. Much has been made in recent years of the concept of projective identification – originally described by Klein (1946) as purely a phantasy, but later developed by other authors, beginning with Bion (1959), as an interactional activity designed to make the other experience the projection. Projective identification consists of the infant's attempt to block the acceptance of the *separateness* of the other – to create an illusion of *controlling* the other, or of *living inside* the other. The transition to the depressive position involves the acceptance of separateness of self and other, the giving up of illusions of omnipotence, and an acknowledgement of ambivalence towards the other. This greater acceptance of reality results in depressive feelings to do with loss and guilt – and an ensuing wish to make realistic reparation.

Rosenfeld's account of the internal mafia was the first description of a destructive mental organisation. A number of other Kleinian authors have described further pathological organisations and complex interrelations between parts of the mind (Spillius, 1988, part 4). No similar descriptions appear in the American psychoanalytic literature, but interestingly there have emerged in recent years some comparable accounts in relation to discussions of multiple personality disorder (e.g. Putnam, 1989) – a concept somewhat controversial but currently in vogue in the USA. Within this framework, which I personally find very useful, it is possible to understand how different subpersonalities or alters may assume highly destructive and malevolent attitudes towards the child parts, or towards the 'host personality'. In my experience, a very common mental state in severely disturbed patients, who cut or otherwise mutilate their body, is an alter which wishes to feel no pain, love or concern, and which hates and attacks the vulnerable child self because it experiences emotional pain.

Bursten

Bursten (1973) distinguishes four types of narcissistic personality: the craving, the paranoid, the manipulative and the phallic narcissist. All have in common the essential task of maintaining and restoring self-esteem associated with the reunion of a grandiose self with an omnipotent object. Moreover all four types share difficulties in separation–individuation on varying degrees of severity. Thus the craving personality shows manifest features of symbiosis, clinging and desparately seeking physical proximity, often showing 'as-if' characteristics, fusing their identity with others. Paranoid personalities represent features of negativism seen when the infant is actively attempting to disengage from symbiosis. The manipulative (lying) personality is more secure in his or her separation. The phallic narcissist is even more secure in his sense of self – the need to be admired represents the reunion motif, but he or she can admire and flatter him- or herself.

Bursten gives importance to the avoidance of shame. He notes that:

What will be shameful and how it will be counteracted depends in great measure on the values the patient has internalised from his family, for it is they who set up his ego ideal and it is the internalised images of them with which he must reunite.

For example, in the case of craving personalities (men), the mother valued her son only as a baby, encouraging him to be openly weak, passive and demanding. Often the father was seen as 'weak'. One of Bursten's craving patients said: 'My mother doesn't concern herself with work. She's intuitive not practical. With her things just happen. My father is practical – it's a whole world I can't understand. I can't write or publish. I just expect to be famous. I never learned how to work.'

In the case of the other three narcissistic personality types, weakness is seen as a *threat* to self-esteem. Bursten describes how in some cases the mother saw the son as her phallus, whilst at the same time denigrating the penis (the father). Such patients are: 'caught between being strong and manly in order to be useful to (acceptable to) mother and yet not really strong and manly because they must be "mamma's boys".' Bursten follows Jacobson (1971) in emphasising a *sadomasochistic* family atmosphere in the family background of paranoid patients – often involving a controlling mother dominating father and son.

Regarding the family background of the manipulative personality, Bursten remarks: 'The public image counted more than the truth.' He implies that the manipulative personality is in less difficulty than the paranoid patient because he or she *knows* he or she is a liar and thus may be less in the grip of an illusion.

The mother of the phallic narcissist has, according to Bursten, placed a high premium on masculinity. Her implicit message is: 'Be a man like I wish your father were.' However, the child has to be *her* man, *her* phallus – thus his true masculinity is undermined because the mother cannot tolerate an independent man.

Several themes in Bursten's account are familiar and link to other authors' views. For example, the difficulties over separation–individuation; the role of the mother in thwarting the child's true independence, often inviting the child into illusions which seduce him away from his real developmental needs – the patient who expected to be famous but who had never learned to work; the ineffectiveness of the father, often denigrated by the mother.

Prominent themes in Bursten's model

- Difficulties in separation–individuation.
- The mother's thwarting of the child's independence and true masculinity.

- The mother's discouraging the child's identification with the father.
- The mother's seduction of the child away from the necessary engagement with reality.
- The ineffectiveness of the father.

Self-disorder categories

1. [Differentiation] Yes.
2. [Subjective self-efficacy] Yes.
3. [Objective self] Yes – by implication the child is trapped in illusory self-images.
4. [Structure–organisation] No.
5. [Balance between subjective and objective aspects] No.
6. [Illusion of self-sufficiency] No.
7. [Sense of lineage] No.

Overview of themes

Although there is a great deal of consensus and overlap of themes, none of the abstracted themes is present in all these models.

Five of the authors see grandiosity or grandiose self-images as a feature of narcissistic disturbance. Rosenfeld gives a slightly different emphasis to the others by focusing particularly on the illusion of omnipotence which is part of the grandiosity. As we have seen, Kohut's grandiose self is an unconscious repressed structure, rather like Winnicott's (1960) 'true self', the emergence of which is feared by the patient – whilst Kernberg's grandiose self is a conscious defensive structure warding off states of helpless rage. Similarly Rothstein emphasises grandiose states of 'entitlement', based on memories of those moments when mother was rewarding, which are enhanced to defend against states of helpless rage. Robbins offers a very similar model in his notion of the possessor–possessed dyad, the 'possessed' being the receptacle of the disavowed and projected helplessness, neediness and inadequacy, allowing the 'possessor' to maintain an illusion of perfection and self-sufficiency.

The illusion of self-sufficiency which may accompany a grandiose state is mentioned by five authors – Kohut, Kernberg, Robbins, Grunberger, Rosenfeld. Again the motive is seen as one of denying neediness and the vulnerability of dependence on the object.

A further area of considerable agreement is in the suggestion that in the childhood of narcissistic personalities, the mother discouraged the child's own initiatives, and failed to recognise and respond to the child's spontaneous gestures. The mother responded to the child in terms of her *own* agenda rather than that of the child. In this way the separateness and potential autonomy of the child has not been recognised; instead the child has been encouraged to adapt to the mother and lose contact with his or her own feelings and impulses. Although there is a good deal of agreement in this area, Kernberg, Rosenfeld and Grunberger do not refer to this at all. This reflects the emphasis of these theorists on the narcissistic anti-developmental forces *within* the child's personality, as opposed to a concern with early *interactions* and experiences of parents that contributed to distorted development. Rosenfeld in particular, through linking narcissism to the death instinct (a biological concept), implies a constitutional, instinctual basis which is not mediated through actual interactions with parents. Kernberg similarly alludes to constitutional factors such as strength of aggression or envy. Grunberger writes as if of an inherent wish to retain a state of fetal equilibrium, again with no reference to early interactions.

It might be expected that the mother's failure to acknowledge the child's separateness and potential autonomy might lead to difficulties in separation–individuation. There is some agreement over this which is emphasised by Rothstein, Bursten and Robbins. Rosenfeld also writes of the narcissistic patient's denial of separateness from the object, but consistently with his ignoring the contribution of the mother to the early interactions, he sees this failure of separation–individuation as defensive on the patient's part – reflecting the patient's wish to avoid an awareness of dependence. Kernberg, Grunberger, Schwartz-Salant and Gear/Hill/Liendo do not refer to difficulties in separation–individuation. Kohut does refer to this in certain of his clinical illustrations, but it does not form a prominent part of his theorising on narcissistic disturbance. Gear/Hill/Liendo, whilst not describing a state of incomplete differentiation from mother, are perhaps referring to a related phenomenon in their idea of the sado-masochistic bind that characterises the narcissistic relationship: the narcissistic personality is trapped and his or her capacity for independent thoughts are severely curtailed. This leads to a further point emphasised by Schwartz-Salant, and also implied in the myth of Narcissus and Echo: the narcissistic patient does not know him- or herself – awareness of self is resticted. Essentially the same insight is represented in Gear/Hill/Liendo's notion of the 'mutilation of psychic space'.

Oedipal issues are focused upon by three of the theorists: Rothstein, Grunberger and Bursten. Grunberger makes the oedipal situation most central, juxtaposing it to narcissistic strivings which he sees as in direct opposition, i.e. he sees the narcissistic desire as being to avoid oedipal struggle altogether, to retreat from the pain of instinctual drives and of painful comparisons between child and parent. Rothstein and Bursten do not draw this dichotomy, but, rather, place narcissistic issues in an oedipal context – among other contexts as well. Thus Bursten and Rothstein consider the impact of the child's sense of self and self-esteem of feeling desired by mother in preference to father, or of feeling rejected by mother as an oedipal lover.

Rothstein suggests that the experiences of oedipal triumph are clung to in order to ward off other feelings of abandonment, helplessness or of exploitation. He suggests that the child dimly senses that although seeming to be favoured by mother, this in itself contains an exploitation – the child's true position and developmental needs are not appreciated. This theme of exploitation of the child by the parent is implicit in several of the theorists: Kohut, Robbins, Schwartz-Salant, Bursten, Gear/Hill/Liendo, Rothstein – even Kernberg hints at it. In various ways the child is described as being treated without empathy, treated as a pawn in a parental drama.

Several aspects of narcissistic disturbance are addressed only by Kohut. These revolve around the concepts of the selfobject functions – of mirroring responsiveness and of availabiltiy for idealisation – and the narcissistic patient's vulnerability to disruption of these functions. Thus Kohut describes the narcissistic patient's proneness to states of 'fragmentation', of loss of the sense of cohesion – the person's mental functions becoming disorganised and disjointed – and states of 'depletion' or empty depression with lowered self-esteem and also states of shame. Kohut's is clearly the most original contribution in that none of the other theorists refers to these phenomena, although Bursten does allude to a proneness to shame in narcissistic disturbance.

Comparison with themes in the myth of Narcissus and Echo

Illusion and captivation by a deceptive image

This theme is not prominent in any of the theorists discussed, although it is perhaps implicit in some. The mother's discouragement of the child's initiatives, described by several theorists, leaves the child in a state of not knowing what he or she really is; insofar as the child is caught up in the mother's desires, it might be inferred that they are trapped in an illusion about their own identity. The grandiose self-images, stressed by five of the theorists, clearly must represent illusions about the self – illusions which, as Rothstein describes, may be fostered by the mother's inappropriate encouragement of the child's fantasy of an oedipal triumph over father.

Lack of self-knowledge and knowledge of origins

The lack of knowledge of the self is implicit in the idea of the maternal fostering of a false self in the child through failing to respond to the child's autonomous gestures.

Reflection and mirroring

Mirroring as a theme in narcissism is explicitly discussed by Kohut, Schwartz-Salant, and Gear/Hill/Liendo. Whereas Kohut emphasises the narcissistic patient's need for mirroring responsiveness from the parent and the analyst, Gear/Hill/Liendo emphasise how the parent may have required the child to be a mirror to *them*. Although not cast in terms of the concept of mirroring, a similar idea is implicit in the descriptions by Robbins, Bursten and Rothstein of the mother's requirement that the child be as she desires rather than what he or she actually is.

Sado-masochism

This is described most explictly by Gear/Hill/Liendo. Whilst it might be inferred that the situations described by other theorists might generate sado-masochistic interactions, this is not explicit.

Fear of being possessed

This is implicit in all those theories that emphasise the narcissistic patient's wish to maintain an illusion of self-sufficiency – although on the whole this wish is not explained in terms of a fear of loss of autonomy, but simply in terms of a wish to avoid the vulnerability of dependence. The theme of 'possession' is most explicit in Robbins' account of the possessor–possessed dyad.

Vanity and pride – and a turning away from object-relatedness

Kohut, Kernberg, Robbins, Grunberger and Rosenfeld all describe a defensive retreat into an aloof stance with an attempt to preserve an illusion of self-sufficiency. Vanity and pride are perhaps related to grandiosity, but they may also be slightly different – they are not in fact explicitly discussed by any of the theorists.

Envy

Narcissism as a defence against envy is given prominence by Kernberg and Rosenfeld. The emphasis is upon the patient's defensive grandiosity and contempt for others which protects against his or her potential experience of envy. By contrast, Schwartz-Salant emphasises the narcissistic patient's anxiety at being the target of envy, i.e. of being subject to an envious attack. Schwartz-Salant suggests that frequently the narcissistic personality has chronically suffered such attacks from parents in childhood.

The dangers of self-absorption and illusion; a developmental cul de sac and death

Narcissus is trapped by an illusion, is unable to move and so dies. This kind of situation could be seen as represented in the description by Rothstein and Grunberger of entrapment in the illusion of oedipal victory and avoidance of the necessary step of engaging in an oedipal struggle.

Origins in a violent primal scene and the absence of a continuing parental couple

This theme is not apparent in any of the theorists.

Overview in terms of the categories of self-disturbance

Differentiation

This is addressed by five of the group of theorists: Robbins; Gear/Hill/ Liendo; Rothstein; Rosenfeld; Bursten. Rosenfeld's emphasis is slightly different from the others because he places the onus on the child's own wish to deny separateness from the mother.

Subjective self: agency/efficacy

This is addressed by five of the group of theorists: Kohut; Robbins; Gear/Hill/Liendo; Schwartz-Salant; Bursten.

Objective self

Disturbances in this category are addressed with varying degrees of explicitness by all the theorists except Grunberger.

Structure–organisation

Only Kohut describes disturbances in this area.

Balance between subjective and objective self

None of the theorists address this kind of disturbance directly, although it is implied in Kohut, Robbins,Gear/Hill/Liendo, Rothstein and Bursten.

Illusions of self-sufficiency

This disturbance is described by five of the theorists: Kohut, Kernberg, Robbins, Grunberger and Rosenfeld.

Sense of lineage

Disturbance in this area is addressed most directly by Grunberger in his model of the narcissistic wish to avoid acknowledging his or her sexual origins. It is also implicit in Rosenfeld's view that the narcissist wishes to believe he has given birth to himself.

Chapter 5
A comprehensive model of narcissistic disturbance

What is required of an adequate model of narcissistic disturbance?

The theorising that I offer here does not derive from an allegiance to any particular grand theory – I am not a Freudian, a Kleinian, a Kohutian or any other kind of devotee, but draw widely from many contemporary psychoanalytic contributions. This leaves me free to consider what criteria an adequate model of narcissistic disturbance should fulfil.

1. It must adequately account for the phenomena of narcissistic disturbance, as described, for example, by Kernberg and Kohut; it must describe a basis for the disturbance of self found in these disorders.
2. As both Kernberg's and Kohut's theories are clearly found to have merit by clinicians all over the world, judging by the range of papers in international journals, an adequate model should subsume aspects of both these theories.
3. In addition it should incorporate recurrent themes emerging in the literature on narcissism.
4. It should be possible to link the model to the various disturbances of self listed in the taxonomy.
5. For this writer, an adequate model must take account of his clinical impressions that a disturbance of oedipal development may be important in these states.

In considering criteria of adequacy of a psychoanalytic formulation, it is helpful to draw an analogy with a psychoanalytic case seminar. In the writer's experience, a well-functioning seminar develops as follows: a case is presented (a 'case' being an account of both the patient and the interaction between the patient and the therapist) and members of the seminar proceed to discuss, each participant drawing attention to particular angles or aspects, and each speaking from a slightly different point of view. Usually each point has some degree of validity, although at an early stage of the discussion, disagreements and incompatibilities of view may be apparent. Gradually, however, a deeper and more holistic understanding emerges, which reorganises and subsumes the earlier more discrete points. Often it is the seminar leader's function to gather together and organise these initially divergent points of view. A seminar discussion concludes satisfactorily – i.e. is accompanied by a shared sense of satisfaction among the participants – when the eventual understanding combines a great many of the earlier formulations – the latter in retrospect then appear like formulations relating to *parts* of the case. The eventual formulation appears more complete and 'deeper' – i.e. addresses deeper structures.

The seminar process may not always develop this way even when the seminar group is working well. Sometimes divergent and incompatible formulations are proposed and there is discusssion of which appears right and which should be discarded as incorrect. This writer's experience is that unless participants or seminar leaders are dogmatically wedded to a particular theory, the latter kind of development is much rarer.

The process parallels that which proceeds during the analytic therapy itself. Numerous impressions and perceptions and part theories of the patient are gradually gathered together and organised into an ever deeper understanding of the patient. Earlier partial understandings are superseded and subsumed by later understandings.

In this writer's view the process of theory development through literature is essentially similar. Initially divergent points of view are gradually combined and reorganised into a deeper formulation. Earlier formulations are not so much disgarded as 'reframed' – i.e. given a different meaning; the phenomena that the theorist was attempting to account for are explained within the new, more holistic, framework.

Thus, a good model of narcissistic disturbance should incorporate as many as possible of the features to which other theories have drawn attention. The 'holistic' nature of psychoanalytic work develops a theoretical 'net' which captures and organises the clinical observations made in the consulting room during the actual treatment of patients. Psychoanalytic knowledge and understanding progress through a continuous interaction between theory and clinical observation.

Thus, here a model is developed that aims to capture and organise clinical observations about narcissistic disturbance. This is then open to exploration and elaboration through clinical psychoanalytic work.

Development of a model – summary

Two stages are proposed in the development of narcissistic disturbance. The first concerns the early communication between mother and child. It is proposed that one basis of the sense of self is the sense of efficacy, based on the experience of being able to evoke a thoughtful emotional response in the mother or early caregiver. Disturbances here relate particularly to categories 2 (subjective self, sense of efficacy) and 4 (sense of organisation).

The second stage concerns the child's entry into the oedipal position – assuming that for both sexes the earliest position is to desire to remain close to mother and to ward off the intruding father. It is argued that the father may play a crucial role in facilitating the child's sense of separateness from the mother, thereby providing the child with a sense of who he or she is in relation to two parents who have a relationship with each other – the child of two parents in intercourse. Failures to enter this position adequately, perhaps with the collusion of the mother, may lead to a variety of disturbances of self – most obviously category 1 (differentiation) and 7 (sense of lineage).

In addition, the child may experience considerable claustro-agrophobic anxieties in relation to the mother – resulting in wishes to avoid dependence (category 6; illusions of self-sufficiency).

The inability to allow, in phantasy, the parental intercourse may be associated with an inability to allow the free intercourse of unconscious parts of the mind – 'free-association'. The relationship between stages 1 and 2 may be understood in terms of the marriage of maternal and paternal elements, a marriage which in the narcissistic state of mind may not be allowed to take place.

There is a further dilemma for the child who has remained too close to the mother and who has failed to allow the father his place in the oedipal position. It is suggested that the problem is not one of inadequate separation from the mother per se, but from the image of the child in the mother's mind. The child feels compelled to be that which corresponds to the mother's phantasy. He or she may thus identify with an idealised image in the mother's mind, resulting in a grandiose self-image – this image may exist alongside a highly negative image corresponding to aspects of the mind that are implicitly rejected by the mother. The additional disturbances here are in terms of category 3 (objective self; self-image) and category 5 (balance between subjective and objective self). Emergence from the false image in mother's mind may result in painful self-consciousness (again category 5).

Thus, disturbances in all categories of the taxonomy are accounted for.

Development of a model

Two stages are proposed. In practice these may be intertwined but conceptually they may be distinguished. Throughout the discussion it may be assumed that where the 'mother' is referred to, this could also in certain circumstances apply to a primary caregiver other than the biological mother.

Failure of early communication; the non-mirroring mother

A first level of disturbance may have roots in the failure of early communication between child and mother. Two theoretical ideas may be
drawn together here: first Broucek's suggestion that the basis of the
sense of self is the experience of *efficacy*, the capacity to have some
effect on the world; secondly the emphasis given by Kohut, Winnicott
and others to the significance of the mother's empathic mirroring
responsiveness in affirming the child's sense of self. Combining these
ideas with the writer's own clinical observations suggests that the basis
of the sense of self is the capacity to evoke a thoughtful emotional
response in the other (originally the principal caregiver).

Failures in this area would seem likely to lead to disturbances particularly in category 2, the sense of efficacy and agency, and category 4,
the sense of organisation – which as Kohut has emphasised is probably
dependent on the formation of an organisation with the caregiver who
provides self-object functions. Thus in Kohut's framework this would
involve a failure to establish an appropriate early self-object relationship. This suggestion may be linked with the emphasis of several theorists upon the tendency of the mother of the narcissistic personality not
to respond to the child's own initiatives, but to respond affirmatively
only to those aspects of the child that are consistent with her own
desires. Essentially this corresponds to Winnicott's (1960) description
of the 'false self' formed when the mother substitutes her own gesture
rather than responding to the infant. In this case the normal situation
of the mother being a selfobject to the child is reversed – the child
being required to function as a selfobject to the mother, to affirm *her*.
In this way the child cannot discover its own desires but only that in
him- or herself that corresponds to the maternal desire – self-knowledge is prevented. The child in this predicament may become other-
oriented, the Me predominating over the I (category 5 of the taxonomy).

*Failure to establish the triadic position: the exclusion of the paternal
dimension*

The disturbances described above can all be understood in terms of an
early *dyadic* relationship with the mother. However, the writer's clinical observations suggest that there is a further aspect to the development of narcissistic disorders. This is the failure to progress from the
dyadic relationship with the mother to the triadic or oedipal position
which allows a place for the father.

The entry into the oedipal position can be seen to involve a radical
restructuring of the self. As the relationship between father and mother
(the primal scene) is recognised, the child must experience a profound
separation from mother, which at the same time allows him or her his

or her own place as the child of two parents who have come together in intercourse, i.e. as the product of the primal scene.

Lacan (1957) has shown how entry into the oedipal position may be associated with entry into the symbolic order – the father being seen as a representative of the outside world, the 'law' and the social order. One of Lacan's achievements is to have pointed out that, although the outward form of the oedipus complex may vary, the necessity to subject one's desires to the law (of society, kinship, family) is universal. Lemaire (1977), in presenting Lacan's position, writes (p. 78):

> Taking up his place in the symbolic register of language and of the family represents for the young child a circumscription of his individuality within his family group and within the global society. It means taking a grip upon himself, a personal realisation ...
> Regardless of its variable forms, the oedipal phenomenon is, as a structure, a radical and universal transformation of the human being; it is the transition from a dual, immediate or miror relationship to the mediate relationship proper to the symbolic, as opposed to the imaginary.

Thus the entry into the oedipal position may be seen to have profound psychic structural consequences. It means a firmer sense of identity and of self-boundaries, both sexually and generationally. This sense of identity rests upon a clearer basis in the social symbolic order, knowing one's place in the scheme of things, and especially in the family; it relates particularly to category 7 of the taxonomy, the sense of lineage. On the other hand, if the child remains predominantly in the dyadic (or narcissistic) position with mother, then his or her boundaries and sense of self are unclear. The child is uncertain about his or her origins and place in the scheme of things, not knowing who he or she is and where he or she comes from. Not having fully separated from mother, a crucial fear will be the loss of differentiation of the self, the fusion of the intrapsychic representations of self and other (category 1 of the taxonomy). A claustro-agoraphobic dilemma seems a highly likely consequence, an oscillation between the twin dangers of fusion with the other and isolation. A proneness to shame and self-consciousness is likely to be associated with this vulnerable sense of self, as outlined in Chapter 3 on these narcissistic affects. It also seems likely that the self boundaries will be relatively fluid as described by Federn (1953) – this state has been reported by Lewis (1971) to be characteristic of shame-prone personalities.

A crucial factor determining the failure to enter the triadic position may be the mother's wish to denigrate the role of the father, which coincides with the child's oedipal wish. This malignant alliance between the mother's wish omnipotently to do without the father, and the child's oedipal desire to remain close to the mother and exclude the father, may trap the child in a developmental cul de sac from which it is increasingly difficult to escape.

Freud (e.g. 1923) noted that the oedipus complex always occurs in both positive and negative forms – thus for both sexes the primary oedipal wish is to remain close to mother and ward off the rival father. This also appears to have been the view of Melanie Klein (1932) studying very young children. Similarly Abelin (1975) considers the core wish for both sexes in the situation of 'early triangulation' to be 'I want Mommy'.

The impossibility of self-knowledge in the dyadic position

It may be that, in the dyadic position, it is fundamentally impossible to know the self, precisely because there is no third dimension to provide a perspective. Thus Narcissisus remained entrapped by the mirror of the pool, unable to separate from his own image and unable to recognise himself. Abelin (1975), discussing his model of early triangulation, has suggested that oedipal rivalry may be necessary for the child to discover his or her own desire. For example, the little boy observes the relationship between his mother and father and sees in his father a being who, like himself, desires his mother. The implication is that without this triadic context the little boy cannot know his own desire. Certainly, the writer's clinical impressions suggest that patients who have not been able fully to negotiate the oedipal position commonly express a puzzlement about who they are.

The primal scene

We might assume that at the level of phantasy the primal scene is the foundation of identity, just as the intercourse of the parents is the concrete origin of the individual's existence. Freud actually outlined several primal phantasies, such as seduction and castration as well as the intercourse of the parents (*the* primal scene). Laplanche and Pontalis (1980) point out that primal phantasies are all related to *origins* – the origin of the individual, of sexuality, of the distinction between the sexes. It seems likely that the primal scene cannot be the foundation of identity if: (1) it is not allowed to take place (this may occur with the collusion of a mother who may like to feel that she produced the child all by herself, denigrating the role of the father); or (2) the phantasy model is too violent – the parents seen as coming together in a purely destructive way. When the primal scene is thus aborted the person seems to be left with a psychic gap where the father should be. Certain phenomena (described later in the section on clinical illustrations) might be understood as attempts to fill this space or to re-engage the foreclosed development and create the missing psychic structure.

Hildebrand (personal communication) has suggested that there may be a further primal phantasy corresponding to death and endings, as opposed to origins. This may be important because origins and death both function as limits to narcissistic aspirations. The narcissistic wish is: (1) not to have originated from two parents, but to have created oneself, to owe nothing to anyone; and (2) to go on for ever (category 6; illusions of self-sufficiency). Becker (1973) has emphasised the ubiquity of the wish to deny death – seeing the narcissistic dream as one of avoiding the vulnerability and limitations inherent in inevitable death. As we have seen the confrontation with the passage of time is a recurrent implicit theme in discussions of narcissism.

These primal phantasies of one's origin and one's death must have an intimate connection with the sense of lineage (category 7 of the taxonomy).

A note on the foreclosure of the father and the denial of the primal scene

It is important to address the question of how to understand the process of the defensive exclusion of the father – to consider whether it corresponds to any commonly described defence mechanism. Clearly, the father is not 'repressed'; the latter term, as used by Freud (e.g. 1915b) refers to the denial of an internal perception (of instinctual need). The attitude to the father in the narcissistic dyad of mother and child seems more akin to what Freud (1918) described as 'disavowal' (*verlangnet*) or 'repudiation' (*verwerfung*) which refers to the dismissal of an external perception (such as the absence of a penis in women). The term 'foreclosure' seems very apt, using its standard dictionary meaning (*Oxford English Dictionary*) of 'to bar, to shut out completely'. In the early narcissistic position we are describing, the father is shut out from the mother–infant dyad. The father is not allowed his normal place in relation to the mother and in relation to the child – the authority of the father, as equal to that of the mother, is not accepted and nor is the father's sexual relationship with the mother with its significance of being the origin of the child.

There may be varying degrees of dismissal of the primal scene. The more complete denial may result in the phantasy that the child was the mother's own omnipotent creation; a less extreme dismissal may not deny the primal scene completely but its continuing significance may be downplayed, so that the person may believe 'they only did it once' or 'they don't do it now' – the mother may foster the view that she was the father's unwilling sexual victim.

The term 'foreclosure' does, however, have a more specific meaning in Lacan's system. He uses it to refer to a development predisposing to psychosis, whereby something that should be symbolised (e.g.

castration) is not given an inner mental representation and the person never properly enters the realm of the symbolic, wherein symbol (signifier) is distinguished from thing symbolised (signified). He links this with the function of the father. In Lacan's view it is through what he conveys by the metaphor of 'Le Nom (Non) du Pere' – the paternal injunction, the 'law' – that a separation is allowed between signifier and signified (as well as between mother and child), thereby permitting entry to language, to names, to the symbolic order.

Such a radical failure of development as Lacan describes is not normally apparent in patients described as narcissistic. Such patients do not normally show the kind of severe thought disorder and failure of reality testing that would ensue from a failure to differentiate signifier from signified. The foreclosure seems to be more partial. Sometimes the impression is of a process similar to what Freud (1927b) described in his account of splitting of the ego in fetishism, whereby one part of the mind accepts the reality of the absence of a penis in women, whereas another part repudiates this – as if part of the narcissistically disturbed person's mind accepts the place and function of the father, whereas another part retains a delusional disavowal. However, the more common situation in narcissistically disturbed patients may be that the father is not completely barred access to the person's mind, the reality of parental sexuality is partially accepted, but it is de-emphasised, not fully acknowledged, or, to use a visual analogy, as if it is pushed out of focus.

Narcissism and the internal primal scene

We can think about the primal scene not only as a phantasy about the relationship of the actual parents, but also as relating to an internal unconscious activity between parts of the mind. This internal intercourse may in some sense be understood as the basis of creativity.

Money-Kyrle (1971) writes (p. 442):

> Remember that in the inner world, parthenogenic creativity is a megalomanic delusion. All you can do, and surely this is enough, is to allow your internal parents to come together and they will beget and conceive the child.

Perhaps another way of stating what Money-Kyrle intends is to say that the conscious 'I' does not do the creating. However, the writer's clinical observations suggest that the narcissistic patient may have as disturbed a relationship to the internal primal scene as to the external one between the actual parents. For example, a somewhat grandiose patient who objected if the therapist made any interpretation that went beyond an empathic elaboration of what the patient was himself conscious of feeling, would also vigorously object to the whole notion of an unconscious mind. The idea that there might be a part of his own mind, a deeper part, that he was not fully aware of, and that he was in a sense dependent on, seemed as intolerable to him as the idea that the therapist might know something about him that he himself did not know, and that he might be in some sense be dependent on the therapist. In a manner characteristic of some of these patients, he could not allow himself to free-associate, but instead would carefully decide upon the content to be discussed in a session, censoring any thoughts that he considered not 'relevant'.

Another patient with similar difficulties would try to decide on what his next mental–emotional development should be – as if maintaining a delusion that his emotional development could be under his own omnipotent conscious control. When this notion was explored in the therapy he began to realise that he did not really allow himself to free-associate but instead kept a conscious control over his discourse. He then went on to speak of his reluctance to accept a legacy from his parents and his wish to be free of all emotional debt to them. It was easy to draw out from this his wish to be self-created, to owe nothing to another or to his unconscious mind. His material in the session immediately subsequent to this focused increasingly on his parents' relationship to each other – and the deeply painful experience of being left as a boy of five for several months with his grandparents while his parents went off together to another part of the country in connection with his father's work; prior to this point he had had a very close relationship with his mother – even as an adult he felt a pull from his mother towards an overintimate relationship with her. Following the moment when he became aware of his delusion of omnipotent control of his own development, he became able to face painful aspects of his relationship to his parents' relationship to each other and to allow his own thoughts to associate creatively.

The notion of an internal primal scene – which may or may not be allowed to take place – need not be thought of specifically in terms of internalised parents. Rather it may be regarded as a paradigm for the creative intercourse of different elements within the mind. In the acceptance of this can be seen the sanity of the 'religious' attitude that recognises a higher or greater creative power than the conscious self.

The paternal function

Insofar as the earliest and closest caregiving relationship is with the mother, the father may be experienced as 'other', as a figure who comes from outside the close dyad, who *impinges* on the dyad and who may therefore be both welcomed and feared. As Loewald (1951) suggested, the father may be the *representative of reality*. Indeed the Jungian author, Neumann (1971), imagines that whatever is prohibitive or frustrating in the mother is experienced by the infant as proceeding from the paternal.

Neumann describes the purely narcissistic state as follows (p. 15):

> In the post-uterine phase of existence in unitary reality, the child lives in a total *participation mystique**, a psychic mother fluid in which everything is still in suspension and from which the opposites, ego and self, subject and object, individual and world have yet to be crystallised. That is why this phase is associated with the 'oceanic feeling' which repeatedly makes its appearance even in adults when unitary reality complements, breaks through or replaces everyday conscious reality with its polarisation into subject and object.

By 'unitary reality' Neumann seems to mean essentially a state in which the differentiation between self and other has not yet been achieved. According to Neumann, the infant does not initially have a differentiated concept of mother and father, of male and female, but gradually as this differentiation is achieved, the disturbances in the primal relationship with mother are experienced as emanating from the masculine – initially the masculine within the mother (p. 104):

> When the child's consciousness is sufficiently differentiated that a disturbing factor is reflected not only by symptoms but also by psychic images it becomes evident that the child's psyche interprets all disturbances of its state of equilibrium, regardless of kind, as emanating from the masculine. In the dreams of children as of grownups, the negative stimulant is often symbolised by terrifying animals or of robbers or burglars. Whether or not they are accompanied by corresponding psychic images, a considerable share of infantile anxieties are connected with this phenomenon of masculine incursion.

In Neumann's scheme this masculine force is the structuring differentiating principle, defining limits and order. The implication is that for the child this principle is gradually felt to be embodied by the father. Different anxieties are evoked by the archetypal (i.e. innate unconscious) maternal and paternal images. The archetype of the 'Terrible Mother' carries anxieties of being devoured or engulfed, of being drawn back into a a state of undifferentiation where there is no masculine principle. On the other hand, the 'Terrible Father' archetype carries anxieties of an overpowering destructive intrusion.

Greenfield (1985) similarly states that 'we may characterise the archetypal masculine as an *intrusive, active* principle that pushes the development of consciousness out of primal undifferentiation and

---

* Although Neumann's concept of 'participation mystique' may apply to certain *aspects* or *periods* of the young infant's state, the newborn certainly has a good deal of differentiated perception from the beginning (see Mollon, 1985; Stern, 1986).

unity with the mother'. Like Neumann, she also describes how the masculine principle is associated in dreams and mythologies with the development of consciousness. Thus here again the masculine or paternal is associated with the awareness of reality, countering *illusions* of undifferentiation.

These accounts of the archetypal masculine seem likely to be related to what is described more concretely in Melanie Klein's (1932) writings as the infant's fear in phantasy of encountering the father's hostile penis inside the mother's body.

In a paper on the missing paternal dimension (Mollon, 1985) the writer described the experience of chaos that may arise when the paternal structuring principle is excluded – in this case by a combination of an ineffectual drunken father and a mother who appeared to lack any capacity to maintain appropriate limits or boundaries. The oedipal situation was distorted by the mother's having allowed the patient, Miss D., to sleep with her until adolescence and her allying herself with Miss D. against the father. Generational boundaries were unclear because the patient felt that her parents did not function as parents – that her father in particular was more like a child. Miss D.'s image of the primal scene, the sexual relationship between the parents, was distorted by her belief that they had not had intercourse since she was born – a belief that found support in the reality of her parents' relationship. Her experience of self was markedly disturbed; as the therapy progressed she complained frantically of not knowing who or what she was, of not knowing what she really thought, felt or believed – in sexual orientation she was bisexual. She showed a tendency to seek out strong idealised paternal figures to attach herself to – for example, a criminal boyfriend, whom she experienced as powerful. It is interesting to note that Miss D.'s disturbed sense of self seemed to have been exacerbated by the fact of her mother's peculiar lack of emotional responsiveness to her – i.e. that she had a non-mirroring mother (stage 1 of the model) as well as a missing paternal dimension (stage 2 of the model).

Clinical illustrations of the search for the paternal function

The writer's clinical impression is that when the father and his paternal function have been excluded from a person's early development, it is common for this foreclosed dimension to be unconsciously sought out, at the same time as it is unconsciously warded off.

Sometimes the third term may be sought in an inanimate form. McDougall (1981), in discussing sexually perverse patients, has described how the fetish may function unconsciously as a 'phallic barrier' between the self and an engulfing mother, with whom the female partner would otherwise be identified. A related example from the writer's practice concerns a male patient, Mr B., whose father died when he was four, resulting in his remaining highly entangled with his mother. During his therapy he described a fantasy that there was a TV camera in every room of the clinic, which would be monitored by someone in a central office. Although this may have the appearence of a paranoid fantasy, for this patient it seemed to have a reassuring function, the camera representing a third party who could potentially intervene in the otherwise dyadic relationship between him and the therapist.

Often there appears to be an attempt to engage in an oedipal struggle that had originally been bypassed as a child. The patient mentioned above, Mr B., would frequently get himself into a situation where he would be confronted by a male figure who would either throw him out of somewhere or bar his access to a woman; he would then feel violently angry with this figure. The impression was that he was attempting actively to create the oedipal situation which had been aborted by his father's death, leaving him engulfed by his extremely 'phallic' mother.

A similar example concerns a young man in group therapy (Toby), who was extremely prone to shame and self-consciousness, his presenting symptom being a fear of sweating in public. He had grown up as an only child with his mother, a possessive woman who had actually hidden his shoes in an attempt to prevent him going out when he first had a girlfriend – his father being an occasional visitor but never part of the household. Very often the patient seemed to perceive the therapy group as a possessive mother who would try to take him over. This had been a recurrent theme in the weeks prior to the following sequence: one session he began angrily to accuse the conductor of being authoritarian and dictatorial, although the basis in reality for these accusations was actually rather slim. It was interpreted to him that he was requiring the therapist to be an intrusive and authoritarian father who could come between him and the engulfing group mother, and with whom he could engage in a rivalrous struggle. He accepted this interpretation and another group member then asked him what he remembered of his father; he produced three memories: the first was of lying in his cot as a baby while his father was 'doing something' to his mother; the second was of father and mother having a violent argument in the car; the third was of his father beating him; thus two of the memories represented a violent primal scene, whilst the third represented a violent engagement between the patient and a largely unavailable father, none of these representing a psychologically viable continuing relationship with a father.

Two more examples concern all-female therapy groups. One of these was a special group run for the mothers in one-parent families (i.e. men were absent both in the group and the background family). The group conductor, also female, in reporting the group described constant fears that the institution, or some external authority, might intrude and stop the group continuing. Thus the institution seemed to carry the paternal dimension for the group. Another all-female group had, throughout most of its two years, referred to men in exclusively negative terms – as incompetent, neglectful, unreliable etc. However, as the group neared its ending date there were recurrent themes relating to psychological birth – e.g. the birth of babies, the discovery of new skills, the creation of more space at home, as well as more negative birth imagery, such as a dream in which a bird crashed against the side of a bulging house and dropped down dead. Concurrent with this development, images of helpful men began to appear – e.g. a builder who helped to create nore space in the home and a man who built a dolls' house for a child. Thus men were eventually allowed their place and were seen as facilitating psychological birth and individuation.

It often appears that the constellation in which the 'paternal dimension' (Chiland, 1982) has been excluded may give rise to the attempt to ressurect the missing father, the phallus, in a degraded and sexualised form, as in the following example: a patient described his mother as very dominant and 'hostile to any self-expression' and his father as an emotionally withdrawn man, incapable of responding to his son. The patient had two sisters but no brothers – thus maleness was not prominent in the family. It appeared that any expression of individuation was discouraged in the family and the patient felt that his 'emotions had to be left on the doorstep before going into the house'. One day, the patient developed the delusional thought that people had seen him masturbating as they walked past the curtained window of his bedsitter. This gradually became a pervasive delusion that people knew about and were talking about his masturbation. When seen some time later, in a consultation, this delusional *belief* had reduced but was still a major preoccupation. It subsided very markedly in response to an interpretation regarding his extreme shame about his masturbation, linking this with his unconscious *wish* for his masturbation to be seen – this latter being an expression of his need to demonstrate that he had a penis, that he *was a man*, and to have that recognised and thus to seek an affirmation of his existence and his maleness which he had not received from his father. (A paranoid delusion of reference may perhaps be partly a defence against the terrifying sense that there is *no* reference or recognition of the self – that there is no-one in whom it is possible to evoke interest; a point which links with stage 1 of the model, and which is discussed at greater length in Chapter 4. Following this interpretation he then reported a recurrent fantasy which apparently he would often have in the presence of men whom he admired; this involved a sensation that he had a penis in his mouth and his anus at the same time. He concluded that this reflected his wish to take in 'potency' from another man – to 'suck it in' through his mouth or to have it 'injected' up his anus. I think it is clear that this fantasy and the delusion regarding his masturbation were neither essentially instinctual nor object-relational; they relate rather to the patient's attempt to build up missing psychic structure relating to his sense of self, and particularly to his sense of masculinity.

The role of the mother in impeding the establishment of a triadic position: the sado-masochistic dyad; the perversion of authority

A frequent contributor to this situation may be the attitude of the mother who denigrates the role of the father and discourages the child from developing an affectionate relationship with him. This may be an expression of the mother's phantasy that she created the child all by herself, or it may give rise to the thought in the child, expressed by one of the writer's patients, that her mother had not given birth to her but had found her. If the father has not been allowed his full place in the mother's mind, it may be more difficult for him to find a place in the child's mind – and in this way the disturbance may be transmitted through the generations.

This kind of foreclosure of the place of the father seems likely to give rise to the sado-masochistic bind which often seems characteristic of narcissistically disturbed patients, preventing change and separation, and making therapeutic endeavours very frustrating to the therapist until the internal closed system is confronted. The point may be illustrated through a consideration of the early power and authority relationship between parent and child. Gear, Hill and Liendo (1981) have described two fundamental modes of excercising authority. In the first, authority defines expectations and rewards or punishes accordingly. Beyond insisting on these rules, authority recognises the child's separate identity. By learning to observe these rules and at the same time learning to assert its own autonomous sphere of identity, the dependent ego is gradually transformed into a partner who cooperates with the significant other and comes to accept a relationship of equality. The other mode of excercise of authority makes any such resolution impossible and leads to a perpetuation of an asymmetrical relationship of dominance and submission – i.e. sado-masochistic. Instead of excercising authority on behalf of the culture the significant other uses this position to exact omnipotent control over the child – impeding the child's development of a sense of agency and autonomy (category 2).

In this latter position, the external order, the symbolic father mediating between the dyad of mother and child, is excluded. Here Lacan's (1957) metaphor of the 'Name of the Father', the 'lawgiver' is relevant. In French, Lacan's phrase contains a pun, 'Le Nom du Pere' can also be heard as 'Le *Non* du Pere'. For Lacan, the entry into language and culture and all aspects of *mediated* reality (a word, for example, being separated from what it signifies, *mediates* between the speaker and the thing itself) can be understood metaphorically as being brought about by a *paternal* function. It is not difficult to see that if the role of the real father is denigrated or denied by the mother then the symbolic father is also likely not to be given due place. The consequence seems to be a basic defect in psychic structure. Moreover, this early interpersonal situation between mother and child becomes inevitably intrapsychic and may account for what seems to be a characteristic therapeutic difficulty in penetrating what appears to be a closed internal system; the therapist is treated either as an excluded and denigrated third term, or else is feared as the engulfing mother, these two positions alternating in the course of therapy.

It would seem probable that it is the attitude of the mother towards the father, rather than the availability of the actual father, that is important in determining whether the child can progress from a dyadic position; it is a matter of to what extent the mother encourages the child to have relationships with the father, or father-substitute – and to what extent she herself has a loving relationship with the father, or at least believes in the *possibility* of a good relationship with men. If the mother conveys to the child the view that anyone other than herself is not to be trusted, or that all men are bad, then the child will feel that a relationship with the father, or a father substitute, is a disloyalty to the mother, which risks the withdrawal of mother's love. On the other hand, if the mother conveys the feeling that loving relationships with men are possible, then the child will find it easier to seek out father substitutes even if the actual father is absent.

The relationship between stages 1 and 2 – the marriage of maternal and paternal functions

Stages 1 and 2 of the model can actually be understood as combined if we think in terms of basic maternal and paternal functions. The emotional receptivity and responsiveness to the child, emphasised as essential in stage 1, might be understood as the feminine or *maternal* function, in partial analogy with the female sexual receptivity. Thus the first stage may be understood as depending on the maternal dimension, whilst the second stage requires the intervention of the paternal dimension, to provide separation, differentiation and structure.

However, the two stages are artificially separated. Structuring, organising and limiting functions are also required from the beginning, even if there is only one main caregiver. We might presume that the optimum development of self in the child depends on an appropriate marriage of maternal and paternal elements in the caregivers – here we might link again to the significance of the primal scene, the sexual relationship between the parents and the narcissistic difficulties associated with the child's denial of this relationship.

One obvious question to be addressed is whether stages 1 and 2 are necessarily connected, and whether stage 1 alone would lead to narcissistic disturbance. It seems very likely that failures in stage 1, the evocation of a thoughtful mirroring response in the mother (or other primary caregiver) would give rise to disturbances in category 2 of the taxonomy (subjective self/sense of agency) and 4 (sense of organisation), but not necessarily in any of the other areas of the taxonomy.

It would be expected that a child feeling unmirrored by the mother would turn to another regular figure, probably the father. However, according to the theory presented here, the crucial pattern contributing to a common syndrome of narcissistic pathology is the absence of a responsiveness in the mother which mirrors the child's authentic self (as opposed to mirroring those aspects of a child that correspond to *her* wishful phantasy of the child) coupled with her discouragement of the child's relationship with the father. In this way the mother imprisons the child in an image in her phantasy – perhaps a highly positive or idealised image, but nevertheless an illusory image rather than the reality of who he or she actually is.

Mr B. – a narcissistically disturbed man whose therapy is briefly described later – told of a story he had once written about a man who was imprisoned in his image on the videotape – a fantasy that captures nicely the experience of alienation from the living self which results from this situation.

Thus the mother's part in excluding the third party, the father, albeit colluding with the child's oedipal wish, can be seen as just one aspect of a maternal failure to recognise the child as a separate and potentially autonomous being – in Kohut's terms, to recognise the child as an independent 'centre of initiative'. The father as a third term perhaps also corresponds to Kohut's 'idealised parent imago'. Kohut (1977) suggests that if the child does not establish a cohesive self in the early mirror relationship with the mother, there may be a second chance if an idealising 'selfobject' relationship can be established with the father. Clearly, this two stage formulation has some similarity to the two-stage model proposed here. The role of the father, as evidenced in Kohut's clinical illustrations but not in his theory, is examined in detail in Chapter 6.

Further discussion of the role of the father in facilitating the emergence of self – survey of relevant literature

Freud's view of the father was largely of a hostile figure who must be fought with or submitted to, in the context of the oedipus complex. This is apparent, for example, in *Totem and Taboo*, *The Future of an Illusion*, and *Civilisation and its Discontents*, where he also refers to his theory, or mythology, of the primal father, the original all-powerful male who kept all the females for himself, castrating or killing any sons who challenged his authority. Freud believed the oedipus complex, involving the wish to possess mother and to kill off father, was universal. In a footnote to the *Three Essays* in 1920, he wrote: 'Every new arrival on the planet is faced with the task of mastering the Oedipus complex.' Much less often Freud did allude to a more positive relationship between son and father. For example, in *Civilisation and its Discontents* he wrote: 'I could not point to any need in childhood so strong as that for a father's protection', and in *Group Psychology* (1921) he wrote:

> ... the little boy manifests a special interest for his father, he wants to become and be like him ... This behaviour has nothing to do with a passive or feminine attitude towards the father (or towards men in general), it is, on the contrary, exquisitely masculine, it is not in opposition to the Oedipus complex but helps to prepare it.

Since then a number of authors have referred to the role of the father in facilitating the child's separation–individuation – the dual strands of separation from the mother and the development of an individuated sense of self (Mahler et al., 1975). Part of this emphasis has been to stress the negative *dread*ful image of the mother and the threat of losing the differentiation from her. One of the earliest of these contributions was that of Loewald (1951), who wrote that 'the original unity and identity, undifferentiated and unstructured, of psychic apparatus and enviroment, is as much a danger for the ego as the demands of the paternal castration threat to give it up altogether'; he proposed that the father played an important role in facilitating ego development, individuation and differentiation. He suggested that in personifying external demands and restrictions on infantile wishes, including oedipal wishes, the father is a representative of reality. Loewald also specifically stressed the father's role in helping the child free him- or herself from 'sinking back into the original unstructured state of identity with her', with an accompanying loss of reality:

It would be justified to look at the defensive function of the ego ... from an entirely different point of view; what the ego defends itself ... against is not reality, but loss of reality, that is the loss of an integration with the world such as exists in the libidinal relationship with the mother, and with which the father seems to interfere in the Oedipus situation (castration threat).

Much of Loewald's paper is concerned with the ego's relationship to reality. This focus occurs again particularly in some of the psychoanalytic writings on perversion. For example, Chasseguet-Smirgel (1985) places the problem of perversion firmly in the context of man's struggle *against* reality – especially the realities of sexual differences, of generational differences between child and adult, the sexual relationship of the parents and the role of the father and the father's penis. According to this strand of theory (which has some similarities to Grunberger's discussion of narcissism), the pervert is attempting to deny that maturation (and the passage of time) is necessary before the child can acquire the same capacities, including sexual capacities, as the father. Chasseguet-Smirgel does not emphasise the other danger, the loss of reality, described by Loewald. McDougall (1981) also discussing perversion from a somewhat similar point of view, emphasises both dangers.

It was Mahler who developed the concept of separation–individuation, the gradual differentiation of the sense of self in the context of the vicissitudes of separation from mother. She also emphasised the father's role in this process (Mahler and Gosliner, 1955). The father is seen as the 'knight in shining armour', uncontaminated by the ambivalence felt towards mother; he represents an 'other than mother' world, a stepping stone from the pull of the symbiotic tie to mother. Mahler (1966) states:

> The mother image evolves by being first differentiated within the symbiotic dual unity complex and then separated out from it; ... the father image comes towards the child from outer space as it were ... as something gloriously new and exciting, at just the time when the toddler is experiencing a feverish quest for expansion.

Whilst Mahler emphasised the uncontaminated pre-oedipal image of the father, a related emphasis has been upon the role of the father as the needed oedipal rival, in the positive and negative versions of the oedipus complex according to the sex of the child. With the exception of Loewald's paper, this focus has come primarily from analysts working in France, especially McDougall, but originally Lacan, drawing on structuralist and linguistic, social-structuralist theorising. Lacan pointed to the necessity of the father's 'castrating' both mother and child – or representing the communication to the mother that she must not reappropriate her product, and to the child that he or she cannot return from whence he or she came. Lacan's insight was that what is universal about the oedipus situation in *every* culture is the necessity of subjecting one's desire to the 'law'. Lacan coined the phrase 'Le Nom du Pere', to refer metaphorically to this law – it is also a pun on 'Le *Non* du Pere', the father's role in imposing restriction, in saying 'No'. Lacan draws on Levi-Strauss's argument that the fundamental laws of society are those of kinship – ultimately the taboo against incest. A parallel is drawn with the child's entry into language, in the broadest sense of entry into the symbolic world whereby desire is mediated through shared symbols including words. Normally the child subject enters into language, finds his or her place within language and is given a name. If the child fails to subject his or her desires to the law, to language, or if the oedipal father fails to intervene effectively in the mother–child symbiosis, then according to Lacan, the result is psychosis – the child has no name and no place.

McDougall (1981) uses some of these Lacanian insights, but in a more orthodox psychoanalytic framework, and with particular reference to perversion. Like her French colleague Chasseguet-Smirgel, she describes the appeal to the pervert of promoting infantile pregenital sexuality as superior to the sexuality of the genital father. Rivalry with the father is bypassed. This often is the case when the mother colludes with the child in giving him or her the impression that they really can be mother's little lover, the sufficient complement to mother's desire. Gratifying though this illusion might be, the child is left without the protection of the father against the danger of reabsorption into mother. The child then feels caught between the two dangers of, on the one hand, the engulfing mother, and, on the other hand, the castrating father. MacDougall describes how the pervert may compulsively require some kind of fetish to represent the missing paternal phallus, and to construct a 'phallic barrier' against the dread of loss of self in mother.

Stein (1985), in his paper 'On being alone with one's mother – the horror of incest', has discussed the dual dread of castration, on the one hand, and of incest on the other. Referring to the incestuous wish, he writes: 'All men nurture such wishes, and the horror of incest impels them to look everywhere for the stays that will guarantee that their desire will never be fulfilled.' He suggests there may be two versions of the interpretation of the conflict: 'The difficulty is that in the version that puts the accent on the primacy of the incestuous wish, the fear is fear of the father; whilst in the one that accents the primacy of the horror of incest, the fear is fear of the mother.' He contrasts the formless horror of incest, the remerger with mother, with the more clearly and easily represented fear of the father's punishment, suggesting the latter may often be used to cover the former:

The horror of incest amounts to the fear of death, such is our conclusion. This horror is without dramatic content. Its content is nothing – the nothingness of death connoted by an abstraction. And we can add, it seems, that the expectation of punishment inflicted by a jealous father or, in transference, the expectation of condemnation by the psychoanalyst is superimposed on this horror and substitutes for it as a representation capable of assuming the form of an image conforming to the logic of a dramatic configuration.

Abelin (1975), working originally in Switzerland and influenced by Lacan and other French analysts, as well as Piaget, developed his model of 'early triangulation' through studying schizophrenic children and their families. Beginning with the idea that schizophrenia is characterised by a breakdown both of symbolic mental functions and of the mental image of the self, he hypothesised that both depend on the existence of a satisfactory relationship *between* the parents:

> ...in normal development, some kind of internalisation of the relationship between the parents takes place around 18 months.... This internalisation somehow leads to the formation of the self-image and of symbolic mental representations in general.

Abelin's argument why this should be so and how it comes about is as follows: drawing on Piaget's work on the sensorimotor world of the young child, he points out that while being at the centre of his own world, the child, before 18 months, knows only about the world and not about himself:

> Indeed before the child is able to construct symbolic mental images of absent objects, he experiences only a succession of scenes ('tableaux') in front of him. He has no concept of himself as a subject like others. His world has only one focus at any one time – prototypically his libidinal attachment object. Even his own motivation is perceived as a quality of the outside object: the child does not desire the object; he sees the object as desirable.

In his emphasis on the infant's experience of a succession of scenes without the capacity to reflect upon, or have a perspective upon these immediate scenes, Abelin appears to be describing Lacan's 'Imaginary' order, which exists prior to the intervention of the father as a third party and the child's entry into language, the 'Symbolic' order.

Abelin argues that the toddler cannot construct a true image of the self as long as he does not realise that *he* is the origin of the desirability of the other, and that self-hood is the acknowledgement of one's core wish. According to Abelin, the child recognises his own desire through feeling reflected in an other, i.e. the father in the oedipal triangle:

... faced with this excruciating experience of exclusion, the toddler recognises for the first time in the rival's wish for the object his own frustrated wish for the same object. His action being suspended (because all his familiar attachment schemata are blocked), what he can do is actively to *imagine* himself as being like his rival: 'There must be an I, like him, wanting her.' Early triangulation is this identification with the rival.

Thus Abelin links the experience of oedipal rivalry with the first awareness of the self, the discovery of desire and entry into symbolic functioning. In his later elaboration of his model, Abelin considers the rival may not only be the father (the primal constellation) but also other children (the Madonna constellation).

Abelin sees early triangulation as leading to the birth of the self. He argues that having disengaged from the mother during the Mahlerian *practising* subphase, the child wishes to reunite with mother in the *rapprochement* subphase. For both boys and girls the core wish is the same: 'I want mummy'.

Only in man does this copernican revolution of the mind take place. In other words, only in man is the father internalised into psychic structure. To be more precise it is the truth of the father–mother relationship that is internalised, the truth about one's origin ... In sexual triangulation, the self is engendered by the father and mother – and with it the explosion of symbolic thought. This is indeed an important step towards the psychological birth of the human infant.

For boys, however, the gender identity may be clearer in the form of I (male) want Mummy (female), whereas for girls the generational difference may be more prominent – I (child) want Mummy (big). Abelin suggests that for girls the father does not form such an important part of the structure of mental representations until later, until the classic oedipal phase around the age of 3 years. From his observations, Abelin draws the perhaps surprising conclusion that boys are conscious of sex differences at an earlier age than girls.

In Abelin's more recent tripartite model of triangulation, he suggests three stages. First the Madonna constellation of mother–baby–self; secondly the primal constellation of mother–father–child; thirdly the classic oedipal triangle, mother–father–child. Abelin's writings are somewhat confusing and it is not at all clear how the second stage differs from the third – for instance, he writes: 'only in the boy is there an early sexual triangulation which is then replicated by the oedipus triangulation on the higher level of symbolic image' (Abelin, 1980). He may be asserting little more than that the little boy is earlier aware of sexual differences than the litle girl. However, it is open to question that this is the case. Edgecombe and Burgner (1975), for example, find both little boys and girls, in the pre-oedipal phallic phase to be preoccupied with bodily sexual differences. Reservations would also be felt by those influenced by Melanie Klein's view that the oedipal concerns arise as early as the first year and that from the beginning the little girl has an awareness of her vagina (Klein, 1932)

Moreover, the view that the father is important for the little girl's gender identity only during the oedipal phase has been criticised, e.g. by Machtlinger (1981). She states:

> Clinical evidence suggests the opposite is true. The fact that the little girl's self-image is implicitly feminine (through her primary identification with her mother) does not mean that the little girl does not need continuous pre-oedipal interaction with a male person (usually the father) in order to *define* her gender ... It is my contention that it is precisely such continuous and affectionate interaction with a father (or father substitute) that makes it possible for her to direct her oedipal wishes towards him in the oedipal situation.

In fact, since Freud's original account of the little girl's change of love object from mother to father to form her positive oedipus complex, the particular role of the father in relation to his daughter has been remarkably neglected in the literature. One notable exception is Leonard (1966) who described various pathological patterns of father–daughter interaction and their consequences for the girl's development. She concludes that what is crucial is the father's availability to his daughter as a love object and his capacity to offer his affection without being seductive or seduced.

In spite of these reservations concerning the details, the importance of Abelin's work is that it emphasises the role of the father and of the relationship between the parents (the primal scene) in the development of the sense of self – in terms of recognition of one's desire, and of differentiation of self generationally and sexually.

Klein's view of the early stages of the oedipus complex raises questions whether there is ever a period of life which should be considered purely dyadic – or whether triadic relationships are present from the start with a differentiation between maternal and paternal elements of the infant's world. For example, Meltzer (1967) speaks of the nipple as the paternal part of the breast; Neumann (1973), a Jungian analyst, describes the infant's experience of the mother's restriction as the intrusive paternal element within the merger, 'participation mystique', with the mother. On the other hand, most American analytic theorising, and that of all those working within the Freudian stream, differentiates a true oedipal phase of jealousy and rivalry beginning around the age of 3.

Rotmann (1978) questions Abelin's assumption that the young child is capable of purely one to one dyadic relationships. He suggests that the child becomes aware soon after the emergence from symbiosis of a pattern of relationships which are *at least* triadic – involving two parents and probably siblings. He proposes that 'early triangulation' is the inherent basic pattern of relationships within the family, forming the background to normal development, and therefore not experienced suddenly as a conflict situation. Rotmann agrees with Loewald (1951), Mahler et al. (1975), Abelin (1971) and Burlingham (1973) that the father plays an important role in helping the child separate and differentiate from mother – but also believes that the father optimally functions as a demonstration that it is possible to have a relationship with mother *and* retain individuality and autonomy. If Rotmann's suggestion is correct, it would presumably follow that a bad relationship between the parents, a distorted primal scene, especially one involving a dominating mother and a passive father, would serve to reinforce the child's fears of an engulfing mother and his or her difficulties in differentiating and individuating.

Herzog (1979, 1980) examines the role of the father through looking at the fantasies, play and dreams of children whose fathers were absent due to divorce. A notable feature of this material was its aggressive content and, on the basis of these observations, Herzog suggests that a particular function of the father is as a modulator of aggression and that the small child experiences the loss of the father as a disruption of his or her *own* control of aggression. These observations also suggest that the child's fear of something inside him getting out of control leads to an intense wish for the father – Herzog coins the term 'father hunger' – and it appears that the mother's attempts to comfort the boy (all this is particulary pronounced in the case of the boy) may only exacerbate the situation by evoking the dread of re-engulfment. One implication of Herzog's findings may be that the litle boy requires a father partly to fight against and to be in rivalry with.

Another author who has emphasised the little boy's positive feelings for his father is Blos (1984). He stresses these isogender experiences associated with the father of the 'dyadic' period, distinguishing this from the oedipal father of the triadic period. He states:

> The oedipal father is by definition the restraining and punitive father under whose threat of retaliation the little boy abandons his competitive strivings as well as his patricidal and incestuous anxieties.

Blos argues that the negative oedipus complex (i.e. the positive feelings for the father) are not recovered until adolescence – that in adolescence there is a wish to be close to the father to counter the dread of the female:

> ... the flight of the adolescent boy to the father, defensively manifested by rising oppositionalism and aggression, is usually commensurate to the intensity and urgency of the son's need for a protective closeness to him vis a vis the magnetic and mysterious female to whom he is irresistibly drawn.

Blos considers that this defensive oppositionalism represents a struggle against passivity. He implies that this is defensive against a more basic wish to be close to the father, which is, in turn, defensive against the pull to the dreaded engulfing female. However, he does not appear to consider the possibility that what the adolescent needs is certainly closeness to the father, but precisely in the form of a battle with him – that it may be through the battle with the father that the adolescent boy affirms his gender identity and his move towards adulthood. Similarly, in discussing the original oedipal childhood situation, Blos makes a distinction between a triadic and a dyadic situation which may be inappropriate. In the present writer's view, the conceptual difficulty arises over the fact that the oedipal father can also be desired and welcomed *as a rival* – that it may not be the case that a dyadic phase, 'preoedipal' father is first loved unambivalently and that this is then followed by the rivalry and hostility of the oedipal period. It may be that part of what the child desires and needs from the father is his availabilty as a rival to be engaged with (Mollon, 1986). Blos seems to hint at this possibility when he states:

> Contemplating the period of the precompetitive son-father attachment, as well as the confidence and security the little boy derives from his father's control and domination, the conjecture presents itself that an indestructable residue of the early father trust carries over into the tumultuous arena of the triadic struggle. This is to say that the restraining and punishing father is also the rescuer of the son from being taken over by infantile delusions; this so called rescuer is the early personification of the reality principle, who makes growing into manhood an attainable expectancy.

Psychoanalytic theorising often seems to draw an artificial distinction between developmental and psychodynamic phenomena – i.e. between pathology due to 'developmental arrests' (e.g. Stolorow and Lachmann, 1980) and that due to conflict. This links with the American tendency to distinguish oedipal and pre-oedipal relationships to the father. Kohut (1977), for example, de-emphasises oedipal conflict and talks instead of the child's need for mirroring and idealised self-objects – often in his clinical illustrations the needed idealised self-object is the father. It does not seem implausible to suggest that the father as idealised self-object, as mirroring self-object and as oedipal rival are intertwined aspects of the relationship to the father – that the child wants to admire his father, wants this admired figure to take an interest in him, and at the same time wants to be able to compete with him and to be admired as a worthy little rival.

To summarise the views discussed in this section: the oedipus complex has been seen as containing a crucial encounter with the realities of the difference between the sexes, the difference between child and adult, and the separation between mother and child. The father's role has been seen as facilitaing this separation from mother and as standing as a bulwark against the threat of regression to an early state of lessened differentiation, the dread of the engulfing mother. In a broader sense the father is seen as standing for reality and the necessity of subjecting one's desires to the law. The encounter with these issues has also been implicated in the development of symbolic functioning and the assumption of one's place within language and culture. The father has been thought to play a crucial role in promoting gender identity, through identification in the case of the little boy, and through being available as a minimally seduced and seductive love object in the case of the little girl.

Model B – the captivation by an illusory image

On reviewing work with a number of narcissistically disturbed individuals, the writer was impressed by the way in which the patients seemed to be in opposition to their own more authentic selves. Instead of desiring their own individuation, they seemed to be more concerned to maintain a particular false image of themselves – i.e. to maintain an illusion. In each case this appeared to be an illusion based on the image in the mother's mind – in three of the four cases, a rather grandiose image. Thus it was not so much a case of a failure to separate and individuate from mother per se, but rather a failure to differentiate from the image in the mother's mind. This image does not permit any growth or development – thus the dimension of time, like that of the father, is excluded. Their own authentic self is regarded with hostility and is feared – feared almost as if it were another person threatening their autonomy. Whilst appearing to, and believing themselves to be, preserving their identity, these patients are actually defending a false illusory identity at the expense of their authentic self; they believe themselves to be what their mother saw in them – thus they are pervaded and captured by the mother's phantasy.

Psychoanalytic therapy is greatly feared by such people because it threatens to destroy the illusion upon which they have based their false self. As described in the first model, the father has been excluded and is felt to be a potential representative of reality, a destroyer of illusion – his intrusion is feared yet is needed if the child/patient is to be freed from the dream-like state of mesmerisation with mother. Similarly, the interpretation of the therapist is both desired and feared. Reality itself is experienced by these people as persecutory in its challenge to illusion.

This elaboration of the model helps to explain further the difference between the narcissistic character and the psychotic individual. The latter may have experienced more difficulty in achieving a sense of separateness from mother per se rather than from the image in mother's mind – a process described by several authors as important in psychotic developments, notably Mahler (1968) and Jacobson (1971). The narcissistically disturbed character seems rather to experience him- or herself not as the *same* as mother, but as a function for mother (more generally, for the 'other'), rather than a separate autonomous agent (category 2 of the taxonomy).

The model and the categories of self-disturbance

Differentiation

The model describes difficulties in separation from mother, fostered by the mother's attitude, the child's oedipal desire and the relative absence of the father. Paternal functions which define boundaries and provide structure and represent reality are excluded. In remaining in a 'dyadic position', the narcissistic personality is unable to reflect upon him- or herself, unable to be truly conscious of self.

The difficulty may not be in separating from mother per se, or from the image of mother per se, but but from the image in the mother's mind.

Agency-efficacy (subjective self)

According to these models, the child's own initiatives towards separation–individuation and autonomy are not encouraged. Thus a deficient sense of agency is expected. Stage one describes how the sense of efficacy, as a fundamental aspect of the sense of self, may be dependent on the capacity to evoke a meaningful emotional response in the caregiver.

Objective self

The model describes how the image the narcissistic person has of him- or herself is derived from the image in the mother's mind; the grandiose aspect of this image may correspond to an image in the mother's mind.

Structure–organisation

Failures of the mother's mirroring functions and unavailability of the father for idealisation, as described by Kohut, are features of the model. These would be expected to lead to deficiencies in the structure and organisation of the self.

Balance between subjective and objective aspects of self

The model describes how this balance is strongly skewed towards objective aspects (the 'Me'). The narcissistic person is preoccupied with being what the other (mother) wants. He or she is out of touch with his or her own inner desires.

Relationship to reality – withdrawal from object relations and illusions of self-sufficiency

The model describes how the father as representative of reality may be excluded. The acknowledgement of separateness, time and the necessity of development is avoided. An illusion of 'perfection now' may be fostered through the attempt to be what mother desires.

Sense of lineage

The obliteration of the primal scene as the origin of the person in the parental intercourse, associated with the narcissistic wish to be self-created, points to an inevitably disturbed sense of lineage.

How is the new model an improvement on other formulations of narcissistic disurbance?

Disturbances in all seven categories of the taxonomy are accounted for. None of the other models of narcissistic disturbance discussed accounts for all categories – most address only one or two.

The model combines the central aspects of the formulations of both Kohut and Kernberg, the two theorists whose views are usually seen as incompatible. The dynamics described by Kernberg of a defensive clinging to a grandiose self-image are included here, but are seen as based on the complexities of the relationship between child and two parents – rather than being explained in terms of Kernberg's simplistic notion of 'oral rage'. In the same way the similar insights of Rosenfeld are incorporated. The oedipal issues highlighted by Grunberger, and also alluded to by Rothstein, but neglected in most models of narcissistic disturbance, are given a crucial place in the model proposed here.

The narcissistic patient's fear of the deeper self, described well by Schwartz-Salant, but not explored in any other earlier theory, is here discussed in terms of the prevention of the internal 'primal scene' and the denial of the dependence of the conscious self on the unconscious mind.

The idea of the overclose relationship to the mother which does not facilitate the child's development of autonomy, emphasised by Robbins, is also a central aspect of the model presented here – but again it is embedded in an understanding of a three-party relationship rather than the merely dyadic as in Robbins's formulation.

The way in which the child may become trapped in a dyadic 'mirroring' relationship characterised by sado-masochism, emphasised by Gear, Hill and Liendo, is also apparent in the model presented here. Like Robbins's model, that of Gear, Hill and Liendo is limited by its failure to take account of the role of the father.

The themes addressed in Bursten's model, such as the difficulties over separation–individuation, the mother's overruling of the child's moves towards independence, the seduction into illusions, the denigration of the father, all find a place in the model developed here.

The theorising presented here can be seen to incorporate and subsume all the insights of the other models discussed. As those other models are a highly representative selection, it is plausible to assert that more or less all the observations and insights that analysts have made about narcissistic patients are incorporated into this model.

Chapter 6
Clinical exploration of the model

To explore and illustrate the model, four cases are described. Each patient showed significant disturbance in several categories of the taxonomy and each complained explicitly of uncertainties in the sense of self. They were treated initially within a brief psychotherapy format, of 15 sessions in two cases and 10 sessions in the other two. These were video-recorded. Each were given further therapy after a follow-up interview.

The material of the therapies is described schematically, the aim being to show the underlying structure of the disturbances.

Mrs A.

The case of Mrs A. illustrates the disturbance in the sense of lineage that can result when a person's actual paternity is obscured. Mrs A.'s attempts to relate to her father and later her step-father were strongly discouraged by her mother. This 'attack on linking' by her mother was internalised, creating difficulty for Mrs A. in making links either with her own authentic self or with other people, especially men. A part of Mrs A., in alliance with this internal mother, was deeply opposed to the work of therapy – it is particularly clear in this case how the therapist may be experienced as the warded off father.

Initial presentation

Mrs A. was 30 years old, divorced, working as a company manager. At the time of referral she complained of feeling tense and depressed, resulting in her turning at times to drink. Reaching this age had prompted her to review her life so far, especially the previous decade which had included a disastrous marriage from age 19 to 23. Her husband, 8 years older than her, had had other girlfriends throughout the marriage and actually had a child by another woman, living with her while still married to Mrs A. She had been living with her current

135

partner for 4 years and had a 13-month-old son by him. They both met
'on the rebound'. Her feelings about him oscillated between content-
ment and extreme dissatisfaction and she felt very uncertain of her
future with him. She wrote in her questionnaire: 'I get very frightened
that we might drift through life with no discussed ideas or plans for the
future.'

She grew up with her mother, an older sister and a younger brother
and a man whom she was allowed to assume was her father. In her late
teens, however, her mother told her that this man was not the father of
the patient or her sister. A few years prior to therapy she had attempted
to explore her own roots but discovered that her actual father had
committed suicide 14 years previously. She described the relationship
between her mother and step-father as stormy and violent, both of
them drinking quite heavily. Her mother threw out the step-father 12
years ago – very brutally the patient felt – as soon as her brother, who
was his son, had left home. The step-father died about a year after this
separation, an early death perhaps associated with his heavy drinking.

In the initial consultation Mrs A. emphasised her fears of repeating
her mother's destructive patterns, relating to men in a callous and
exploitative way. This anxiety was highlighted by her recent thoughts of
leaving her current partner. She spoke of her fear of becoming 'one in
a line of funny ladies who've raised children without fathers'.

Summary of psychodynamics as revealed in the brief psychotherapy

Mrs A.'s difficulties were understood as organising around her struggles in separation–individuation from her mother – her failure to establish a clear sense of her own identity (category 1). Her mother appeared
to have discouraged the patient's awareness of her own thoughts and
feelings, attempting to maintain her daughter as the 'same' as her –
with the result that Mrs A. experienced a kind of perverse 'guilt' about
having thoughts and desires of her own, and about seeking therapy. A
particular focus of her mother's hostility towards separation–individuation was her discouragement of her daughter's relationship to her step-
father – and indeed to any men. Mrs A. was not told the truth about her
paternity and its significance was denied (leading to a disturbance in
her sense of lineage – category 7). Thus she was denied access to the
father/step-father who might have facilitated separation–individuation.
She experienced anxiety and 'guilt' about her contact with the male
therapist.

Based partly upon these characteristics of her actual mother, Mrs A.
developed an internal object with the characteristics described by Bion
(1959) in his discussion of 'attacks on linking'.This internal structure
was hostile to emotional linking, especially to men (father/step-

father/partner/therapist) and to linking past and present. If Mrs A. made emotional contact with herself, or with another person, especially a man, she then experienced an internal reaction whereby she feared a terrifying revenge and felt alone and abandoned; for example, following sessions in which a number of important links were made, including between past and present, she would often experience an overwhelming anxiety that her children would disappear or die, or that her peace of mind and her enjoyment of her relationship with her children and her partner would be destroyed. These anxieties were very clearly free-associatively linked with an extremely destructive maternal imago; her mother was ill with cancer and Mrs A. expressed a terror that her mother would take her with her to the grave. During one session in which she appeared emotionally very cut off and when little of emotional meaning seemed to be emerging, she remarked that something inside her told her she had no right to make links with the past.

The other position she would take up at other times was to ally herself with this internal mother and, in an ego-syntonic way, she then became the one who was opposed to linking – wishing to cut off relationships and opposed to her own authentic feelings (category 6). She would be emotionally cut off, detached and unable to think. In this state, no work could be done in the session until released from it through interpretation; she would be hostile and rejecting towards the therapist who seemed to represent the excluded father. She was then faced with her anxiety and guilt over repeating her mother's destructive pattern. However, she would then feel a curious kind of 'guilt' about feeling guilty – also associated with a similar 'guilt' about feeling upset or sad. She was able to see this 'guilt' in terms of her mother's communications forbidding emotional links. She seemed to be describing what might be termed a 'perverse superego' which forbade appropriate guilt over destructivenes and substituted a kind of 'anti-guilt'. Thus, in her therapy sessions she was predominantly in one of two staes of mind: she would be in alliance with the therapist, making links, but then fearing a terrible retribution from her internal mother; or she would be in a state of great resistance to therapy, allowing no meaningful linking, or thinking, to take place – a position in which she was identified with the hostile-to-linking mother.

In struggling to separate and individuate Mrs A. encountered claustro-agoraphobic anxieties, feeling either trapped and taken over, or alone and abandoned. Her conflicting feelings and states of mind were not brought together in consciousness, as in a state of ambivalence, but were kept actively split – so that she alternated between moving towards and away from her relationships, whether with the therapist or her partner. As a result of the therapy she became more capable of holding conflicting attitudes simultaneously, more capable of ambivalence. The splitting in her mind, and its lessening, was illustrated particularly by her eventually telling the therapist about a secret other relationship with a man at work. She referred to this disclosure as 'something fundamental left out at the beginning (of her therapy)'; clearly this repeated the way in which her potential relationship to her father had been foreclosed in the beginnings of her development. This other relationship was often felt to her to be 'unreal' and she stated that she felt she was living part in reality and part not in reality – a clear statement of an ego split. Various functions may have been served by this, perhaps particularly (1) a means of avoiding investing all of herself in *one* man and thus feeling more vulnerable; (2) a means of preserving an area of herself protected from her mother's intrusion (both her actual mother and internal mother); and (c) a means whereby, when feeling claustrophobic in relation to one, she could run to the other.

A further major issue concerned her narcissistic vulnerability and narcissistic resistances. She referred to a vulnerable core of herself associated with feelings of shame – this core 'cannot be prized open', but had to be protected. Her narcissistic vulnerability seemed to derive from her having felt her emotions were ridiculed, especially those towards her step-father. She resisted what she perceived as the therapist's threatening efforts to change her, to turn her into someone else – she felt the 'deeply formed' parts of herself should not be changed. The irony of the conflict was that these deeply formed parts of herself were in their very structure determined by the others from whom she was trying to free herself.

Mrs A. – categories of self-disturbance

1. *Differentiation* – she experienced a considerable struggle to differentiate from her mother.
2. *Subjective self-agency* – she felt herself to be 'a collection of impulses' rather than as a director of herself; she definitely lacked a sense of autonomy.
3. *Objective self* – her self-image was poor; her self-esteem was low.
4. *Structure–organisation* – she often felt frighteningly lacking in a sense of inner structure and coherence – she struggled to hold on to the 'protected core' of her.
5. *Balance between the I and the Me* – this was markedly skewed. There was too much Me and not enough I.
6. *Illusions of self-sufficiency* – she would often retreat to illusions of self-sufficiency – she was afraid of any sense of needing the therapy or the therapist.
7. *Sense of lineage* – Mrs A.'s sense of lineage was markedly deficient – she had not known her father and the message from her family was that it was not important to know who her father was.

Themes of narcissism

1. *Illusion* – this theme was reflected in her not knowing who or what she was, in being captivated by her mother's false propaganda, and in her struggles to free herself from her mother's illusions.
2. *Lack of self-knowledge and knowledge of origins* – this was a central issue. Knowledge of her origins had been concealed from her – she felt that she did not know who she was.
3. *Reflection and mirroring* – this was not a prominent theme except in its negative – an absence of mirroring of who she is.
4. *Sado-masochism* – Mrs A. experienced herself as being in the 'victim' role. She had an expectation of relationships being characterised by cruelty, exemplified by her mother's treatment of men.
5. *Vanity, pride, turning away* – she would often retreat to an aloof withdrawn state – a turning away from the object when she felt threatened by feelings of dependency.
6. *Fear of being possessed* – this was a prominent theme. She was quite consciously afraid of being repossessed by her mother.
7. *Envy* – this was a prominent theme, in the form of a fear of her mother's envious attack.
8. *Dangers of self-absorption* – this did not seem to be a prominent issue here. Mrs A. seemed more object-related than Narcissus of the myth.
9. *Violent primal scene and an absence of a continuing parental couple* – this was a very prominent theme. There was no image of a loving relationship between her mother and father; there was no continuing couple.

Mr B.

The case of Mr B. illustrates how a person may be quite alienated from his own feelings and lost in the images and fantasies of the other (his mother). This is a situation that can evoke enormous rage, which, for Mr B. was expressed in self-destructive behaviour and sado-masochistic sexual fantasies and activities. This state of alienation seemed to have developed in the context of an oedipal victory – he was his mother's little lover – but behind his hostility to his father emerged clear longings for an idealised paternal figure.

Initial presentation

Mr B. was a 37-year-old, flamboyant and entrepreneurial businessman in the fashion world. He was separated from his wife. His career had progressed well until in his late twenties he had dropped out and travelled the world living as a hippy. After a few years he had returned and took up his career again and had been moderately successful in recreating his business. He had, however, tended to sabotage his chances and generally behave self-destructively – including from time to time drinking heavily. He sought help because he was concerned about this pattern.

He wrote in his questionnaire of feelings of confusion and uncertainty about his goals in life and of finding difficulty in facing reality. Narcissistic concerns with self-image and self-aggrandisement were apparent in his responses to the questionnaire, as well as in the assessment consultation. For example, he wrote of his hopes from therapy: 'I hope to realise my potential as a human being so that I can have a warm loving relationship, good friends, a sparkling career, wealth and be a reliable, responsible, organised, clear and lovely man'.

In the initial consultation interview he came across as seductive and entertaining, a performer, but he conveyed the impression of enormous suppressed rage. Mr B. seemed to become momentarily aware of this rage when the interviewer commented on his apparent feeling that as a child he had felt valued only for his performance and not for himself – he had been speaking of his mother's pride in his performances when she had put him in for local variety shows. Although fleetingly in touch with anger he quickly became unaware of it, lighting a cigarette and forgetting what he had just said. This manoeuvre seemed to constitute what he referred to as his 'going unconscious'. When this issue was explored he spoke of a 'terror of consciousness'; he thought that he was very cut off from his feelings and very frightened of experiencing them. He thought he would 'drink, smoke, fuck, anything in order to not see how I am feeling'. In talking of his repression of his anger he associated to his having sometimes felt very depressed.

He spoke of feeling phoney and of being manipulative – the impression was that he felt trapped in a world of mutual manipulation and exploitation. This and accompanying rage seem to find expression also in sado-masochistic sexual fantasies and practices which he referred to. He spoke of a preoccupation with sexual conquests, an avoidance of real intimacy and the feeling that his relationships were essentially shallow. His narcissistic sensitivity was apparent in his accounts of how easily he can feel rejected or offended. He also described his constant proneness to acute self-consciousness – a terrifying feeling that he would struggle to suppress when his work required him to be something of a performer.

He described his early relationship with his mother as blissfully happy – 'a love affair' – he would often run indoors just to tell her he loved her. However, he described his later feelings towards her as more complicated and less trusting. He recalled jealous hostility towards his father and described mixing a plate of kitchen 'poison' in order to kill him! Apparently his father, a writer, was often absent, and when at home locked himself away with his typewriter. As well as having little relationship with his father Mr B. was also deprived of contact with other males through being sent to a school predominantly for girls – he recalled wanting to be out fighting among the boys.

At the time of this consultation his mother was still alive. His father had died some years previously.

Summary of psychodynamics as revealed in the brief psychotherapy

This seemed to organise into two main interrelated areas. First his distrust and paranoid feelings, stemming from his relationship to his mother, and his split images of self and other. Secondly, his wish for his father as an alternative trustworthy figure.

Mr B. assumed he must perform for the other, fulfil the other's ambitions. This was particularly apparent in relation to the therapist whom he felt he must please. The necessity then of sacrificing his own desires evoked pain and rage which he could not let himself be aware of, and which he defended himself against by detachment. In terms of category 5 of the taxonomy, the balance between the 'I' and the 'Me' was radically skewed towards the 'Me'. He could not reconcile perceptions of his mother as exploitative with images of the mother he had had the love affair with. The split images of his mother and his accompanying paranoia were illustrated by a childhood dream in which his mother had been taken by 'them' and replaced with a replica. Thus, his self-image of basking in mother's love remained unintegrated with the image of an enraged self in relation to an exploitative and abandoning mother. Whilst feeling close to his mother, he had 'ignored' his father and had made conscious plans to poison him. His oedipal wishes deprived him of more contact with his father, exacerbating his father's relative absence. During the course of therapy he became aware of how he had also wanted closeness to his father as an alternative to the controlling dyadic relationship with his mother. Part of what he was deprived of in trying to fulfil mother's ambitions was contact with other males – he was sent to a girls' school and clearly felt feminised. This may have increased the intensity of his need for contact with males, ultimately for contact with his father. During the therapy this need for a paternal figure often took the form of attempts to identify with powerful, strong or 'ruthless' idealised selfobjects, for example a martial arts teacher and Christ.

A particular kind of relationship that developed in the transference, which presumably repeated an earlier one with his mother, was a highly restrictive 'monitoring' relationship – the patient felt either closely and oppressively observed and monitored by the therapist, or else he was monitoring the therapist. As a child he seemed to have identified with the observer, developing a 'self-monitor', always looking on at himself. In the ensuing world of mirrors and monitors his subjective 'I' became lost – embedded in the immediacy of the dyad he could not locate or reflect upon himself, a situation portrayed in a fantasy of being videoed while watching the video of his therapy. The father could have potentially offered an alternative, a mediating perspective, but again was unavailable, partly due to Mr B.'s oedipal exclusion of him.

Further therapy

The feelings and the transference evoked by the therapy could not be contained within the ten sessions. Mr B. denied the significance of the ending until it actually came; he then wanted to be seen again soon. In spite of this limitation of the ten-session format, positive features of the therapy were that his paranoid fears of exploitation and his rage and his sadness of the lack of relationship with his father were more deeply felt and understood in historical context.

He was seen for a follow-up two months later and, as had been promised to him, he was allowed to see some of the video-tapes. Although initially claiming that he could not say that he had really learned anything from the therapy, on looking at the tapes he felt that he had learned a lot, but that the insights gained had become part of him, integrated into his self-awareness rather than consciously held. Other comments he made at this point concerned how anxious and unreal he appeared in the early sessions and also how he liked himself in those parts of the last session where he was sad and seemed to him to be more authentic.

At Mr B.'s request he was seen for further therapy, once per week, for about eight months until the therapist left the clinic. During this time, changes in his mood and behaviour became apparent.

The initial sessions of this further phase of therapy became focused on his sadistic and violent impulses, particularly towards women. It became apparent that if someone got emotionally close to him, he would attack them. This appeared to stem from his profound fear of exploitation and violation – his defence was to attack, violate or pervert the other. He spoke of his sexual excitement over the 'innocent' child-like appearance of his current girlfriend and of his impulse to violate this innocence. An interpretation, that he was actively repeating his own experience of violation and perversion of his childhood by being required to perform for his mother, seemed to have meaning for him. Master–slave, mutually controlling features of relationships were apparent in his enacted beating fantasies. To some extent the sado-masochism served to protect against intimacy – it seemed that greater potential intimacy with his girlfriend led to an intensification of his sadistic sexuality. Overall he appeared to be warning that his sado-masochistic impulses would become engaged in the therapy, particularly if the therapist were able to make emotional contact with him. Mr B. added the information that with his wife he had been unable to enagage her as victim – she was the master and he would impotently attack her by staying out late and drinking heavily. At this stage of the therapy Mr B. was drinking a great deal, and arriving rather late for his sessions and the parallel in the transference seemed clear.

As Mr B. became more aware of the extent of his destructive impulses he became more concerned about his excessive drinking and was able to give it up. Having done so, it became apparent that a further motivation behind his drinking and violence was his need for excitement and his profound fear of an empty lethargic unstimulated state – he was, to use his own words, a 'drama queen'.

The therapy moved on to become increasingly concerned with his homosexual fantasies, his wish and fear of being raped by powerful men and his need for idealised strong male figures. At times his concern would be with spiritually or morally ideal figures and, at other times, more concretely and regressively with large penises. It was clear that he was increasingly turning toward the therapist as father in the transference. He began to feel his father could have offered him something 'quiet and subtle' in contrast to the drama and excitement he associated with his mother. A pattern became apparent, that he tended to miss a session after he and the therapist had talked about his father; he complained of feeling confused and disoriented when he tried to think about his father, feeling there was a 'hole' in his mind. Eventually in the hole he located feelings of anger and sadness about his father's unavailability. A small piece of acting out highlighted this: one day he ignored the receptionist's instructions and walked straight to the consulting room, arriving there before the therapist. The receptionist, a woman, tried to telephone the therapist to inform him that the patient was on his way up, but the patient answered the phone in the consulting room and refused to leave the room. In the subsequent session, Mr B. produced material about never having been allowed in his father's room – the room where he wrote and spent most of his time. The receptionist reminded him of 'all the powerful women in my life'.

After some weeks, Mr B. announced that he was beginning to feel differently about himself. He said he felt 'like a man is emerging', and that physical objects were looking more three-dimensional. He also spoke of feeling more able to be himself with the therapist. This was contrasted with how he felt meeting his ex-wife when he had felt squeezed out by her egocentricity. The therapist suggested that, in view of recent material, perhaps it was his father who was the third dimension, allowing him to emerge as a man from the dyad with his mother. This interpretation seemed to have meaning to him. He disclosed that it had been while with the martial arts teacher, a clearly idealised paternal figure, that the world had begun to appear three-dimensional. He then produced more material about having felt he had no real place or role with his wife – he had felt himself to be a 'toy', a 'clown performer', in his wife's house.

The impression he gave was of having been squeezed into two dimensions with no substance or autonomy of his own. The therapist was reminded of a fantasy reported some time before of being reduced to a two-dimensional image on a video film. The general trend of the material suggested that the presence of a paternal figure, a third dimension, was associated with Mr B.'s own emergence into a three-dimensional state. Mr B. went on to talk about his uncertainty about himself as a man and his taking up Aikido as something very masculine, concerned with fighting and confronting. He also at this point expressed concern about his own inadequacies as a father and spoke of his wish to read books about fathering.

A further phase, which continued to the end, concerned the increasing emergence of what he referred to as his 'serious side' which he had hitherto normally kept hidden. He referred to his childhood 'Little Buddha' self, quiet and contemplative, which had been covered by his extroverted 'naughty' public persona. He spoke with regret of how while with a friend on holiday he had behaved in quite a false way, being cynical and joking as the friend expected him to be. His mood and manner in the sessions became more and more relaxed, thoughtful and seemingly more authentic. At the same time he talked increasingly of his religious and spiritual interests, continuing the 'Little Buddha' theme. He dreamt that he was a wealthy man and associated to thoughts of spiritual wealth.

His spiritual interests were clearly linked with the idealised selfobject of the martial arts teacher who was clearly a paternal *spiritual* figure to him as well as representing masculine strength and power. At the same time his dreams reflected a concern with the size of penises and with physical sexual power. These seemed to represent a concrete sexualised version of his idealised spiritual concerns. He associated to a childhood curiosity of looking at his father's penis and thinking that his own would never be that big. It was possible to arrive at a plausible reconstruction that what was being represented here was his childhood disappointment in his father's failure to stand up for him against his mother – his disappointment in his father's lack of potency as protective father, and his compensatory fascination with the size of his father's penis.

Increasingly Mr B. seemed to value the therapy as a setting in which he could be himself – where, as he described it, he and the therapist could each have their separate thoughts, meeting together rather than one imposing thoughts on the other. He began to feel that he would miss the therapy very much when it ended. On the other hand, he feared degenerating into the old pattern becoming destructive and self-destructive with his anger over the ending.

In the final session, an old theme re-emerged – his difficulty in having a perspective on himself. He wanted the therapist to tell him how he was, how he had changed etc., commenting on the absence of a video to give him a picture of himself this time. Again he seemed to be looking for himself in the picture someone else had of him. He also reaffirmed his continuing wish for a 'guru', a spiritual selfobject. He expressed profound gratitude for the therapy, saying that he now felt more solid and more real.

Mr B.'s categories of self-disturbance

1. *Differentiation* – Mr B. existed primarily in a state of 'being for the other', a performer filling an assigned role. He was quite out of touch with his own feelings and markedly unable to reflect upon himself.
2. *Subjective self: agency* – consciously Mr B. did not complain of feelings of powerlessness; however, his fears of being exploited, manipulated and controlled soon became apparent. One of the ways he appeared to have tried to deal with this anxiety was by means of G. Klein's 'reversal of voice' – he became the one who actively controlled himself and his feelings.
3. *Objective self* – overtly grandiose self-images were apparent.
4. *Structure–organisation* – this was not a notable manifest area of disturbance to begin with, except in his narcissistic vulnerability to rejection, slights etc. Later as the therapy progressed, and particularly in the longer further therapy, his great need to feel linked to an idealised paternal selfobject became apparent, his desire to obtain masculine 'hardness', to strengthen what he felt to be his soft feminine self. At the end of his therapy he spoke of feeling more solid, an aspect of experience of self which may be included in this category.
5. *Balance between the I and the Me* – this balance was markedly skewed towards the Me. He tended to be quite out of touch with the I.
6. *Retreat to illusions of self-sufficiency* – in a rather non-specific way, Mr B. seemed to experience difficulties in facing reality – both external reality and the internal psychic reality of his own feelings.
7. *Sense of lineage* – Mr B. did not appear notably disturbed in this area.

Mr B. – themes of narcissism

1. *Illusion and captivation by a deceptive image* – Mr B. was trapped in the illusion of his mother's fantasy that he should be a beautiful

performer on the stage. He spoke evocatively and concretely of feeling trapped in the image – his fantasy of being a prisoner of the video-tape.

2. *Lack of self-knowledge* – this captivation in his mother's fantasy meant that Mr B. was strikingly out of touch with his own feelings and desires. He looked for himself in the image presented by the other – more concretely he looked for himself in the image on the video screen.

3. *Reflection and mirroring* – Mr B. was greatly dependent on the other's reflection for his sense of self.

4. *Sado-masochism* – sado-masochism pervaded Mr B.'s relationships. His sexual fantasies and activities were strongly sado-masochistic. Tremendous rage underlay his relationship to women.

5. *Fear of being possessed* – whilst this anxiety might be expected, in view of Mr B.'s general mental state and early development, it was not prominent, although it might be inferred from his difficulties in relationships with women.

6. *Vanity and pride* – Mr B. was overtly 'narcissistic', somewhat vain, egocentric and exploitative and preoccupied with his body.

7. *Envy* – this did not appear to be a prominent theme.

8. *Dangers of self-absorption and illusion – developmental cul de sac and death* – his mother's narcissistic use of him (using him to satisfy her own needs) and Mr B.'s own 'narcissistic' conduct meant that his development had been restricted. He had achieved little of substance either in his career or his relationships.

9. *Origins in violent primal scene and absence of a continuing parental couple* – this was not a prominent theme. Mr B. knew who his parents were and he seemed quite able to acknowledge his origins. However, there seemed to be no *continuing* strong parental couple in his early experience; his mother was the dominant figure and his father relatively absent.

Mr C.

The case of Mr C. illustrates how profoundly incapacitated a person can be if *inappropriately* narcissistically gratified by his mother by being given the impression that he need not strive or develop because he is already perfect. For Mr C. this illusion was supported also by his mother's denigration of his (step)father in contract to her idealisation of Mr C. The narcissistic illusions offered to Mr C. by his mother were initially gratifying but had become a trap, grossly restricting his further development. He longed for more involvement with a father who could have provided more of a route into reality.

Initial presentation

Mr C. was a 39-year-old man who appeared much younger. At the time of assessment he had done one year of a foreign language degree course as a mature student, but having failed the examinations was taking a year off with a view to returning to college later. He was experiencing difficulties in studying and had been seeing a counsellor at the college. Prior to enroling as a student he had worked for a number of years as an insurance salesman.

In the assessment consultation he complained of difficulties in making relationships and of lacking self-confidence. These had been particularly apparent while at college. More generally he described feeling that he drifted through life with no purpose. He had been married for two years in his twenties but had no children. More recently he lived with a woman for a couple of years, but at the time of attending the clinic he was living alone and had no girlfriend and gave he impression of a rather limited social life.

His marriage had fallen apart, he felt, through mutual disinterest. He thought that there was a pattern in his relationships in that they started off well, each partner attempting to present his or her 'best side' to the other, but he would be afraid of the other person seeing what he was really like – eventually there would be a mutual disillusionment. The theme of his presenting the best side of himself recurred in his talking of how accommodating he can be, often finding himself altering his views in order to fit in with the other person.

Another area he described was his tendency to feel self-conscious, looking in mirrors a lot and often feeling people were looking at him. He thought he easily felt offended and often reacted as if feeling that people were trying to put him down.

With regard to his childhood he placed particular importance on having been told at the age of 21 that he was illegitimate, his mother having had him before she met his step-father. He had been unaware of this fact, but the knowledge had seemed to link with a chronic sense of his having occupied a strange position in relation to his 'parents'. He recalls hating his mother for always seeming inappropriately to stand up for him against his step-father. One example he gave was that as an adolescent he would sometimes come home late and his mother would offer to make him sandwiches; however, if his step-father requested a sandwich she would scornfully refuse. On the other hand, Mr C. felt that his step-father was not particularly interested in him, preferring his step-brother. He recalled an incident from his primary school days: a number of parents had gathered to complain about a teacher who assaulted the children; in the case of every other child it was the father who turned up, but in the case of the patient it was his mother. Thus it seemed that a sense of illegitimacy existed alongside a feeling of being in a rather privileged position.

After a wait of some months Mr C. was offered ten sessions of therapy with a possibility of a review and further therapy later. Mr C. was asked to clarify with his student counsellor that this did not conflict with her involvement with him – this seemed to become a signficant influence on the material of the first session, in which he appeared preoccupied with the implied deference of the male therapist (father) in relation to the female counsellor (mother). The counsellor in fact was seeing Mr C. only occasionally at this point.

Summary of psychodynamics as revealed in the brief psychotherapy

Mr C.'s mother was over-protective and over-indulgent, shielding him inappropriately from reality, especially from his step-father as a representative of reality and discipline. The latter was denigrated by his mother whilst the patient was the favoured one in his mother's eyes; she appeared to have identified him with her idealised image of his biological father, whom she had known only briefly. As a result Mr C. felt that something was missing from his psychic resources; he lacked the capacity for self-discipline and tolerance of frustration, qualities that he might have otherwise acquired through identification with his step-father. He described a tendency to retreat from reality into an omnipotent world of fantasy, which seemed to represent his clinging to the over-gratifying relationship with his mother (category 6 of the taxonomy).

On the other hand, the closeness to his mother had its alarming aspects, particularly when he reached adolescence. He dreamt of a phallic mother, literally his mother with a penis, whom he wished to run away from. His mother's love began to seem engulfing. His efforts to disengage from his mother in adolescence were illustrated by his having become immersed in his image in the mirror, finding a reassuring confirmation of himself in the thought that he was 'an ugly sod' – an image that perhaps he felt to be himself, contrasting with the idealised image of him in his mother's mind (struggles in the area of category 1 of the taxonomy). He longed for a father in whom he could see a reflection of himself, particularly a reflection of his maleness, father and son mirroring each other. During the therapy he experienced a degree of calm and well-being which seemed to be the result of the presence of the interested therapist, functioning as a paternal selfobject.

His father hunger was clearly very strong, directly related to his sense of the absence of interest in him from his step-father. In the absence of a father who would mirror *him*, be a selfobject for him, it seemed that he attempted to merge his identity with that of his step-father. He described how he had attempted to become a reflection of his stepfather by 'twisting and turning' to fit into his views. Thus, his identification with this step-father's views became part of a false self which he later consciously sought to disengage from. It was perhaps as if he strove to escape the captivation by the image in his mother's mind by attempting to become a likeness of his father. Recognition of his own authentic self was missing.

His inability to evoke an interested response from his father, as a mirroring or idealised selfobject, appeared to have contributed to his proneness to narcissistic rage when the world did not respond as he wished; he would smash objects that thwarted his wish for omnipotence and his tolerance of frustration could be extremely low. The impression was that his primary helplessness and rage was the helplessness of being unable to gain his father's interest – the narcissistic supplies necessary for him to feel affirmed in himself, to experience himself as a 'centre of initiative'.

Further therapy

The ten sessions could not be said to have achieved more than limited therapeutic success. The gains were that a good deal was clarified of his psychopathology and he seemed to become more aware of, and have an understanding of, his narcissistic tensions – his needs to be responded to, and his father hunger, and the impact on his sense of well-being of the presence of an interested paternal figure. He also may have become more aware of his repressed anger about the absence of his father's interest. However, there was little evidence of any real structural change or resolution of conflict; in the final session he appeared withdrawn and resentful and to feel tht he had achieved little benefit. It seemed likely that if the therapy had been longer Mr C. may have been more able to use the therapist as a paternal selfobject around whom to organise a more authentic sense of self. However, there was a way in which the transference never really came alive in this brief therapy, as if the therapist as an intrusive oedipal figure had to be warded off. It seemed possible that a more overt oedipal struggle would have achieved more.

Mr C. was seen for a follow-up three months later. At this point he said he had gained a lot of understanding from the therapy, but that putting into practice what he had learned was a different matter. In particular he had realised how much he shut off his awareness of his emotions. He also reported that fantasy had less appeal to him now; he still would drift off into day-dreams at times, but these no longer provided the same gratification.

However, the dominant impression he conveyed was of stagnation.

He appeared to be spending his days doing very little other than read novels, had no plans for the future and moreover seemed remarkably unconcerned about his situation; indeed it was initially difficult to get him to address the present reality of his life. When asked to imagine his life 10 years on he said he imagined it would be 'just the same'. He talked about the difficulties he had had in his college courses; he thought that he had given up the work whenever any effort or struggle was involved, whenever he could not write or understand *immediately*. It occurred to the therapist that he was describing a delusion that no learning need be involved, that knowledge, understanding and skills should be present instantly. Mr C. acknowledged that this seemed to be the case and he recalled how as a child he liked to make plastic models; he would smash them if they were not perfect – they usually were not, because he would never read the instructions, as if assuming he should have no need to take in information but should have the necessary knowledge present already. A little later in the interview he complained of 'people who tell you you should act your age', mentioning a friend who played guitar in a rock group and whose wife told him he was too old for this. The therapist commented on his apparent efforts to maintain an illusion of the obliteration of time, of development, maturation, change and the necessity of learning. Mr C. responded by saying he had sometimes thought that he is like Peter Pan; all his friends had grown up, their lives had changed, they had married and had children, while he had stayed *the same*. It was then possible to link this material with his efforts to maintain the illusion of remaining mother's partner, obliterating the necessity of growing up and acknowledging father's superior age. Mr C. appeared to accept this, but then seemed to return to his previous stance, this time complaining of how people might get married just because their parents had got married, and how boring, empty, conventional and depressing most people's lives were. The therapist commented that whilst rejecting a certain way of life associated with parents or fathers, he did not appear to be forging a satisfying lifestyle of his own. Mr C. replied 'Yes I sometimes wonder whether when I go on about conventional things, people's possessions and so on, whether I'm really rejecting them simply because they are things which go with being older and grown up'.

In a second interview it became clearer how he maintained an ego split, rather like that described by Freud in connection with fetishism (1927b), one part adopting a realistic stance and the other maintaing illusions. He talked again about his difficulties in studying, but talking as if he was still a bona fide student, seeming to ignore the reality that he had been expelled from the course. Exploration of this revealed his efforts to maintain an uncertainty in which everything can seem possible, rather like an adolescent not yet ready to decide on a path. Returning again to his difficulties with essays, Mr C. described how he needed what he wrote to be 'perfect' and that even an alternative point of view would constitute an imperfection. It became understandable how Mr C. had been severely incapacitated in his college work through his efforts to avoid the whole area of comparison, competition and authority.

As the therapist knew that he could offer Mr C. more therapy if necessary, he felt free to interpret and confront Mr C.'s difficulties. Although Mr C. initially appeared rather unconcerned about his situation, the therapist felt *very* concerned. The role the therapist seemed called upon to play was that of the intruding father – 'father time' – destroyer of infantile delusions and representative of reality. Mr C. was offered further therapy which he accepted, remarking that he would like to be helped to make the transition from adolescence to adulthood.

Mr C. – categories of self-disturbance

1. *Differentiation* – Mr C.'s image of himself was undifferentiated from his mother's idealised image of him. Another aspect of this was that his image of his actual self was not fully differentiated from his image of his ideal self.
2. *Subjective self-agency* – Mr C. was strikingly passive. This seemed to relate to his mother's excessive indulgence and protection of him from the reality of the need to work. The paradox was that his excessive impact on his mother seemed to have prevented from engaging his sense of agency *realistically* with the world – thus without his mother's fostering of his illusion of omnipotence he was left quite passive and impotent.
3. *Objective self* – Mr C.'s self-esteem was low. He aspired towards self-images of perfection, of knowing everything already and therefore not needing to learn.
4. *Structure–organisation* – Mr C. was vulnerable to disorganising narcissitic rage when feeling ignored or unrecognised. He was also prone to disorganising self-consciousness.
5. *Balance between the I and the Me* – this was skewed towards the Me. Mr C. was very self-conscious, and the theme of his false self was an important one.
6. *Illusions of self-sufficiency* – Mr C. would frequently retreat from reality into grandiose daydreams.
7. *Sense of lineage* – Mr C.'s sense of lineage was disturbed. He had not known his father and was puzzled about his origins.

Mr C. – themes of narcissism

1. *Illusion* – Mr C. was caught up in an illusory identification with his mother's idealised image of him. This fostered his tendency to turn

away from painful realities and retreat to grandiose illusions. A central illusion which became apparent involved the belief that it was not necessary to grow up.

2. *Lack of self-knowledge* – being trapped in illusion, Mr C. was partly blind to who and what he was. He feared to discover his own capacities or lack of them, preferring grandiose day-dreams. His lack of knowledge of his own paternity, his own origins, was a significant theme.

3. *Reflection and mirroring* – Mr C.'s need for mirroring and the absence of it from his father was a major focus in the therapy. His preoccupation with mirrors and his own reflection was also apparent.

4. *Sado-masochism* – Mr C. indicated that he was aware of intense latent anger within himself. He referred in one session to such feelings being evoked by seeing a film in which a man was humiliated – he linked this to witnessing his mother's humiliation of his stepfather. The sadomasochistic pattern appeared in two forms: (1) his mother masochistically submits to Mr C.'s wishes, attempting to prevent him suffering any frustration – overtly she was his victim, but as is often the case in sado-masochistic dyads, the pattern was covertly the reverse – he is trapped by her submission to him and so is her victim; (2) his mother sadistically denigrates and humiliates his father.

5. *Fear of being possessed* – there were numerous allusions to Mr C.'s conflicts in relation to his mother's over-possessiveness – for example, he spoke of his feeling that she made him a 'little mother's boy'.

6. *Vanity, pride, turning away* – generally Mr C. seemed to prefer his idle grandiose day-dreams to a real engagement with others.

7. *Envy* – envy was not a particularly prominent theme.

8. *Dangers of self-absorption and illusion* – this was quite a central theme. Mr C. retreated from painful reality and his own imperfections, escaping to illusory grandiose day-dreams. Although attempting to maintain the illusion that the passage of time can be arrested, his life seemed to stagnate.

9. *Violent primal scene and the absence of a continuing parental couple* – this was a significant theme. Mr C.'s biological father was absent and unknown to Mr C. – thus there was no continuing parental couple. The relationship between his mother and stepfather was represented as a sado-masochistic one.

Mr D.

The case of Mr D. illustrates how, when an accommodating 'false self' (taxonomy category 5) is prominent, many aspects of a person's feelings, especially anger, may be lost from awareness. Mr D. projectively located many such feelings in his twin brother, who was known as the 'bad one' – Mr D. himself was known as the 'good one'. A particularly interesting point is the way in which Mr D.'s anger (and other unacceptable feelings) and his father both had to be warded off because they threatened his state of partial psychological merger with his mother. It becomes apparent in this therapy that Mr D. needed his father's oedipal intervention (represented by his wife's having an affair with a rival man) in order to allow him to separate and individuate out of this 'cocoon' with his mother. One of the reasons why his father had not been affectively present for Mr D. was because he was belittled by the rest of the family.

Initial presentation

Mr D. was in his mid-forties, born in northern Scotland, a tall cerebral looking man with a pleasant engaging manner. He sought psychotherapeutic help as his second marriage was breaking up. He worked as a teacher at a private school.

An uncertainty about his identity and sense of self were conveyed in his opening remarks on his questionnaire (a standard form sent to all patients attending the clinic for assessment consultations – it asks for factual information and for a personal description of the patient's difficulties):

> Who am I? What do I like and dislike? I am extremely timid. I lack courage. I wear masks, mostly which hide this lack of courage, even from myself, particularly when other people accept the mask.

In the consultation he described a proneness to acute self-consciousness and also shame:

> When I'm teaching, particularly if I have read to something from a book, I become so appallingly self-conscious I have to stop – as if what I'm afraid of is dramatising and acting, exhibiting myself, where I would be the centre of attention – it's to do with attracting attention to *me* rather than to what I'm saying.
>
> To be frank I probably do wish for attention, I wish for interest to be shown in me – I both want and don't want attention – as if I feel myself to be a bit invisible – I felt invisible at school, I melted into the background.
>
> I feel I have the power to draw attention to myself – I think of it in terms of acting – I'm afraid of it – it makes me very uncomfortable – a dishonesty, as if a huge vanity is at work.

Mr D. had a non-identical twin brother. His brother was regarded as the 'bad one' whilst Mr D. was regarded as the 'good one'. He described his mother as warm and attractive but rather remote because of chronic illness – perhaps a rather idealised figure. His father was often absent due to his career in the army, was a strict disciplinarian, but was somehow considered 'irresponsible' by the family.

Mr D. felt that he had squandered his early twenties in a 'puerile rejection of a middle-class background that achieved nothing'. He had rebelled but had not achieved a clear identity and direction of his own. His current wife apparently complained of what she saw as his passivity.

He presented two early memories in the consultation, both seemingly referring to his being favoured by his mother over his brother. The first is of being taken to the railway station to meet his mother returning from hospital; he ran enthusiastically to meet her but his brother did not and was crying. The second memory is of a collection of stones, objects which had been found and which he preferred to the toys he had been given. One day he decided that one of the stones had to die, he took one and dropped it down the drain. The fact that he associated to the two memories sequentially suggested that the stone that had to die represented his brother.

Mr D. was seen for several assessment consultations before settling on and beginning the 15-session brief therapy.

Summary of psychodynamics as revealed in the brief psychotherapy

A striking feature of Mr D. was the way he endeavoured to agree with the therapist all the time and to present an image of himself as endlessly amiable and accommodating. Behind this facade of a false self his resentment and aggression were apparent, but these had to be repudiated. He despised his own dishonesty; he once remarked to the therapist: 'If you said black and the chap outside the door said white, I would agree with each of you, in private – and if you were both together I would sit on the fence.' He complained that he could not confront others nor assert himself. He was greatly prone to feelings of shame. When challenged about his tendency always to agree with the therapist he experienced considerable discomfort and spoke of feeling cornered. On the other hand, there was evidence of his secret sense of triumph in 'fooling' people with his false self.

For Mr D. the process of separation–individuation had been arrested (category 1). He had remained partially identified with a delicate and idealised mother. In order to maintain this partial merger he had to repudiate aspects of himself which he felt to be incompatible with his mother's desires. These unwanted aspects were projectively located in his twin brother (the bad one) and in his father – both of whom he looked down upon. In this way he could maintain a gratifying illusion of continuity with his mother, or of being the perfect complement to his mother's desire, of being the desired phallus. This must have been partly determined by his mother's perception of him as the 'good one' (category 3). A further threat to his continuity with mother was his father's presence as an oedipal rival. His father had to be warded off – as did certain of his own feelings and impulses. This pattern was precisely repeated in the transference; Mr D. constantly attempted to ward off his own threatening feelings and also to keep the threatening therapist at bay. He also acknowledged a 'secret belittling' of the therapist that repeated a similar childhood belittling of his father.

The result of these processes was that Mr D. was left with a depleted and uncertain sense of self (category 4) – constantly preoccupied with how he is appearing to the other person, striving to accommodate the other's wishes, lacking a sense of his own agency (category 2), and prone to the narcissistic affects of self-consciousness and shame. This predicament evoked chronic rage at the need to reject his own self. Yet the rage itself was unacceptable. He feared that his anger might further endanger his sick mother. Moreover, he feared that separation–individuation would mean death to both of them – falling into the abyss with no father to catch him. Thus he had both wished for and feared the intrusion of the father, who would separate him from mother and allow him to become his own self.

Further therapy

Eighteen months later Mr D. was seen for a follow-up interview and was offered further therapy. This was accepted, he said, not so much out of a sense of urgent need but because he knew the therapist would be leaving in a few months. Mr D. had by this time fully separated from his wife and appeared to entertain no hope of rapprochement. His mood appeared sober but not depressed; his general manner seemed somehow older and less boyish. He had developed one or two cautious relationships with new women, but indicated that he was not yet ready to open himself to another deeply emotional relationship; this reserve clearly also extended into the therapy, although useful clarificatory work was nevertheless done. He appeared at this point to be in the process of modifying his belief in God, although he feared that that left him with 'no-one to turn to'. Generally, he indicated that he felt himself to be in a profoundly different state to when he was first seen, more at ease with himself and less frightened – in particular he seemed to feel less frightened of confrontation. He gave an example of how he had recently directly accused a student of plagiarism in an essay; he felt that previously he would have been afraid to do so. This stand against falsehood and pretension became a central theme in the therapy that followed – it was apparent that he was also trying to confront his *own* dishonesty.

In the subsequent sessions he spoke of his 'dread of donning false garments', of presenting a false image. He talked of wanting to be clear and honest about what he was, both to himself and to others. He described his awareness of how he engaged in what he called 'fencing' in the sessions – meaning that he would appear to be open, whilst revealing as little as possible; he wanted to stop this. Exploring this, it became apparent that if the other is taken in by his manoeuvre (e.g. a woman, or the therapist in the transference), they then become a devalued and contemptible figure whom he wishes to escape from. He also conveyed his anxiety that he has to live up to the false image he presents. On the other hand, he indicated that he found the idea that he was deceitful and dishonest difficult to tolerate – it was not consistent with his preferred image of himself (his 'narcissistic image of perfection'). Full acknowledgement of his 'false self' was painful to him. It was apparent that he had hitherto been far more concerned with maintaining images of himself than with authentically being himself.

Another metaphor illustrated a further aspect of his emergence from his false self. He recalled that as a schoolboy he had, during a boring lesson, on occasion read Dostoeyevsky hidden behind his physics book. He also recalled an incident when he had broken into his aunt's house. As these memories were explored he expressed his longing for the 'delinquent side' of himself to be recognised – for his release from the prison of being the 'good one'.

Indications did become apparent of his gradual release from this assigned image of the 'good one'. For example, he reported in one session that he had been 'taken aback' recently while driving to find himself cursing other drivers and *swearing like his brother*. Previously it was only his brother – the 'bad one' who swore. The therapist commented that the patient had been 'taken aback' by finding himself 'taking back' some of his own projected aggression that had been located in his brother. The emergence of such spontaneous anger and aggression marked the continuing gradual release of Mr D. from his state of captivation by false images and the emergence of a more authentic self.

Mr D. – categories of self-disturbance

1. *Differentiation* – Mr D. was incompletely differentiated from his mother and by his own description was uncertain of who and what he was.
2. *Subjective self-agency* – Mr D. was intensely passive and seemed to lack initiative or a sense of his own direction.
3. *Objective self* – Mr D.'s self-esteem was low. At the same time, more hidden grandiose images were apparent – e.g. his image of himself as the 'good one'.

4. *Structure–organisation* – Mr D. suffered disorganising experiences of shame and self-consciousness.
5. *Balance between the I and the Me* – this was skewed very much towards the Me.
6. *Retreating to illusions of self-sufficiency* – Mr D. would attempt to retreat secretly to illusions of self-sufficiency. This would be concealed behind an outwardly accommodating and engaged kind of stance.
7. *Sense of lineage* – this was not a major area of disturbance for Mr D., but clearly he did not have a comfortable sense of himself as the product of two parents. He seemed to prefer illusions of self-sufficiency to an acknowledgement of his dependence on others.

Mr D. – themes of narcissism

1. *Illusion* – Mr D. attempted to maintain a gratifying illusion of continuity with his mother, of being the 'good one'.
2. *Lack of self-knowledge* – Mr D. seemed unaware of many of his feelings.
3. *Reflection and mirroring* – this was not a prominent theme.
4. *Sado-masochism* – Mr D. tended to accept a passive masochistic position, particularly in relation to women. His sense of having to be what the other required also could be seen as masochistic, especially when it was associated with an excessively ingratiating manner.
5. *Fear of being possessed* – this was not overtly a central theme, but it was perhaps implicit in his preserving a secret area of himself behind his outwardly compliant self.
6. *Vanity, pride, turning away* – one of Mr D.'s characteristic positions was an aloof stance, contemptuous of his father – repeated in the transference as a secret belittling of the therapist. Pride and vanity were also apparent in the 'tyranny of the narcissistic image', his preoccupation with his self-image which was quite psychologically constricting.
7. *Envy* – envy was not a particularly prominent theme.
8. *Dangers of self-absorption and illusion* – Mr D. was very preoccupied with his self-image and with preserving the illusion of being the perfect complement of the other person – originally preserving the illusion of being the 'good one'. Maintenance of these illusions prevented him from becoming more authentically himself.
9. *Violent primal scene and the absence of a continuing parental couple* – Mr D. appeared not to have an inner image of a loving relationship between his parents.

Varieties of false self illustrated by the four cases

All four cases demonstrate versions of a 'false self' (a concept introduced into psychoanalysis by Winnicott, 1960). They demonstrate structures which are more complex than that described by Winnicott. Further examination of the concept of false self is required.

Mr B. assumed he must perform for the other (the therapist in this instance) and clearly felt quite out of touch with himself and his feelings such as his rage. For example, it became clear that he assumed he was required to fulfil the therapist's expectations and aspirations by accomplishing a miraculous change. During the course of the therapy he became aware that he had spent his life trying to be a good boy, trying not to be a disappointment. It was apparent that behind this desire, and as a result of feeling himself to be under this pressure, he felt an angry wish to *be* a disappointment, to frustrate the other, originally his mother, and, in the transference, the therapist. Whilst much of the time he was unaware of his rage, cutting himself off from his feelings, this nevertheless did find expression in, first, his sado-masochistic sexuality and his generally sadistic relations with women and, secondly, his self-destructiveness in his career. However, as his career was based upon his fulfilling his mother's ambitions for him, the apparent self-destructiveness could be seen as actually his attempt to destroy his *false self*. His 'dropping out' in his early twenties, travelling round the world and experimenting with hallucinogenic drugs, can also be understood as part of his efforts to throw off a false identity, to destroy through drugs a psychic structure based upon accommodation to the other, and to recover a more authentic self.

Mr D. also assumed that the purpose of his having therapy was to gratify the therapist rather than to get help for himself. He was preoccupied with saying the right thing and with being what he thought the therapist wanted, continually accommodating himself to the other. However, in his case it was apparent that the false self was in the service of control – secret control of the other in order to protect his vulnerability. Thus his false self-accommodation seemed somewhat more conscious than Mr B.'s – he consciously feared that if he relinquished his false self he would become vulnerable and not in control of himself and the other person.

Mr C.'s false self, on the other hand, seemed to stem from his fear that his real self would be an enormous disappointment and would evoke no interest – a fear that related particularly to his experience of failure to evoke his stepfather's interest. Having failed to evoke his stepfather's mirroring selfobject response to him, it appeared that he had attempted to become a reflective selfobject to his stepfather, 'twisting and turning' to identify with the latter's views. During the therapy he represented his false self through a metaphor of a 'mask' –

describing a fantasy of himself as a 'masked character', presenting himself as he sensed the other required. The culmination of this fantasy was that he would aggressively tear off the mask and reveal his true identity.

Mrs A., like the others, showed a predominance of the 'I' over the 'Me', associated with her failure to separate–individuate from her mother. Her experiences with her mother, whom she felt was 'committed to trying to get me to think the same way as she does' contributed to the development of an internal mother who was hostile to her separation–individuation and to her making too deep a contact with herself – thus she feared being honest and any expression of authentic feelings seemed to lead to internal punishment. Another contribution to her false self seemed to be the lacunae in her knowledge of her origins which appeared to have led her to identify with the false position she was placed in by her family. Her choice was of either facing a psychic void regarding her origins, or of accepting a false identity offered by her mother and sisters. Her internalisation of her mother's attitudes, and her rejection of her father and of her authentic self, as well as her general resistance to change, seemed to have become a very fundamental part of her 'self' – as though the rejection of her self had in some paradoxical way become part of her 'nuclear self', like a fifth columnist taken into the very heart of her psychic structure. Thus her accommodation to the therapist was less apparent than in the three other cases. It was more that she clung to an identification with her mother in rejecting the therapist's attempts to relate to a more authentic part of her. In this way she actively struggled to preserve her 'self' but was actually preserving something false.

In reviewing the false self aspects of the four cases, a further common phenomenon becomes apparent. Although the patients had internally compromised their integrity, taking in others' attitudes and making them part of their own psychic structure to suppress their more authentic self, this internal threat to the self, to autonomy, was in each case projected – with the result that other people, including the therapist, were experienced as threatening to violate. This was particularly apparent with Mrs A. and Mr D. The latter, for example, repeatedly talked of his experience of prohibitory commands as emanating from outside himself, from society or from the therapist as representative of society. He seemed to demonstrate a curious clinging to, and identifying with, a certain moral stance, while experiencing its prohibitory aspect as emanating from outside himself. Broadly two varieties of false self can be discerned: first the false self of compliance, described by Winnicott (1960), in which the locus of initiative is surrendered to the other; secondly what might be termed a 'manic false self' – involving a manic denial of psychic reality, a person's deeper authentic feelings, and perhaps a bypassing of the necessity of mental development.

Further discussion of the concept of false self in the light of this material

Brief review of literature on the false self – Winnicott, Deutsch and Khan

In view of the subtle differences among the false self structures of these patients, it is appropriate to review briefly earlier descriptions of false self in the literature.

Winnicott (1960) introduced the term 'false self' into psychoanalysis. He saw this as a part of the personality based on *compliance* to an environment which did not respond to the infant's own inner initiative. For example, he remarked (Winnicott, 1960, p. 145):

> ... the mother who is not good enough ... repeatedly fails to meet the infant's gesture; instead she substitutes her own gesture which is to be given sense by the compliance of the infant. This compliance on the part of the infant is the earliest stage of the False Self and belongs to the mother's inability to sense her infant's needs.

Winnicott saw this false self as having a positive caretaking function of protecting the true self until such time as it might have an opportunity to give expression to itself.

A much earlier description of a false self was provided by Deutsch (1942, 1955) in her papers on the 'as-if' personality and the 'imposter'. Deutsch, 1942) referred to (p. 265):

> ... a completely passive attitude to the enviroment, with a highly plastic readiness to pick up signals from the outer world and to model oneself and one's behaviour accordingly. The identification with what other people are thinking and feeling is the expression of this passive plasticity and renders the person capable of the greatest fidelity and the basest perfidity (sic).

Deutsch considered that such a person can rapidly exchange one love object for another if abandoned – and similarly in the moral sphere (p. 265):

> Completely without character, wholly unprincipled, in the literal meaning of the term, the morals of the 'as if' individual, their ideals, their commitments are simply reflections of another person, good or bad.

Deutsch related the aetiology of the 'as-if' personality to 'a devaluation of the object serving as a model for the development of the child's personality'. She argued that as a consequence of this the individual fails to appropriately internalise and identify with the parent. She implies, but does not state explicitly, that this is in the context of the oedipal situation, where, according to the classical model, the child ultimately internalises the same sex parent to form the superego (p. 276):

> Conflict with the superego is thus avoided because in every gesture and every act the 'as if' ego subordinates itself through identification to the wishes and commands of an authority which has never been introjected.

In a later paper (1955), Deutsch described a related personality structure – 'the imposter'. These are characters who actively assume a false identity and attempt to persuade others of its validity. Whereas the 'as if' personality may dissolve in numerous identifications with external objects, the imposter seeks to 'impose on others a belief in his greatness'.

Regarding her main example of an imposter, Deutsch writes:

> Jimmy was overloaded with maternal love. I knew the mother very well and I know that she was one of those masochistic mothers who, loving and warmhearted, completely surrender themselves for the benefit of others ... Her child's every wish was granted. Any active striving he had was paralysed through premature compliance ...

Thus here she is describing excessive compliance on the part of the *mother* as opposed to the compliance of the *child* described by Winnicott. Deutsch comments (Deutsch, 1955, p. 335):

> I believe that the emotional overfeeding of a child is capable of producing very much the same results as emotional frustration. It contributes to an increase of infantile narcissism, makes adaptation to reality and relationships to objects more difficult.

Deutsch considered that the decisive precipitating factor for this boy's development was a traumatic disillusionment with his father who became chronically ill when Jimmy was age 7: 'Jimmy was no longer able to feel himself to be part of a great father.'

Thus Deutsch described the bypassing of an identification with the father and a consequent difficulty in accepting and engaging with reality (p. 337):

> ... he behaved as if his ego ideal was identical with himself; and he expected everyone else to acknowledge his status.

In this respect, Deutsch's account has some similarity to the model proposed here of failure of triangulation, and also to Kernberg's model of narcissistic personality in which there is a fusion of ideal self and actual self.

Whilst Winnicott placed emphasis on the false self as a protective, outward compliance that conceals and protects the true self, Khan (1972), the major interpreter of Winnicott, emphasised, like Deutsch, a more omnipotent and manic quality – describing the false self as an 'omnipotent defensive self-cure'. He described how an exploitation of intellect may be a basis of a false self-organisation, referring to this precocious mental functioning as 'a special type of manic defence'.

What is meant by the distinction between 'true' and 'false' self?

Whilst concepts of 'true' and 'false' self are easily and frequently used, defining what is really meant by these terms is more difficult. Moreover, whilst 'true' sounds good and 'false' sounds bad, one might wonder what a pure true self with no trace of false self would be like – would it for example be some kind of totally unsocialised 'noble savage' being?

In some ways it seems to be easier to describe and point to a false self. We can think in terms of the idea drawn from Mead, as discussed in Chapter 3, of the balance between the 'I' and the 'Me', the question of the locus of personal initiative and spontaneity – whether the person is actually more aware of the other's needs and desires and fantasies than of his or her own. A person with a predominantly false self would be distinguished then by a strong tendency to be accommodating and responsive to other people, while tending to be unaware of his or her own feelings and desires. By contrast then, a true self perhaps has something to do with spontaneity and, to use Kohut's (1977) phrase for describing a healthy self, being a 'centre of initiative'.

A phenomenon that is perhaps related to the true self is the spontaneous emergence of new mental–emotional growth as artificial identifications are undone during the process of psychoanalysis – growth that is *not* dependent on gross identification with the personality of the analyst. An example is the emergence of *Mrs L.'s* love of writing, her giving up a career of acting which she felt was to do with 'suppressing one's self' and forging a new career involving writing, which she felt was to do with 'expressing one's self' (discussed in Mollon 1984, 1986). Whilst this kind of development depends on internalisation of the analyst's *functions*, just as the child's development depends on the gradual appropriation of the parents' caretaking functions in order to achieve a relative independence, it is subtly different to a gross identification with the *person* of the analyst or parent. The healthy process of gradual 'microinternalisation', which is perhaps akin to digestion at the physiological level, may thus be distinguished from unhealthy 'macrointernalisation', which seems more like a foreign body lodging inside the mind.

As Khan (1972) points out, there is a danger of the concept of a true self being romanticised and idealised as a state free of all influence of others. However, this process of gradual microinternalisation, or, as Kohut (1977) terms it, 'transmuting internalisation', describes how aspects of others (essentially the parents) and their functions are utilised to form the basis of the self. Kohut places particular emphasis upon the parents' 'mirroring' functions and their availability for idealisation. This process, although clearly involving the influence of others, is not based on a wholesale identification with the other – the latter may mean a bypassing of the authentic possibilities, whereby the other is substituted for the self.

One interesting question which derives from the differing accounts of the false self from Winnicott and Deutsch is whether the initiative for a false self-development comes from the self or the other (the parent). Does the development stem from a wish to escape from painful aspects of being oneself (e.g. vulnerability, shameful weakness or dependence etc.) by identifying with the other who is perceived as stronger – a process sometimes termed 'projective identification' (see Ogden, 1982) – or does it stem from pressure from the other for compliance with the other's desires? Actually these two processes may not be so distinct because it seems very likely that, if the child is not sympathetically understood for what he or she truly is, it is difficult for him or her to be tolerant of his or her own authentic development – the child's vulnerable self is not supported. This seems to be the way in which the manic false self, described by Deutsch, and Winnicott's false self of adaptation are related – both serve to conceal a vulnerable authentic self.

Manic aspects of false self in the four cases

None of the four cases showed a simple Winnicottian false self structure, the false self of compliant accommodation based on the absence of a supporting enviroment for the 'true self'. All showed manic aspects involving denial of imperfection, depression, vulnerability or dependence, as well as a general alienation from his or her own feelings. For three of the four – *Mr D.*, *Mr B.* and *Mr C.* – this defensive organisation corresponded partly to Kernberg's 'grandiose self' which functions to deny potential infantile feelings of helplessness; in the case of *Mrs A.*, whilst tending to deny her own feelings there was no grandiose element to this. In all four cases there was evidence of a collusion between patient and mother to deny the true self. In the three cases involving a grandiose element the mother's perception or fantasy of her child appears to have been grandiose – thus the false self of compliance to mother's desire was also a 'grandiose self'.

An analogy can be drawn with Lacan's (1937) account of the infant's 'mirror stage'. According to Lacan, the child of perhaps 18 months becomes delighted by the *coherence* of his or her image in the mirror and jubilantly identifies with it – thereby denying a prior sense of bodily incoherence, a sense of fragmentation and incoordination. In Lacan's account, this illusory image is seen as bigger, stronger, better than the actual self and so is eagerly embraced, but at the cost of alienation from the true lived self. It is an identification with an image 'out there' which is mistakenly confused with the self. This prepares the way for further alienation in identification with the images offered by human mirrors. In the four cases discussed here, the individuals seemed to have identified with the images presented by their mothers in such a way that contact with their own authentic self was severely compromised.

The four cases also demonstrate how the false image can be misperceived as the true self and be vigorously defended against perceived threats to its autonomy. At the same time the true self is actually feared as threatening the false organisation that has been established. Thus it appears that the threat to autonomy, which is really an *internal* threat deriving from the alienating identification, is projected so that it is experienced as emanating from outside. It is as if the recognition of an emotional 'fifth columnist' is felt to be intolerable.

The manic destructive alliance against the father, the therapist and the authentic self

As we have seen, all four cases showed manifestations of a false self organised in rejection of the more authentic self. In addition, all four demonstrated an alliance with the mother (strictly speaking, the *internal* mother) not only against the authentic self, but also against the father.

This was shown most clearly by *Mrs A.*. She described how she felt worse, i.e. very anxious – if she had allowed herself to be allied with the therapist in examining her relationship with her mother. In these states of mind she feared some kind of catastrophe would befall her, particularly involving loss of her children. Frequently she appeared to be allied with her mother (both actual and internal) in an aloof scornful rejection of the therapist, which seemed to mirror her reports of her mother's rejection of her father.

Similarly, *Mr D.* subtly rejected the therapist, attempting to ward the latter off in a manner similar to his childhood warding off of his father – his 'secret belittling' which linked with his mother's belittling of the father. Also associated with this state of mind was a hidden grandiose stance of looking down on 'mere mortals'.

Mr B. appeared to experience the therapist more clearly as the *mother* to whom he must accommodate, at the same time as ragefully resenting this. However, gradually he came to experience the therapist more as the *father* whose presence he needed in order to free him from the mother. Although initially he appeared to assume that he must collude with the therapist to deny his authentic self, during the course of the therapy he seemed gradually to become more genuine in his presentation.

In the case of *Mr C.* the collusion with the mother appeared to have taken the form of her encouragement of him in maintaining the 'Peter Pan' stance, the illusion that he need never grow up and face reality. The impression was that, as an adult faced with frustration, he would retreat to an internal mother who encouraged him to feel that he need not grow up, learn or work, and to feel that he was quite satisfactory as he was (i.e. that there was no differentiation between his ideal self and his actual self).The therapist's attempts to confront this illusion had little effect much of the time – in this respect he was regarded like the father who had been treated with contempt by the mother.

The absence of the father and the failure of triangulation in Kohut's clinical illustrations

Although the role of the absence of the father is not emphasised in Kohut's theory of narcissistic disturbance, most of his clinical illustrations indicate that this is a crucial factor. Almost all his published cases are consistent with the model presented here.

Mr Z.

Kohut's most extensive published case history is that reported in his paper 'The two analyses of Mr Z.' (1979). It is worth examining this in some detail because it is entirely in line with the proposed model of failure of triangulation.

Kohut describes a patient, Mr Z., who had an analysis with him some years prior to the development of 'self-psychology'. During this original analysis, meanings were attributed to the patient's material in accordance with the classical psychoanalytic model which focused on oedipal conflict. This appeared initially to have been completed successfully and plausibly. However, some years later, Mr Z. reapproached Kohut, indicating that subtle problems still troubled him. Kohut conducted a second analysis, this time in accord with the understanding of his 'self-psychology'. In this paper, Kohut describes how this newer psychoanalytic framework allowed deeper and more fundamental problems to be worked through. His retrospective view was that the first analysis was based upon an incorrect and invalid theory.

Kohut describes the patient as follows. Mr Z., a graduate student in his twenties, complained of mild somatic symptoms, social isolation and a feeling that academically he was functioning below his capacities. He was an only child. At three and a half years his father had been ill and hospitalised, and following this went off with another woman, a nurse, eventually returning to the patient and his mother when Mr Z. was five years. A continuing closeness to his mother was indicated by the fact that as an adult, Mr Z. had one close man friend with whom he would sometimes go to the theatre, concerts etc., but often the two of them would be accompanied by his mother. Mr Z. described recurrent and long-term masturbation fantasies with masochistic content – he would imagine that he was forced to have sex by a strong, demanding and insatiable woman. Thus, clearly in the opening description of the patient there are the themes of a demanding and overwhelming mother, represented in the masturbation fantasies, and of an absent father.

Kohut writes that a prominent feature of the transference was the patient's grandiosity. He refers to (Kohut, 1979, p. 5):

> ...his unrealistic, deluded grandiosity and his demands that the psychoanalytic situation should reinstate the position of exclusive control, of being admired and catered to by a doting mother who – a reconstruction with which I confronted the patient many times – had, in the absence of siblings who would have constituted pre-oedipal rivals, and, during a crucial period of his childhood, in the absence of a father who would have been the oedipal rival, devoted her total attention to the patient.

Thus, Kohut was at this earlier time formulating the patient's difficulties in terms of a wish to reinstate early exclusive possession of the mother and to ward off the father as a feared oedipal rival. He did not, however, address the patient's likely dread of remaining in the dyadic position with mother and *wish for* the father's intervention. Kohut emphasised a fear of taking a competitive stance towards the father – and specifically his castration anxiety. He interpreted the patient's fantasy of a phallic woman in terms of a denial of castration – the woman with a penis – and in terms of the presence of a powerful woman who would protect him against the rival father (p. 6):

> I attempted to demonstrate to him that he had, from way back, denied the fact that his father had indeed returned home when the patient was only four and a half or five years old and that his insistence – as enacted in the transference – that he did not have an oedipal rival, that his preoedipal possession of his mother had remained total after the father's return, was a delusion. In other words I interpreted the persistence of defensive narcissism as it protected him against the painful awareness of the powerful rival who possessed his mother sexually and against the castration anxiety to which an awareness of his own competitive and hostile impulses towards the rival would have exposed him.

Kohut also notes Mr Z.'s preoccupation with the primal scene. Details of early masturbation fantasies emerged (age 5–11): 'he imagined himself as a slave, being bought and sold by women and for the use of women, like cattle, like an object that had no initiative, no will of its own' (p. 6).

In this first analysis there was some investigation of a homosexual relationship which had taken place during Mr Z.'s adolescent years – an affectionate relationship with a summer camp counsellor whom Mr Z. idealised. With the onset of puberty, this relationship had ended, but Mr Z. had not developed much interest in girls. He had become 'more and more tied to his mother. The father so far as we learned in the first analysis, remained a distant figure for him' (p. 8).

Kohut mentions a particular dream which occurred about half a year before termination of the first analysis: the father arrived loaded with gifts; the patient was intensely frightened and attempted to close the door to keep the father out. At this time Kohut interpreted the dream in terms of the patient's ambivalence towards the father as an oedipal rival.

Apparently the outcome of this analysis had seemed satisfactory at the time. However, four and a half years later, Mr Z. recontacted Kohut, indicating that he still experienced difficulties – his relationships still seemed emotionally shallow and he also conveyed the impression that his masochism had shifted from his sexual fantasies to his work which he now found burdensome. During this second analysis, Kohut listened and observed, informed by the insights of self-psychology which he had by then begun to develop. He noted that the patient initially developed an idealising transference, followed quickly by a mirror transference, in which he behaved in an arrogant grandiose way which also revealed despair and masochism. Kohut was more impressed with the despair and masochism this time, in its implication that his demandingness was not simply a desire for gratification (p. 12):

> When we now contemplated the patient's self in the rudimentary state in which it came to view in the transference, we no longer saw it as resisting change, or as opposing maturation because it did not want to relinquish its childish gratification, but on the contrary, as desparately – and often hopelessly – struggling to disentangle itself from the noxious selfobject, to delimit itself, to grow, to become independent.

A different picture of the patient's mother emerged. Mr Z. began to recognise that his mother had required total domination of him (p. 12):

> What had been missing from his reports was the crucial fact that the mother's emotional gifts were bestowed on him under the unalterable and uncompromising condition that he submit to total domination by her, that he must not allow himself any independence, particularly as concerning significant relationships with others.

Mr Z. also began to realise that he had experienced his father's move from home as a flight from the mother and an abandonment of his son.

Gradually Mr Z. became aware of disavowed perceptions of his mother, recognition of her psychotic core, and his compliance with this. The emergence of awareness of these perceptions was accompanied by great anxiety – 'disintegration anxiety', fears concerning 'the loss of the mother as an archaic selfobject'. He recalled his mother's intense preoccupation with his faeces, his possessions and with blemishes on his skin – which 'constitute representative aspects of her attitude towards him – an attitude which, as we came to see more and more clearly, manifested her uneradicable and unmodifiable need to retain her son as a permnanent selfobject' (p. 14). It was also recalled that Mr Z. enjoyed no privacy from his mother, even as an adolescent – she insisted that his door be kept open at all times and would suddenly and unexpectedly disrupt whatever might be going on between Mr Z. and a visiting friend. In the analysis, Mr Z. shifted from a preoccupation with his mother to talking more about his father. Kohut noted that now he talked about the parents' sexual relationship with reference to the father's role, whereas previously 'he had hardly considered his father's participation – and my attempts to emhasise that mother *and* father had been engaged in intercourse had evoked no significant response from him'. In particular, he became preoccupied with the idea that his father was weak and that his mother had dominated him. At the same time the patient expressed curiosity about the analyst, particularly about his relationship to his wife. Interpretations in terms of infantile sexual curiosity resulted in the patient complaining of feeling misunderstood. Kohut eventually interpreted 'that it was a need for a strong father that lay behind his questions, that he wanted to know whether I too was weak – subdued in intercourse by my wife, unable to be the idealised emotional support of a son' (p. 18). The result of this was a 'dramatic lessening of his depression and hopelessness'. Thus, the analysis now focused on the patient's need for an idealisable man, an image of masculine strength with which to merge or identify. The earlier dream of the father's arrival bearing gifts was given a deeper meaning – as reflecting a traumatic state of psychoeconomic imbalance evoked by the intensely wished for return of the father:

> Having been without his father during the period when the male self is phase appropriately aquired and strengthened via the male selfobject, the boy's need for his father for male psychological substance was enormous .... so he had been exposed to ... a traumatic state by being offered with overwhelming suddenness, all the psychological gifts for which he had secretly yearned, gifts which indeed he needed to get.

Kohut concludes that: 'His most significant psychological achievement in analysis was breaking the deep merger tie with his mother.'

Kohut's reformulation of Mr Z.'s difficulties in terms of the new framework of self-psychology is impressive, as is the apparent result of conducting the anlysis along these lines. However, it seems implausible that the first analysis was entirely wrong – unless Kohut is suggesting that all his pre-self-psychological work, and that of other analysts, was based on a completely invalid theory and thus achieved its results purely by suggestion. It seems more likely that Kohut's first interpretation must have been *partially* correct. In fact, Kohut's two analyses can be seen to reflect two sides of the same coin; the first the wish to ward off the father in the oedipal situation; the second dealt with the *need for* an oedipal *defeat* – i.e. the need for a strong father who would be an effective oedipal rival, thereby reinforcing the son's sense of separateness from mother at the same time as representing an image of masculine strength. The essential conflict could be understood as that between the wish for an oedipal triumph and the need for an oedipal defeat – the latter being necessary to liberate the son from the merger with mother.

Thus, Kohut's main clinical illustration of the application of his 'self-psychology' clearly demonstrates the crucial role of the father in narcissistic disturbance – in particular his function of aiding in the separation from mother is apparent. Kohut's *theorising*, however, does not reflect this emphasis.

The remainder of Kohut's published clinical illustrations are more briefly considered in order to show that in the majority of these the father – or rather his absence – appears to have a similarly crucial role.

Most of Kohut's clinical illustrations can be shown to be consistent with the theory proposed here of a failure of triangulation due to the literal or affective absence of the father, and the consequent remaining in a dyadic position with mother. In order to demonstrate this, Kohut's twenty other published cases, from *The Analysis of the Self* and *The Restoration of the Self* are summarised below; all are included for the sake of completeness, although some are very brief and contain little or no historical material.

Cases from the 'Restoration of the Self'

Mr U.

This case is interesting here because Kohut stresses a maternal contribution to the aetiology, but what is emphasised in the treatment is the need for the father.

Mr U.'s chief symptom was a fetishistic perversion:

> ... arisen in reaction to a primary structural defect in his grandiose self due to faulty mirroring by his oddly unempathic, unpredictable, emotionally shallow mother ... From the traumatic unpredictability of his mother he had retreated early to the soothing touch of certain tissues (such as nylon stockings, nylon underwear) which was readily available in his childhood home. They were reliable and they constituted a distillation of maternal responsiveness.

Having explained the patient's disturbance essentially in terms of failures on the mother's part, Kohut then states that the therapeutic work essentially involved recognition of the role of the father:

> The crucial work in the analysis was not done with regard to the substitution of the maternal selfobject, the fetish, however – it concerned the idealised imago, the father.

Kohut explains that:

> ... in early childhood the patient had tried to secure his narcissistic balance by turning away from the attempt to obtain confirmation of his self with the aid of his mother's unreliable empathy to the attempt to merge with his idealised father ... But Mr U.'s father ... could not respond appropriately to his son's needs. He was a self-absorbed, vain man, and he rebuffed his son's attempt to be close to him, depriving him of the needed merger with the idealised selfobject.

Kohut then goes on to state explicitly that the cure involved the introduction of the father into the patient's psychic structure (p. 57):

> The transference ... never reinstated the earliest preoccupations with soothing selfobjects for sufficiently long periods; a thorough working through of the structural defects in the self resulting from the deprivations from the mother's side was therefore not achieved. But despite this the patient made a satisfactory recovery; he lost interest in the fetish, and after the disappointment with regard to the idealised father's responses to him had been worked through for a number of years, he was able to devote himself intensely to his professional activities...

Miss V.

This is another case in which the father's role appeared crucial in rescuing the patient from enmeshment with the maternal psyche. Again Kohut states that the most important transference revivals concernd the father (pp. 59–62):

The primary defect in Miss V.'s personality structure – dynamically related to the periods of protracted enfeeblement of her self when she was lethargic, unproductive, indeed felt lifeless – referred genetically to the interplay with her mother in childhood. Her mother who, like the patient, was subject to periodic depression, was emotionally shallow and unpredictable ...

Whatever the exact diagnostic category may have been into which her mother's disturbances fall, it is clear that as a small child the patient had been exposed to traumatic disappointments from the side of her mother, whose mirroring responses had not only been deficient much of the time (either altogether absent or flat) but also frequently defective (bizarre and capricious) because they were motivated by the mother's misperceptions of the child's needs or by the mother's own requirements, which were unintelligible to the child ...

The propensity towards the periodic enfeeblement of Miss V.'s self was thus established in early childhood in the pathogenic matrix of her relation to the mirroring mother. Miss V. had, however, been a vigorous and well endowed child who did not quite give up the struggle for emotional survival. Trying to extricate herself from the pathogenic relation with her mother, she had attached herself with great intensity to her father, a successful manufacturer with frustrated artistic talents and ambitions who, on the whole, responded to his daughter's needs. Her relation with the father thus became the matrix from which she developed those interests and talents ... those compensatory structures ... which ultimately led to her career ... The relation to her idealised father ... provided her with the outlines of an internalised structure – a paternal ideal – which was a potential source of sustenance for herself ... [D]uring the most important phases of the analysis, the focus of working through was not directed, as one might expect, at the primary structural defect of herself (psychopathology correlated to the mother's flawed responsiveness to the child), but, during a secondary idealising transference, at the insufficiently established compensatory structures (psychopathology correlated to the father's failures) ... Specifically, the crucial transference revivals concerned events in childhood when the father himself appeared to be so severely disappointed by his wife's frustrating emotional flatness and lack of empathy that he too seems to have become temporarily depressed and thus emotionally unavailable to his daughter ... from the patient's transference reactions ... we could reconstruct that he retreated, principally by staying away from home, ... at the very time his daughter needed him most, when the mother was depressed and the daughter expected her idealised and admired father to be a bulwark against the pull of lethargy that emanated from the mother and threatened to engulf the child's personality.

Mr M.

Kohut describes this case in terms of the patient's experience of a non-mirroring mother and his attempts to turn towards an idealised father. The patient's identification with his father's skill with words is used as an example of a *compensatory structure*, making up for the primary defect in the self.

Mr I.

Kohut states:

> ... the father to whom the child attempted to turn in his search for a sustaining merger with the idealised parent imago was not sufficiently available to the child.

Mrs Y.

(This is not one of Kohut's own cases.) The transference appeared to be largely in terms of a *maternal* mirroring selfobject.

Mr W.

The role of the father was not particularly in evidence here.

Cases from the 'Analysis of the Self'

Mr A.

This case again illustrates the need for the father as a rescuer from the maternal disturbance.

Mr A. complained of homosexual preoccupations and a tendency to feel vaguely depressed; he also showed a vulnerability and sensitivity to criticism, to a lack of interest in him, or an absence of praise. He tended to seek guidance from authority and experienced homosexual fantasies of control over men of great bodily strength and perfect physique. Kohut related these needs for idealised male figures to the patient's having felt repeatedly 'abruptly and traumatically disappointed in the power and efficacy of his father' – the father had apparently repeatedly enthusiastically shared his business plans with his son, but each time these had ended in disaster. Mr A.'s mother was deeply disturbed. Although seemingly quiet and calm, she tended to disintegrate with extreme anxiety and unintelligible excitement when exposed to pressure.

Mr K.

This is a major case example which Kohut uses as a paradigmatic illustration of the idealising transference. The patient had suffered an 'enmeshment with his ... mother'. He attempted to 'attach himself to his father as to an admired, idealised parent imago' which failed 'in consequence of his mother's subtle but very effective interference'. The father was depreciated by the mother and moreover 'could not tolerate the son's idealisation and withdrew from him'.

Mr B.

The role of the father is not apparent from Kohut's description. However, the patient had experienced an intense enmeshment with his mother who 'had supervised and controlled him in a most stringent fashion. His exact feeding time ... and in later life his eating time, were determined by a mechanical timer which the mother had used as an extension of her need to control the child's activity – and thus the child felt increasingly that he had no mind of his own ...'. In later childhood he withdrew to his room and locked the door; his mother's response was to have a buzzer installed. Kohut adds:

> From then on she would interrupt his attempts at internal separation from her whenever he wanted to be alone; and she would summon him to her, more compellingly (because the mechanical device was experienced as akin to an endopsychic communication) than would have been her voice, or knocking, against which he could have rebelled.

Thus, from this brief description, it is apparent that Mr. B remained mired in a dyadic enmeshment with his mother – although an absence of his father is not mentioned, it is certainly implied.

Miss F.

Miss F. suffered from 'diffuse dissatisfaction ... and sudden changes in her mood which were associated with a pervasive uncertainty about the reality of her feelings and thoughts'. Kohut explains the roots of her disturbance as follows:

> During decisive periods of her childhood, the patient's presence and activity had not called forth maternal pleasure and approval. On the contrary, whenever she tried to speak about herself the mother deflected imperceptibly the focus of attention to her own depressive self-preoccupations ... Her father, to whom ... the patient had turned ... in search of a substitute for the narcissistic approval which she had not obtained from her mother ... had further traumatised the child by vacillating between attitudes of fetishistic love for the girl and emotional disinterest and withdrawal over long stretches.

The following cases are discussed only briefly in the *Analysis*, often simply a short vignette illustrating an aspect of transference.

Mr C.

Kohut describes mainly the transference, with little reference to the patient's early life, except to refer to a 'narcissistically enmeshing mother' who withdrew from him when a new baby was born.

Mr E.

Early separation from mother and rejection by the father are referred to. The patient engaged in perverse activities – voyeuristic behaviour in public lavatories during which he achieved a feeling of merger with the man at whom he gazed. Kohut focuses mainly on the mirror transference.

Mr J.

The patient shows overt grandiosity. Kohut refers to the mother who 'would value the patient only as a vehicle to her own aggrandisement'. There is no reference to the father.

Mr D., Mr G., Mr H., Miss L., Mr N., Mr O., Mr P., Mr Q. and Mrs Y.

These are all very brief vignettes with no historical material.

Theoretical impressions from Kohut and Wolf (1978)

Thus, most of Kohut's cases of narcissistic disturbance, with any degree of historical material, indicate that the absence of an appropriate response from the father has been crucial. Almost all suggest a background of enmeshment with a mother who did not facilitate separation, who did not recognise the child's separateness.

It might be assumed from this that Kohut emphasises the role of the father and of a move from a dyadic position to a triadic position, in his theorising. This is *not* the case. An examination of the theoretical summary by Kohut and Wolf (1978) makes this particularly clear. Various narcissistic disturbances are clarified and explained in terms of rather direct responses to failures of the primary selfobjects (for example, Kohut and Wolf, 1978, pp. 418 and 419):

> *The understimulated self*: this is a chronic or recurrent condition of the self, the propensity to which arises in consequence of prolonged lack of stimulating responses from the side of the selfobjects in childhood. Such personalities are lacking in vitality. They experience themselves as boring and apathetic, and they are experienced by others in the same way.

> *The fragmenting self*: this is a chronic or recurrent condition of the self, the propensity to which arises in consequence of the lack of integrating responses to the nascent self in its totality from the side of the selfobjects in childhood.

> *The overstimulated self*: the propensity towards recurrent states during which the self is overstimulated arises in consequence of unempathically excessive or phase inappropriate responses from the side of the selfobjects

of childhood ... Closely related to the overstimulated self is the *overburdened self*. But while the overstimulated self is a self whose ambitions and ideals had been unempathically responded to in isolation, without sufficient regard for the self in toto, the overburdened self is a self that had not been provided with the opportunity to merge with the calmness of an omnipotent object.

The notion of conflict is strikingly absent from these descriptions. Although they are original formulations with some clinical plausibility, the phenomena they describe do not appear to be mediated by the unconscious mind and they do not involve any of the oedipal issues that are seen as central to the model of failure of triangulation. The only *dynamic* aspect in the formulations in the Kohut and Wolf paper is the description of defences *against* these primary states. Of particular significance to the argument here is the fact that the specific contribution of the father is not mentioned at all in this theoretical summary of Kohutian self-psychology.

Max Forman

The same issues concerning the role of the father in narcissistic disturbances are strikingly apparent also in a paper by Forman (1976), who writes from an essentially Kohutian point of view. Forman discusses the characteristics and diagnostic features of narcissistic personality disorders, specifically distinguishing them from patients with oedipally based problems. He then gives three clinical examples of the former.

In the case of one patient, he describes a number of diagnostic criteria: hypochondriacal fantasies, homosexual fantasies, feelings of emptiness, and an urgent need for responses from the analyst. There was evidence of sensitivity to separations, resulting in hypochondriasis and homosexual fantasies. Forman states that all of this was 'indicative of a non-cohesive self requiring the analyst to help him to regulate his self-esteem.' In the context of the present argument, the important points concern the historical background. Apparently the patient's mother 'always praised him as having great talents but she insisted that all his good qualities were inherited from her'. She also deprecated his father. Forman refers to the father's lack of empathy and emotional distance. Altogether the patient 'felt he was a toy for his mother'. Thus in this example there are the ingredients of the proposed model of failure of triangulation: an omnipotent mother who deprecated the father and unrealistically praised her son – plus the unavailabiltiy of the father.

In the second example, Forman states that the mother had regarded the patient as a genius, but had taken no interest in his actual activities. Of particular interest is the observation that she would sit on the patient's bed and comfort him whenever he had an argument with his father. The father himself was distant and unresponsive. Thus here is an example of a mother perceiving the patient in terms of an ideal image from her own psyche, whist showing no interest in the actual child and his activities; in addition she appears to have colluded with the son to denigrate the role of the father.

In the third example, Forman notes that 'the patient and his mother were very intensely involved with each other ... his mother was domineering and oppressive and did not encourage the patient's aggressiveness'. The patient's father 'had practically no relationship with him'.

Thus in each case there is a variation on the theme of an enmeshment with mother and a failure of the father effectively to come between child and mother – a failure to assist the child in a move from a dyadic to a triadic position.

Chapter 7
The healing process: self-psychology and beyond

Kernberg's model of the curative process

Kernberg sees the narcissistic patient as attempting to preserve a pathological grandiose self-structure in order to avoid experiences of helplessness and rage. As we have noted, Kernberg's account of the origins of the noxious, warded off experiences has an almost biological quality when he writes, for example, of 'oral rage'. The analyst's task in this model is to interpret the patient's defences so that the narcissistic position is undermined. Thus, schematically the process is extremely simple.

Kohut's model of the curative process

Kohut's view is somewhat more subtle. He regards the narcissistic patient as attempting to engage the therapist as an empathic self-object in order to resume the arrested narcissistic development. The mode of cure is not so much through insight per se as through the process called 'transmuting interpretation'. According to this concept, through the analyst's interpreting empathically the disruptions in the patient's sense of self brought about by inevitable break-ups of the mirror and idealising selfobject transferences, the patient is enabled gradually to transform and reinternalise the narcissistic components of self which had been invested in the selfobject analyst.

The therapeutic process implied by the new model

The clinical approach stemming from the comprehensive model presented here finds a role for both Kohut's and Kernberg's techniques, but the process is more complex than either of these theorists describes. The patient's defences must be interpreted, as in Kernberg's model, but in addition the patient's needs for mirroring and idealisation must be addressed. Oedipal issues as well as selfobject issues must also be attended to. The patient is seen as in *conflict* in relation to the therapist – both wishing for and fearing the therapist's intervention to free the patient from illusion.

The narcissistic patient may be disturbed in any, and most probably, all the categories of the taxonomy. Thus the patient may have an incompletely differentiated sense of self, a weak sense of personal agency, a poor self-image, perhaps coupled with a grandiose self-image, a tendency to mental disorganisation, a preoccupation with the other's view of the self at the expense of his or her own experience, a tendency to retreat to illusions of self-sufficiency and finally an uncertain sense of origins and lineage. All these aspects may be organised as a function of the particular structure of internal object relations. This structure is externalised in the transference to the therapist. Thus the patient experiences the therapist as (1) the mother who must be accommodated to, and (2) the father who must be warded off – either alternately or simultaneously as a mixture of the two. Oppressive aspects of the internal mother, as well as unwanted aspects of self, are projected onto the therapist, who is then experienced as both possessive–controlling and potentially intrusive. Schematically the following process seems a likely pattern:

1. The therapist carries projected images of the controlling mother and the feared denigrated father. Outwardly the patient is compliant, presenting a false self, whilst being covertly denigrating – Mr D.'s 'secret belittling'.
2. The therapist withstands the denigration. By functioning effectively analytically, he demonstrates that he is not in reality belittled and beaten off.
3. The patient briefly, from time to time, switches from the pathological alliance with the internal mother and forms a therapeutic alliance with the therapist. At this point there is a feeling in the therapy of insight being achieved and work being done.
4. The patient fears hostile attacks from the internal mother as punishment for switching allegiance to the therapist-father.
5. The patient retreats to an alliance with the internal mother; again the therapist is experienced as controlling or intrusive.
6. This process is worked over many times. Gradually this clears the way for a selfobject transference to emerge as the patient begins to feel (unconsciously) that it is safe enough. The position that is eventually arrived at is that of an authentic self in relation to a mirroring selfobject – a mirroring selfobject which may also be idealised. (This selfobject transference is never pure but is always mixed with other elements stemming from object-relational conflict.) The selfobject

transference is transformed and worked through in the process of Kohut's 'transmuting internalisation'.

One of the major tasks for the therapist is to resist the patient's attempts to form a collusive false self alliance with the therapist – secretly accommodating to what he or she senses the latter wants, in such a way as to ward off the unwanted impulses, experiences and images of the self. The narcissistic patient will assume that this is what the therapist requires. If the therapist attempts interpretively to penetrate this false veneer, the patient organises him- or herself more firmly against him as if he were the father intruding on the dyad with the mother.

An important function of the therapist in penetratively intervening in the patient's dyad with the internal mother is to release the patient from illusions – to release him or her from entrapment in *images*. Inherent probably in any analytic process of reflection is the patient's coming to see that he or she is not identical with his or her image or self-representation – the discovery that there is a subjective self, an experiencing 'I', Kohut's 'centre of initiative' which is not confined by the image. The process of analytic reflection is itself freeing; that which the patient was embedded in, or identical with, becomes transcended in the act of reflecting upon it – there is an I which reflects upon the image. Freeing the patient from narcissistically protective illusions exposes him or her to warded off images and experiences of self as unmirrored and enraged. However, these images too are ultimately distinguished from the subjective self which is able to reflect upon them.

Through the therapist's interpreting past the images, illusions and false self-organisation, the patient gradually acquires confidence that his or her subjective self, the experiencing 'I', can find expression and mirroring recognition in the therapist's responses. In this way, as described by Kohut, the patient comes to feel more of a 'centre of initiative'; anxieties about the danger of feared and warded off aspects of self intruding on the dyadic illusion are replaced by the pleasure of discovery of the deeper self – the emergence of what Schwartz-Salant has described as the 'Joyful Child' within the personality.

Further consideration of technique inspired by self-psychology

Whilst Kohut's teachings have provided a potent new perspective on the analytic process, with empathy and a focus upon subjective experience as its new vantage point – complementary to other traditional perspectives which placed unconscious conflict and phantasy in the foreground – his framework was limited by its being cast in the narrow narcissistic realm of grandiosity and idealisation. Since that time, others – post-Kohutians such as Atwood and Stolorow – have recognised that the selfobject concept can encompass many more areas of the child's need for empathic attunement which have only a remote connection with narcissism. People need empathic responses. When we are in distress, we all need someone to be available who will show empathic understanding. This soothes us and restores our equilibrium and capacity to cope with the stresses and challenges of life.

Working in a psychiatric inpatient setting with some severely damaged and disturbed patients, it is apparent to me that for people in profound suicidal despair, often the most important function I can offer is an empathic understanding of this despair. This is not easy. Utter despair and hopelessness is difficult to tolerate and the temptation is somehow to talk the patient out of it or to interpret it away; but, in fact, any attempt to interpret underlying mechanisms behind the despair may be experienced as unempathic and an indication that the therapist cannot bear to know the pain. What is more fruitful is examination of the way the patient attempts to protect others from encountering the full extent and intensity of their despair. This is countered by a desperate wish to communicate the pain. The paradox is that, if the communication is received and tolerated by the therapist, and the patient is allowed to know this, then the despair is transmuted into hope.

Mrs Y. shows a typical mental structure. She is consistently seriously suicidal, following a deterioration in her marriage, and has been detained in hospital under the Mental Health Act for over a year. She has made a number of serious attempts to take her own life. On one occasion she took a large quantity of paracetamol and made her way to her mother's house in another town some distance away, depositing herself on her mother's doorstep in a semi-conscious state. A recurrent theme in her communications in her therapy has been that of not being heard properly, of not getting through to someone. This is her experioence in relation to a variety of people, including the therapist. Sometimes she has experienced me as the one person who does know about her despair and sometimes she feels that I too do not want to know. She remarked once that she felt that the only way she would get me to understand how she felt would be by killing herself. She acknowledged that behind her depositing herself in a state close to death on her mother's doorstep was the thought that surely now at last her mother would understand; when her mother began to cry, Mrs Y. felt considerable relief.

Mrs Y.'s feelings of despair become most lethal when she feels that they are not received and understood. It is on those occasions when she has attempted to communicate, but has felt rebutted, that she has become most determined to escape and kill herself.

The following brief vignette is illuminating. She told the therapist she had been very upset about some news she had received and had created a disturbance on the ward, but complained 'they just put me in seclusion'. This prompted me to ask 'How do you think your mother dealt with a distressed child?'. She replied 'Well my brother cried all the time but my mother coped with that'. 'How did she cope?' I asked. 'By switching off' was her reply.

At other times it has been Mrs Y. herself who was switched off from herself – actively opposing any emotional communication with the therapist. She would sit in silence, declare that she had nothing to say and resent the therapist's attempts to reach her. She would assert that she did not wish to know about her own feelings. In this state she would be identified with the rejecting object, the object hostile to emotional communication. Thus the structure of her disturbance is as follows – she can be in one of two positions:

1. She experiences an object rejecting of emotional communication – essentially an internal object modelled on her early experience of her mother.
2. She identifies with this rejecting object – in opposition against her distressed child self and against the therapist's attempts to make contact with the distressed child.

Depression in a schizophrenic patient

The crucial role of empathy with extreme states of despair and loneliness is also illustrated in the following work with a schizophrenic patient whom I have been seeing for 4 years. She is in her mid-twenties, lives with her parents and siblings, and manages to hold down a responsible job in spite of being at times floridly psychotic. My work with her forms part of her general psychiatric care which also includes a small amount of major tranquilliser.

I will not attempt to describe comprehensively her various mental states and the therapeutic process, but will highlight some issues relevant to my theme. She was referred to me by a psychiatrist because she was clearly very anxious and troubled, but she had great difficulty explaining the nature of her distress and would speak in a whisper as if afraid someone might hear; she often sat for long periods in silence. She appeared terrified of human contact; while waiting for her session she would stand outside the building or would hide behind a large pot plant. Only gradually did she reveal to me the very private, autistic thoughts and fantasies in whose grip she was held – often these were of a very destructive nature. She told me, for example, of how she might walk down the street imagining she was dripping with blood and that she was Joan of Arc. She felt in the grip of powerful non-human beings, and forces and scenarios in which she was often assigned a position of supreme importance, for example, as the 'Son of God'. She often felt her body was being transformed in some way, turning to plastic – a process she termed 'holy plastification'. This psychotic area of her mind appeared to exist alongside another part of her mind which dealt tolerably well with the external world; she would no doubt have appeared odd to others but she did manage to maintain her work.

There came a point when she began to incorporate me into her delusional system – believing that I was talking to her constantly in her mind and that we were not separate but really one person. She proposed that we should go away to set up house together in Iceland, desparately pleading with me to agree to her plan. Although this was alarming to me at the time, in retrospect the apparent deterioration in her mental state appears to have been a positive step which formed a bridge between her autistic inner world and another person in the external world – a step of great unconscious courage. For some time she became preoccupied with the fact that it was easier for her to talk to the version of me in her mind than to the therapist she found in the consulting room. Realising the difference between us was a slow and painful process for her.

When she was not floridly psychotic she could appreciate that she had been ill and that this illness corresponded to schizophrenia. However, she often mentioned that when asked to indicate the nature of her illness, on official sickness forms, for example, she preferred to call it 'depression'. Eventually I realised that this was not simply an attempt to avoid the greater stigma of 'schizophrenia' but also contained an important truth. We began to appreciate that the deepest core of her illness was a state of immense loneliness, emptiness and despair – a state of depression in its most terrifying extreme.

In many ways Miss G.'s experience of the world corresponded to Stern's (1985) account of the 'emergent ego' when different aspects of perceptual experience are brought together into a coherent whole. Her perceptual world was at times incoherent; she would look at a person talking to her and not be able to connect the sights and sounds, so that her perception would be fragmented and cross-channelled. For example, she would 'see' words coming out of the person's mouth. Her 'stimulus barrier' was poor; sensory input would often seem to penetrate her violently. As well as this deriving perhaps in part from a defect in her capacity to organise her perceptions, we were able also to understand that this reflected active defensive activity. We began to appreciate that she would dismantle her perception in this way when under stress, an attempt to lessen the impact of the encounter with the other person. A talking human being was terribly complex and confusing for her. One aspect of my way of being with her that she greatly valued was that I was relatively still, and spoke calmly and simply to her, with well-formed sentences.

The origins of her perceptual dismantling appeared to lie in her experience of her emotionally confusing mother who was excitable and passionate, alternating between great affection and hostility. Miss G. reported that her mother would often come into her bedroom, even when Miss G. was asleep, and bombard her at length with criticisms. Miss G.'s way of dealing with this was to dismantle her perceptual experience and dissociate herself, so that she felt she was observing a scene on TV.

It became clear that the problem for her had been that as she had withdrawn in the face of her mother's onslaughts, she had then increasingly been in a state of terrified inner isolation. The isolation had also been exacerbated by a chronic lack of affect attunement from any significant figure in her family; nobody recognised her extreme state of depression, and her mother's excitable temperament was quite alien to her. She had no experience of what Kohut would have termed 'twinship'. This absence of early affect attunement was emphasised by her indication of the immense importance to her of the therapist's quiet and calm attentiveness to her. Her terrifying inner loneliness had necessitated the construction of a psychotic restitutive world inhabited by non-human and omnipotent figures. An increasing divorce took place between her outer social self and her hidden autistic psychotic self.

The process of therapy has been one of bridging the lonely inner self and the outer world through the therapeutic relationship. Although at one time she incorporated the therapist into her delusional system – a first step towards bridging inner and outer worlds, and perhaps a kind of transitional area, as described by Winnicott, between reality and autistic fantasy – she later talked of a wish to be *like* the therapist, a state which she distinguished clearly from that of being the *same* as the therapist, as she had believed in her delusional phase. She made it clear that the therapist's recognition of her lifelong inner loneliness which lay behind her psychosis was the crucial healing factor. It seems to have been this connection with the lost inner self, through being recognised and accepted by the therapist, that has allowed her to feel that she can join the human family. She describes how she no longer feels surrounded by non-human forces but is aware of other people as real people and increasingly enjoys relating to people. She expresses enormous gratitude that she has been enabled to feel like a human being. At the same time she describes a nostalgia for the excitement of psychosis, and a profound dread of falling back into her 'depression' – a decathexis of the human world which she is aware could come about if she were prematurely deprived of the selfobject functions provided by the therapist. The work continues.

The search for mirroring: clarifying the patient's developmental needs in brief analytic therapy

A self-psychological perspective can lead to a style of work in which interpretation of defence and of the historical transference is not prominent. The focus is upon describing and clarifying the patient's developmental needs – articulating what kind of response the patient is seeking from the therapist.

In order to illustrate this point I will describe aspects of a brief 10-session psychoanalytical psychotherapy conducted in a clinic setting. The patient was a young man of 21, in many ways well functioning, with a responsible job and maintaining a relationship with his girlfriend. He sought help because of an obsessional anxiety that he could become a 'Yorkshire Ripper' (a mass murderer) type of figure – an anxiety he had had ever since the Ripper case emerged in the news some years previously. He was an only child of parents whom he described as caring and affectionate. It became apparent that there were reasons why he was enraged with his mother, but I will not deal with these except to say that he had at times experienced her as humiliating and feminising. What emerged during the therapy was that he had felt there to be no place for aggression in the family, either between his parents or between him and his parents. A theme developed to do with 'conning' people – his anxiety that he could quite literally get away with murder. We came to understand that he was afraid that people did not know about his aggression, and that he needed me to know about it.

Soon he began to tell me about secret sadistic activities from his childhood – his pleasure in making spiders fight by putting one on another spider's web, and an ingenious device he constructed for torturing wasps. In retrospect he felt guilty about these activities. I commented on the importance of the fact that instead of 'conning' he was now confessing and therefore being truthful to himself and to me about his sadism which had originally been secret. He then spoke of how he could imagine being a football thug, thumping someone and disappearing back into the crowd. He went on to tell me how he never saw his father being aggressive – and how disappointed he felt when his father did not retaliate when a man insulted him in a pub – he complained that his father had given him nothing to rebel against. In the transference I became a father who knew about his aggression and who provided a firm confronting presence, a sparring partner – he liked to shake my hand, rather like two men shaking hands after a competitive aggressive game.

At one point he came to his session in some agitation, saying he felt that maybe he and his girlfriend would have to split up. Apparently they had had an angry row and this had never happened before. We looked at his assumption that relationships could not survive an expression of anger, including, by implication, his relationship with me.

Halfway through the therapy he reported a dream in which the 'Ripper' was dancing in a boxing ring and the audience was applauding. This seemed to represent his new feeling that aggression could be contained, made safe, playful, and could be approved of. He looked to me to be a paternal figure who would encourage his assertiveness and masculinity. He described how sporting activities were never encouraged by his father and how anything adventurous or rebellious was positively discouraged. During one session he asked if I thought he should join a football team; he wondered whether this might be a good way of repairing his masculinity. Commenting on the significance of his asking me, I suggested that if I said 'Yes, great idea!', he would be pleased, feeling that I was giving him the encouragement he had not received from his father . At this point, he interjected with a comment about how he always used to ask his mother for advice, for example, about whether he should take his plastic mac. I went on to say that if I had said 'Oh I wouldn't do that' (mimicking the discouraging tone he had often ascribed to his father), he might then rebelliously think 'Well hell I will!'. He responded enthusiastically saying that he should have taken more of a 'hell I will' attitude when his father was not encouraging. I replied that his remarks about his mother's advice suggested that he may have felt he got too much response from his mother, along the lines of 'Don't forget your plastic mac dear' – which may have left him feeling somewhat feminised – and not enough encouragement for his masculinity from his father. He agreed and went on to talk of the significance to him of football being an all-male sport – and his fantasies of seeking admiration from other men for his sporting prowess and masculinity. Thus, during most of the ten sessions he was bringing his latent aggression and masculinity to me for recognition and mirroring.

The final session was interesting in its shift to a different tack. He told me that his 'Ripper' worries had more or less faded away, but he did find himself now worried about homosexuality. He reported a homosexual dream about a friend. He also dreamt that his brother had died. With some embarrassment he eventually mentioned that he had had a dream about me – that he came to see me in a hospital room where I was lying on a bed naked. His association was to a wishful fantasy of his father lying in bed having a fatherly chat with him about life. He mentioned that his brother had had a closer relationship with his father than he had. I told him that his dream was clearly expressing his wish to be closer to me, standing for his father – perhaps with an allusion to a deathbed scene evoked by the ending of his therapy – and that he was telling me about his jealousy of his brother and his wish to take his place. This all made sense to him and he seemed relieved. He then went on to speak of his worries about whether his job in a bank was really very masculine, compared, for example, to someone working on a building site. He added that he had always been rather sensitive, easily moved to tears at school where he would struggle to hide this – he had already described being bullied and teased at school. I remarked that I expected he probably wondered about how masculine my job was – and that I thought the question he was raising for himself was whether it is possible to be masculine *and* sensitive. There then followed a clarification of his assumptions regarding masculinity; we saw, for example, how some of his assumptions led him to the conclusion, which he recognised as absurd, that a violent psychopath, without compassion or sensitivity, was the epitomy of masculinity.

Finally I said to him that although most of the therapy had been concerned with recognising his aggression and masculinity, now at the end he was bringing his sensitivity to me for recognition. He agreed with this construction. He indicated convincingly that he had found the 10 sessions extremely helpful. Follow-up a year later revealed that his anxieties had not returned.

Although there were other important determinants of the 'Ripper' fantasy which we came to understand, the relationship to his father was the main emerging focus.

In this brief and successful analytical psychotherapy, there was little or no interpretation of anxiety in the transference. Nor was there any interpretation of defence. More or less all my remarks to him were in terms of his need for mirroring in the paternal selfobject transference – his bringing his masculinity to me for recognition and repair. Thus I seemed for him to be not at all a *historical* transference figure, but rather represented the *missing* paternal selfobject, a new figure whom he could temporarily use as a means of integrating hitherto split off parts of his personality. I suspect that the manner and focus of interpreting facilitated his using me in this way, and that if I had referred to myself as a historical transference figure, and particularly if I had attempted to locate perverse and sadistic impulses towards me in a maternal transference, the therapy would not have taken the brief and benign course it did; the patient may have felt dragged back to the past, rather than experiencing the therapy as going with and facilitating the developmental initiative. Of course in longer analytical psychotherapy or analysis, a thorough working through of the historical transference would need to take place alongside the elaboration of the selfobject dimension.

The selfobject dimension as the curative factor in psychoanalysis

Freud saw the curative process of analysis as coming about through the increased dominance of the reality oriented ego within the mind resulting from the increased insight offered by analysis. Thus, in his last major work (1940) he wrote (p. 181):

> ... we have done the best for him [the patient] if, as analysts, we raise the processes in his ego to a normal level, transform what has become unconscious and repressed into preconscious material and then return it once more to the possession of his ego.

Strachey (1934) added a further dimension to the Freudian explanation in his account of the modification of internal objects, such as the superego, through projection onto the analyst; through the analyst's failing to behave as a punitive superego, the patient was offered a more benign figure for reintrojection. Thus, Strachey was addressing the projective dimension of transference. Alexander and French (1946) took this model a step further in advocating a deliberate manipulation of the superego by the analyst. Most analysts considered that this recommendation went beyond the bounds of psychoanalysis. From a Kleinian point of view, Segal (1962) considered insight as the basis of analytic cure, but emphasised the process of integration of split-off parts of the self – drawing on projective and historical dimensions of transference. One of the few in earlier years to emphasise the curative value of the discovery of the analyst as a new and real object was Loewald (1951) – thus being closer to addressing the selfobject dimension of transference.

Kohut's (1977) reformulation of the analytic cure was in terms not of insight but of 'transmuting internalisation'. This takes place through the analyst's optimal *failures* as a new object. Each tolerable failure in the analyst's understanding allows the patient to establish a little more internal structure by taking over some of the functions previously located in the analyst. Kohut's emphasis on the role of the analyst's empathy is comparable to Rosenfeld's (1987) and Langs' (1978) focus on the analyst's state of mind – the idea that the quality of the analyst's interpretation conveys to the patient something about the analyst's state of mind. When good – i.e. accurate and deep – interpretations are given, especially ones that relate to the patient's experience of the analyst, the patient feels that there is a healthy and truthful aspect of the analyst to identify with. It is important to note that, for Kohut, Rosenfeld and Langs, among others, the analyst's mental and emotional functioning are seen as a crucial aspect of the analytic cure. This was clearly not Freud's view. For Freud, the cure proceeded through insight provided by the analyst, which then led to a purely intrapsychic resolution of neurotic difficulties. There is absolutely no indication in Freud's writings that the patient turns to the analyst in search of a developmentally *needed* response.

In Britain, it is common for analysts to speak of a process of 'containment' (e.g. Casement, 1985). What is usually meant by this is that, through feeling the analyst has sufficiently understood the nature and degree of the anxiety or emotional pain, the patient feels soothed and able to think more clearly without having to resort to acting out. Undoubtedly such a process occurs and is an important part of analytic work, especially with the more disturbed patient. But from what theory of psychoanalysis does this concept arise? There is certainly no idea remotely like this in Freud.

The notion of containment seems to stem most directly from Bion's modification of Klein's (1946) concept of projective identification. Whereas Klein described an intrapsychic phantasy of intruding a part of the self into others, from a variety of motives, Bion (1962) described an *inter*psychic communicative exchange, whereby the mother is receptive to the baby's distress, applies her thoughts to it and, through her thoughtful action, returns the projected pain in a modified and meaningful form. In this way the baby's evacuative reflex is transformed into a meaningful communication. Thus, through this simple paradigm, Bion drew attention to the significance of the mother's mental functions – in addition to her significance as an *object* of the baby's love and hate. Similarly the use of Bion's notion of containment in the analytic process draws attention to the quality of the analyst's mental functions, as does Kohut's concept of the selfobject. There are, in fact, considerable points of contact between Bion and Kohut (Mollon, 1986). Bion emphasised *receptiveness* to the patient's communications (projective identification), whereas Kohut emphasised empathy, which implies an active *reaching out* in imagination into the other's experience. These seem to be two related aspects of grasping the patient's pain.

All these theorists who focus on the significance, for the patient's state of mind, of the analyst's state of mind can be said to be referring to the selfobject dimension of transference. They are recognising the patient's dependence on the actual responsiveness of the analyst, the patient's need for certain responses from the analyst in order for development to proceed – just as the child is dependent on the availability of development-enhancing responses from parents and other important early figures. Resolution of internal conflict is not sufficient. Although this point reflects an emerging trend, it has generally been made insufficiently explicit in conceptualising the analytic process.

In conclusion

So where have we got to? We have examined the need to clarify the geography of the self and the person's relationship to the self – in juxtaposition to theorising about the relationship to others. It has been possible to construct a provisional taxonomy of disturbance of self, and we have seen that different theories of narcissism address different categories of this taxonomy. We have looked at those experiences such as shame, embarrassment, self-consciousness and humiliation – the narcissistic affects – which inherently concern injuries to, and disturbances in, the self. From there we attempted to explore a more comprehensive model of narcissistic disturbance that highlights a combination of failures in the availability of mirroring and idealised selfobjects (the domain described by Kohut) with disturbances in oedipal development. Some final reflections, following leads by Stolorow and other post-Kohutians, have elaborated on the clinical use of the selfobject dimension of the relationship between patient and therapist, the consistent and disciplined application of empathy, and understanding of the patient's needs in this dimension.

Is this theorising helpful? I personally find it so. Increasingly, I talk to my patients about their self-image, their self-esteem, sense of agency and other aspects of the experience of self. My patients respond to this, become more engaged, less anxious and 'resistant', and ultimately emerge happier and more free. I hope that the reader may find something of value in it too.

References

ABELIN, E.L. (1971). The role of the father in the separation–individuation process. In J.B. McDevitt and C.F. Settlage, Eds, *Separation–Individuation*. New York: International University Press.

ABELIN, E.L. (1975). Some further observations and comments on the earliest role of the father. *International Journal of Psycho-Analysis* 56, 293–302.

ABELIN, E.L. (1980). Triangulation, the role of the father, and the origins of core gender identity during the rapprochement subphase. In R. Lax, S. Bach, and J.A. Burland, (Eds), *Rapprochement. The Critical Subphase of Separation–Individuation*. New York: Aronson.

ADLER, A. (1917). *Study of Organ Inferiority and its Psychical Compensations*. London: Nervous and Mental Disease Publishing.

ADLER, A. (1929). *Problems of Neurosis*. London: Kegan Paul, Trench, Trubner.

ALEXANDER, F. and FRENCH, T.M. (1929). *Problems of Neurosis*. London: Kegan Paul, French, Trubner.

ALEXANDER, F. and FRENCH, T.M. (1946). *Psychoanalytic therapy*. New York: Ronald Press.

AMSTERDAM, B. and LEVITT, M. (1980). Consciousness of self and painful self-consciousness. *Psychoanalytic Study of the Child* 35, 67–83.

ARIETI, S. and BEMPORAD, J. (1980). *Severe and Mild Depression*. London: Tavistock.

ANDREAS-SALOMÉ, L. (1962). The dual orientation of narcissism. *Psychoanalytic Quarterly* 31, 1–30.

ATWOOD, G. and STOLOROW, R.D.. (1984). *Structure of Subjectivity. Explorations of Psychoanalyytic Phenomenology*. Hillsdale, NJ: Analytic Press.

BACH, S. (1980). Self-love and object-love: some problems of self- and object-constancy, differentiation and integration. In R. Lax, S. Bach and J.A. Burland (Eds), *Rapprochement: The Critical Subphase of Separation–Individuation*. New York: Aronson.

BALINT, M. (1960). Primary narcissism and primary love. *Psychoanalytic Quarterly* 29, 6–43.

BASCH, M.F. (1975). Towards a theory that encompasses depression. A revision of existing causal hypotheses in psychoanalysis. In E.J. Anthony and T. Benedek (Eds), *Depression and Human Existence*, pp. 485–534. Boston: Little Brown.

BECKER, E. 91973). *The Denial of Death*. New York: Free Press.

BETTLEHEIM, B. (1983). *Freud and Man's Soul*. London: Chatto and Windus.

BION, W.R. (1959). Attacks on linking. *Second Thoughts*. London: Heinemann.

BION, W.R. (1962). *Learning from Experience*. London: Heinemann.

BLOS, P. (1984). Son and father. *Journal of the American Psychoanalytic Association* 32, 301–324.

BOWLBY, J. (1980). *Loss, Sadness and Depression*. London: Hogarth.

BRADSHAW, J. (1988). *Healing the Shame that Binds you*. Deerfield Beech, FL: Health Communications.

BRAZELTON, T.TB., KOSLOWSKI, B. and MAIN, M. (1974). The early mother infant interaction. In M. Lewis and L. Rosenblum (Eds), *The Effect of the Infant on its Caretaker*. New York: Wiley.

BRENMAN, E. (1980). The value of reconstruction in adult psychoanalysis. *International Journal of Psycho-Analysis* 61, 53–60.

BRENMAN-PICK, I. (1985). Working through in the countertransference. *International Journal of Psycho-Analysis* 60, 311–316.

BROMBERG, P.M. (1983). The mirror and the mask. *Contemporary Psychoanalysis* 19, 359–387.

BROUCEK, F. (1979). Efficacy in infancy: a review of some experimental studies and their possible implications for clinical theory. *International Journal of Psycho-Analysis* 60, 311–316.

BROUCEK, F. (1982). Shame and its relation to early narcissistic developments. *International Journal of Psycho-Analysis* 63, 369–378.

BROUSSARD, E. R and CORNES, C.C. (1981). Early identification of mother–infant systems in distress. What can we do? *Journal of Preventive Psychiatry* 1, 119–132.

BUBER, M. (1937). *I and Thou*. Translated by R.G.Smith. Edinburgh: T. & T. Clark.

BURLINGHAM, D. (1973). The pre-oedipal infant-father relationship. *Psychoanalytic Study of the Child* 28, 23–47.

BURSTEN, B. (1973). Some narcissistic personality types. *International Journal of Psycho-Analysis* 54, 287–300.

BUSS, A.H. (1980). *Self-consciousness and Social Anxiety*. San Francisco: Freeman.

CASEMENT, P. (1985). *Learning from the Patient*. London: Routledge.

CHASSEGUET-SMIRGEL (1985). *Creativity and Perversion*. London: Free Association

CHILAND, C. (1982). A new look at fathers. *Psychoanalytic Study of the Child* 37, 361–380.

COOLEY, C.H. (1902). *Human Nature and the Social Order*. New York: Schocken Books 1964.

DETRICK, D. and DETRICK, S. (1989). *Self Psychology. Comparisons and Contrasts*. Hillsdale, NJ: The Analytic Press.

DEUTSCH, H. (1942). Some forms of emotional disturbance and their relationship to schizophrenia. In *Neurosis and Character Types*. New York: International Universities Press, 1965.

DEUTSCH, H. (1955). The imposter. Contributions to ego psychology of a type of psychopath. In *Neurosis and Character Types*. New York: International Universities Press, 1965.

DODDS, E. (1951). *The Greeks and the Irrational*. Berkeley: University of California Press.

DURUZ, N. (1981). The psychoanalytic concept of narcissism. Part I: Some neglected aspects in Freud's work. Part II: Towards a structural definition. *Psychoanalysis and Contemporary Thought* 4, 3–67.

EDGECOMBE, R. and BURGNER, M. (1975). The phallic narcissistic phase: a differentiation between preoedipal and oedipal aspects of phallic development. *The Psychoanalytic Study of the Child* 30, 161–180.

EMDE, R. (1988). Development terminable and interminable! Innate and motivational factors from infancy. *International Journal of Psycho-Analysis* 69, 23–42.

EPSTEIN, S. (1987). A cognitive self theory. In *Self and Identity. Psychosocial Perspectives*. London: Wiley.

ERICKSON, E. (1959). *Identity and the Life Cycle*. New York: International Universities Press.

FAIRBAIRN, W.R.D. (1952). *Psychoanalytic Studies of the Personality*. London: Tavistock.

FENICHEL, O. (1946). *The Psychoanalytic Theory of Neurosis*. London: Routledge.

FEDERN, P. (1953). *Ego Psychology and the Psychoses*. London: Imago.

FLEGENHEIMER, W.V. (1982). *Techniques of Brief Psychotherapy* New York: Jason Aronson.

FERENCZI, S. (1913). Stages in the development of the sense of reality. In *First Contributions to Psychoanalysis*. London: Hogarth Press, 1952.

FORMAN, M. (1976). Narcissistic personality disorder and the oedipal fixations. *Annual of Psychoanalysis*, Vol. IV.

FRANKL, V.E. (1973). *The Doctor and the Soul. From Psychology to Logotherapy*. London: Penguin.

FRAZER, J.G. (1963). *The Golden Bough. Taboo and the Perils of the Soul*. New York: St Martin's.

FREUD, A. (1966). *The Ego and the Mechanisms of Defence*. London: Hogarth.

FREUD, S. (1905). Three essays on the theory of sexuality. *The Complete Psychological Works of Sigmund Freud*, standard edition, vol. 7. London: Hogarth Press, 1953.

FREUD, S. (1909). Analysis of a phobia in a five year old boy. *The Complete Psychological Works of Sigmund Freud*, standard edition, vol. 10. London: Hogarth Press, 1955.

FREUD, S. (1910). Leonardo da Vinci and a memory of his childhood. *The Complete Psychological Works of Sigmund Freud*, standard edition, vol. 11. London: Hogarth Press, 1957.

FREUD, S. (1911a). Psycho-analytic notes on an autobiographical account of a case of paranoia (dementia paranoides). *The Complete Psychological Works of Sigmund Freud*, standard edition, vol. 12. London: Hogarth Press, 1958.

FREUD, S. (1911b). Formulations on the two principles of mental functioning *The Complete Psychological Works of Sigmund Freud*, standard edition, vol. 12. London: Hogarth Press, 1958.

FREUD, S. (1913). Totem and taboo. *The Complete Psychological Works of Sigmund Freud*, standard edition, vol. 3. London: Hogarth Press, 1962.

FREUD, S. (1914). On narcissism: an introduction. *The Complete Psychological Works of Sigmund Freud*, standard edition, vol. 14. London: Hogarth Press, 1957.

FREUD, S. (1915a). Instincts and their vicissitudes. *The Complete Psychological Works of Sigmund Freud*, standard edition, vol. 14. London: Hogarth Press, 1957.

FREUD, S. (1915b). The unconscious. *The Complete Psychological Works of Sigmund Freud*, standard edition, vol. 14. London: Hogarth Press, 1957.

FREUD, S. (1918). From the history of an infantile neurosis. *The Complete Psychological Works of Sigmund Freud*, standard edition, vol. 17. London: Hogarth Press, 1955.

FREUD, S. (1921). Group psychology and the analysis of the ego. *The Complete Psychological Works of Sigmund Freud*, standard edition, vol. 18. London: Hogarth Press, 1955.

FREUD, S. (1923). The ego and the id. *The Complete Psychological Works of Sigmund Freud*, standard edition, vol. 19. London: Hogarth Press, 1961.

FREUD, S. (1925). Some psychical consequences of the anatomical differences between the sexes. *The Complete Psychological Works of Sigmund Freud*, standard edition, vol. 19. London: Hogarth Press, 1961.

FREUD, S. (1927a). The future of an illusion. *The Complete Psychological Works of Sigmund Freud*, standard edition, vol. 21. London: Hogarth Press, 1961.

FREUD, S. (1927b). Fetishism. *The Complete Psychological Works of Sigmund Freud*, standard edition, vol. 21. London: Hogarth Press, 1961.

FREUD, S. (1929). Civilisation and its discontents. *The Complete Psychological Works of Sigmund Freud*, standard edition, vol. 21. London: Hogarth Press, 1961.

FREUD, S. (1936). A disturbance of memory on the Acropolis. *The Complete Psychological Works of Sigmund Freud*, standard edition, vol. 22. London: Hogarth Press, 1962.

FREUD, S. (1937). Constructions in analysis. *The Complete Psychological Works of Sigmund Freud*, standard edition, vol. 23. London: Hogarth Press, 1964.

FREUD, S. (1940). An outline of psycho-analysis. *The Complete Psychological Works of Sigmund Freud*, standard edition, vol. 23. London: Hogarth Press, 1964.

GEAR, M.C., HILL, M.A and LIENDO, E.L. (1981). *Working through Narcissism.,Treating its Sado-masochistic Structure*. New York: Jason Aronson.

GEDO, J. (1979). *Beyond Interpretation*. New York: International Universities Press.

GEDO, J. (1981). *Advances in Clinical Psychoanalysis*. New York: International Universities Press.

GILL, M. (1982). *Analysis of the Transference*. Vol 1. *Theory and Technique Psychological Issues*, Monograph 53. New York: International Universities Press.

GIOVACCHINI, P.L. (1986). Schizophrenia: structural and therapeutic considerations. In D. Feinsilver (Ed.), *Towards a Comprehensive Model for Schizophrenic Disorders*. Hillsdale, NJ: Analytic Press.

GOLDBERG, A. (1973). Psychotherapy of narcissistic injuries. *Archives of General Psychiatry* **28**, 722–726.

GLYNN, S. (1984). The eye/I of the paradox. Paper presented to the Self and Identity Conference. Cardiff.

GRAVES, R. (1955). *The Greek Myths*. Harmondsworth: Penguin.

GREEN, A. (1982). Moral narcissism. *International Journal of Psychoanalytic Psychotherapy* **7**, 243–269.

GREEN, B. (1979). The effect of distortions of the self. A study of the Picture of Dorian Gray. *Annual of Psychoanalysis* **VII**, 391–410.

GREENFIELD, B. (1985). The archetypal masculine: its manifestation in myth and its significance for women. In A. Samuels (Ed.), *The Father*. London: Free Association Press.

GREENWALD, A.G. (1980). The totalitarian ego: Fabrication and revision of personal history. *American Psychology* **35**, 603–608.

GREENWALD, A.G. and PRATKANIS, A.R. (1984). The self. In R.S. Wyer and T.K. Srull (Eds), *Handbook of Social Cognition*. Hillsdale, NJ: Lawrence Erlbaum.

GROSSMAN, W. (1982). Self as fantasy: fantasy as theory. *Journal of the American Psychoanalytic Association* **30**, 919–937.

GROTSTEIN, J. (1981a).Who is the dreamer who dreams the dream and who is the dreamer who understands it? In *Do I Dare Disturb the Universe?* Beverley Hills: Caesura Press.

GROTSTEIN, J. (1981b). *Splitting and Projective Identification*. New York: Aronson.

GROTSTEIN, J. (1986). The psychology of powerlessness: disorders of self-regulation and interactional regulation as a newer paradigm for psychopathology. *Psychoanalytic Inquiry* 6, 93–118.

GRUNBERGER, B. (1971). *Narcissism*. New York: International Universities Press.

GUNTRIP, H. (1961). *Personality Structure and Human Interaction*. London: Hogarth.

GUNTRIP, H. (1968). *Schizoid Phenomena, Object Relations and the Self*. Hogarth: London.

HAMILTON, V. (1982) *Narcissus and Oedipus*. London: Routledge & Kegan Paul.

HARTMANN, H. (1950). Comments on the psychoanalytic theory of the ego. In *Essays in Ego Psychology*. New York: International Universities Press, 1960.

HAVENS, L. (1986). A theoretical basis for the concepts of self and authentic self. *Journal of the American Psychoanalytic Association* 34, 363–378.

HEIMANN, P. (1952). Certain functions of introjection and projection in early infancy. In *Developments in Psychoanalysis*. London: Hogarth.

HEIMANN, P. (1962). Notes on the anal stage. *International Journal of Psycho-Analysis* 43, 406–414.

HERZOG, J. (1979). The father's role in the modulation of aggressive drive and fantasy. Paper presented to the meeting of the American Psychoanalytic Association, December, New York City.

HERZOG, J. (1980). Sleep disturbance and father hunger in 18–28 month old boys: the Erlkonig syndrome. *Psychoanalytic Study of the Child* 35, 219–233.

HILDEBRAND, P. (1987). Brief psychotherapy. *Psychoanalytic Psychology* 3, 1–12.

HOLLAND, N. (1985). *The I*. New York: Yale University Press.

IZARD, C. (1977). *Human Emotions*. New York: Plenum.

JACKSON, H. (Ed.) (1991). *Using Self Psychology in Psychotherapy*. New York: Aronson.

JACOBSON, E. (1964). *The Self and the Object World*. New York: International Universities Press.

JACOBSON, E. (1971). *Depression*. New York: International Universities Press.

JAMES, W. (1890). *The Principles of Psychology*. Reprinted 1983. Cambridge, MA: Harvard University Press.

JAMES, W. (1900). *The Principles of Psychology*. New York: Holt.

JOFFE, W. and SANDLER, J. (1967). Some conceptual problems involved in the consideration of disorders of narcissism. *Journal of Child Psychotherapy* 2, 56–66.

KAGAN, J. (1981). *The Second Year. The Emergence of Self-Awareness*. Cambridge, MA: Harvard University Press.

KAUFMAN, G. (1980). *Shame. The Power of Caring*. Cambridge, MA:. Schenkman Books.

KAYE, K. (1982). *The Mental and Social Life of Babies*. London: Harvester.

KEGAN, R. (1982).*The Evolving Self*. Cambridge, MA: Harvard University Press.

KERNBERG, O. (1974). Further contributions to the treatment of narcissistic personalities. *International Journal of Psycho-Analysis* 55, 215–240.

KERNBERG, O. (1982). Self, ego, affects and drives. In *Severe Personality Disorders*. New York: International Universities Press.

KHAN, M. (1972). The finding and becoming of self. In *The Privacy of the Self*. London: Hogarth.

KINSTON, W. (1980). A theoretical and technical approach to narcissistic disturbance. *International Journal of Psycho-Analysis* 61, 383–394.

KIRSHNER, L. (1991). The concept of self in psychoanalytic theory and its philosophical foundations. *Journal of the American Psychoanalytical Association* 39, 157–182.

KLEIN, G. (1976). *Psychoanalytic Theory: An Exploration of Essentials*. New York: International Universities Press.

KLEIN, M. (1932a). The effects of early anxiety situations on the sexual development of the girl. In *The Psycho-Analysis of Children*. London: Hogarth, 1975.

KLEIN, M. (1932b). The effects of early anxiety situations on the sexual development of the boy. In *The Psycho-Analysis of Children*. London: Hogarth, 1975.

KLEIN, M. (1946). Notes on some schizoid mechanisms. In *The Writings of Melanie Klein*, Vol III. London: Hogarth, 1975.

KOHUT, H. (1966). Forms and transformations of narcissism. *Journal of the American Psychoanalytic Association* 14, 243–272.

KOHUT, H. (1971). *The Analysis of the Self*. New York: International Universities Press.

KOHUT, H. (1972). Thoughts on narcissism and narcissistic rage. *Psychoanalytic Study of the Child* 27, 360–400.

KOHUT, H. (1976). Creativeness, charisma, group psychology. In *Self Psychology and the Humanities*. New York: Norton.

KOHUT, H. (1977). *The Restoration of the Self*. New York: International Universities Press.

KOHUT, H. (1979). The two analyses of Mr Z. *International Journal of Psycho-Analysis* 60 (3), 3–27.

KOHUT, H. (1983). Selected problems of self psychological theory. In J.D. Lichtenberg and S. Kaplan (Eds), *Reflections on Self Psychology*. Hillsdale, NJ: Analytic Press.

KOHUT, H. (1984). *How Does Analysis Cure?* Chicago: University of Chicago Press.

KOHUT, H. and WOLF, E. S. (1978). The disorders of the self and their treatment: an outline. *International Journal of Psycho-Analysis* 59, 413–425.

LACAN, J. (1937). The looking-glass phase. *International Journal of Psycho-Analysis* 18. Reprinted as 'The mirror stage as formative of the function of the I.' In *Ecrits*. London: Tavistock, 1977

LACAN, J. (1957). On a question preliminary to any possible treatment of psychosis. In *Ecrits*. London: Tavistock, 1977.

LAMB, M.E. (Ed.) (1981). *The Role of the Father in Child Development*, 2nd edition. London: Wiley.

LANGS, R. (1976). *The Bipersonal Field*. New York: Jason Aronson.

LANGS, R. (1978). *The Listening Process*. New York: Jason Aronson.

LAPLANCHE, J. and PONTALIS, J.B. (1973). *The Language of Psychoanalysis*. London: Hogarth.

LASCH, C. (1978). *The Culture of Narcissism*. New York: Norton.

LEE, R. and MARTIN, J. (1991). *Psychotherapy after Kohut. A Textbook of Self Psychology*. Hillsdale, NJ: Analytic Press.

LEMAIRE, A. (1977). *Jacques Lacan*. London: Routledge & Kegan Paul.

LEONARD, M. (1966). Fathers and daughters: the significance of 'fathering' in the psychosexual development of the girl. *International Journal of Psycho-Analysis* 47, 325–334.

LEVIN, S. (1971). The psychoanalysis of shame. *International Journal of Psycho-Analysis* 52, 335–362.

LEWIS, H. (1963). A case of watching as a defence against an oral incorporation fantasy. *Psychoanalytic Review* 50 (5), 68–80.

LEWIS, H. (1971). *Shame and Guilt in Neurosis*. New York: International Universities Press.

LEWIS, M. and BROOKS-GUNN, J. (1979). *Social Cognition and the Aquisition of Self*. New York: Plenum.

LICHTENBERG, J. (1983). *Psychoanalysis and Infant Research*. Hillsdale, NJ: Analytic Press.

LICHTENSTEIN, H. (1961). Identity and sexuality. A study of their interrelationship in man. *Journal of the American Psychoanalytic Association* 9, 179–260.

LICHTENSTEIN, H. (1964). The role of narcissism in the emergence and maintenance of a primary identity. *International Journal of Psycho-Analysis* 45, 49–56.

LICHTENSTEIN, H. (1971). The malignant No. Instinctual drives and the sense of self. In *The Dilemma of Human Identity*. New York: Jason Aronson, 1977.

LICHTENSTEIN, H. (1977). Identity configuration and developmental alternatives. *The Dilemma of Human Identity*. New York: Jason Aronson.

LOEVINGER, J. (1966). Three principles for a psychoanalytic psychology. *Journal of Abnormal Psychology* 71, 432–443.

LOEWALD, H. (1951). Ego and reality. *International Journal of Psycho-Analysis* 32, 10–18.

LOVLIE, A-L. (1982). *The Self. Yours, Mine or Ours*. Arlov: Universitetsforlager.

LYND, H. (1958). *Shame and the Search for Identity*. New York: Science Edition.

MCDOUGALL, J. (1980). *Plea for a Measure of Abnormality*. New York: International Universities Press.

MACHTLINGER, V. (1981). The father in psychoanalytic theory. In M.E. Lamb (Ed.) *The Role of the Father in Child Development*. London: Wiley.

MACKINNON, D.W. and DUKES, W.F. (1964). Repression. In L. Postman (Ed.) *Psychology in the Making*. New York: Knopf.

MAHLER, M. (1966). Discussion of Dr Greenacres's 'Problems of the overidealisation of the analyst and of psychoanalysis'. Abstracted in *Psychoanalytic Quarterly* (1967) 36, 637

MAHLER, M. (1968).*On Human Symbiosis and the Vicissitudes of Individuation*. Vol. 1, *Infantile Psychosis*. New York: International Universities Press.

MAHLER, M. and GOSLINER, B.J. (1955). On symbiotic child psychosis: genetic, dynamic and restitutive aspects. *Psychoanalytic study of the Child* 10, 195–212.

MAHLER, M., PINE, F. and BERGMANN, A. (1975). *The Psychological Birth of the Human Infant*. London: Hutchinson.

MALAN, D. (1963). *A Study of Brief Psychotherapy*. New York: Plenum.

MARKUS, H. (1977). Self-schemata and processing information about the self. *Journal of Personality and Social Psychology* 3, 63–78.

MASSERMAN, J.H. (1955). *The Practice of Dynamic Psychiatry*. Saunders: Philadelphia.

MASTERSON, J.F. and RINSLEY, D.B. The borderline syndrome. The role of the mother in the genesis and psychic structure of the borderline personality. In Lax, R.J., Bach, S. and Burland, J.A., Eds, *Rapprochement*. New York: Jason Aronson, 1980.

MEAD, G.H. (1934). *Mind, Self and Society*. Chicago: University of Chicago Press.

MEISSNER, W.W. (1984). Differential diagnosis: the narcissistic disorders. In *The Borderline Spectrum*, Chap. 5. New York: Aronson.

MEISSNER, W.W. (1986). Can psychoanalysis find its self? *Journal of the American Psychoanalytic Association* 34, 379–400.

MELTZER, D. (1967). *The Psycho-Analytic Process*. Perthshire: Clunie Press.

MERLEAU-PONTY, M. (1964). *The Primacy of Perception*. Evanston, IL: Northwestern University Press.

MILLER, A. (1979). The drama of the gifted child and the psychoanalyst's narcissistic disturbance. *International Review of Psycho-Analysis* 60, 47–58.

MILLER, S. (1985). *The Shame Experience*. Hillsdale, NJ: Lawrence Erlbaum.

MITTERAUER, B. and PRITZ, W.F. (1978). The concept of the self: a theory of self-observation. *International Review of Psycho-Analysis* 5, 179–188.

MODELL, A. (1980). Affects and their non-communication.*International Journal of Psycho-Analysis* 61, 259–267.

MODELL, A. (1984). *Psychoanalysis in a New Context*. New York: International Universities Press.

MOLLON, P. (1984). Shame in relation to narcissistic disturbance. *British Journal of Medical Psychology* 57, 207–214.

MOLLON, P. (1985). The non-mirroring mother and the missing paternal dimension in a case of narcissistic disturbance. *Psychoanalytic Psychotherapy* 1, 35–47.

MOLLON, P. (1986). An appraisal of Kohut' contribution to an understanding of narcissism. *British Journal of Psychotherapy* 3 (2), 151–164

MOLLON, P. (1987). Self-awareness, self-consciousness, and preoccupation with self. In K. Yardley and T. Honess (Eds), *Self and Identity: Psychosocial Perspectives*. London: Wiley.

MOLLON, P. (1988a). What kind of infant does the therapist reconstruct? The view from the vantage point of self psychology. *British Journal of Psychotherapy* 4, 173–182.

MOLLON, P. (1988b). An appraisal of Kohut's contribution to an understanding of narcissism. *British Journal of Psychotherapy* 3, 151–164.

MOLLON, P. and PARRY, G. (1984). The fragile self: Narcissistic disturbance and the protective function of depression. *British Journal of Medical Psychology* 57, 137–145.

MONEY-KYRLE, R. (1971). The aim of psycho-analysis. In *The Collected Papers of Roger Money-Kyrle*. Strath Tay: Clunie Press, 1978.

MOORE, B.E. (1975). Toward a clarification of the concept of narcissism. *The Psycho-analytic Study of the Child* 30, 243–276.

NEUMANN, E. (1973). *The Child*. London: Hodder & Stoughton..

NOY, P. (1979). The psychoanalytic theory of cognitive development. *Psychoanalytic Study of the Child* 34, 169–216.

OGDEN, T. (1982). *Projective Identification and Psychotherapeutic Technique*. New York: Jason Aronson.

OLINER, M. (1982). The anal phase. In D. Mendell (Ed.), *Early Female Development*, pp. 25–60. Lancaster: MTP.

ORNSTEIN, P. and ORNSTEIN, A. (1980). Formulating interpretations in clinical psychoanalysis. *International Journal of Psycho-Analysis* 61, 203–211.

PAO, P-N. (1979). *Schizophrenic Disorders*. New York: International Universities Press.

PIAGET, J. (1951). *Play, Dreams and Imitation in Childhood*. London: Routledge.

PIERS, G. and SINGER, A. (1953). *Shame and Guilt*. Springfield, IL: Thomas.

PINE, F. (1985). Formation, expansion and vulnerabilities of the self experience. In *Developmental Theory and Clinical Process*. New Haven: Yale University Press.

PINES, M. (1982). Reflections on mirroring. *Group Analysis* 15 (suppl.), 1–26.

PINES, M. (1987). Shame. What psychoanalysis does and does not say. *Group Analysis* 20, 16–31.

POPPER, C. (1962). *Conjectures and Refutations*. New York: Basic Books.

PRITZ, W.F. and MITTERAUER, B. (1977). The concept of narcissism and organismic self-reference. *International Review of Psycho-Analysis* 4, 181–196.

PULVER, S. (1970). Narcissism. The term and the concept. *Journal of the American Psychoanalytic Association* 18, 319–341.

PUTNAM, J. (1989). *Diagnosis and Treatment of Multiple Personality Disorder*. New York: Guilford.

PYSZCYNSKI, T. and GREENBERG, J. (1986). The causes and consequences of a need for self-esteem: a terror management theory. In R.F. Baumeister (Ed.), *Public and Private Self*. New York: Basic Books.

PYSZCYNSKI, T. and GREENBERG, J. (1987). The role of self-focused attention in the development, maintenance and exacerbation of depression. In K. Yardley and T. Honess (Eds), *Self and Identity*. Chichester: Wiley.

RADO, S. (1928). The problem of melancholia. *International Journal of Psycho-Analysis* 9, 420–438.

RICHARDS, A.O. (1982). The supraordinate self in psychoanalytic theory and the self psychologies. *Journal of the American Psychoanalytic Association* 30, 939–957.

RICOEUR, P. (1970). *Freud and Philosophy*. New Haven: Yale University Press.

RICOEUR, P. (1981). The question of proof in Freud's psychoanalytic writings. In *Hermeneutics and the Human Sciences*. New York: Cambridge University Press.

ROCHLIN, G. (1973). *Man's Aggression. The Defence of the Self*. Boston: Gambit.

ROGERS, T.B. (1981). A model of the self as an aspect of the human information processing system. In N. Cantor and J. Kihlstrom (Eds), *Personality, Cognition and Social Interaction*. Hillsdale, NJ: Lawrence Erlbaum.

ROBBINS, M. (1982). Narcissistic personality as a symbiotic character disorder. *International Journal of Psycho-Analysis* 63, 457–473.

ROSENFELD, H. (1964). On the psychopathology of narcissism: a clinical approach. *International Journal of Psycho-Analysis* 45, 332–337.

ROSENFELD, H. (1971). A clinical approach to the psychoanalytic theory of the life and death instincts: an investigation of the aggressive aspects of narcissism. *International Journal of Psycho-Analysis* 52, 241–251.

ROSENFELD, H. (1987). *Impasse and Interpretation*. London: Free Association Press.

ROTHSTEIN. A. (1979). An exploration of the diagnostic term 'narcissistic personality disorder. *Journal of the American Psychoanalytic Association* 29, 893–912.

ROTHSTEIN. A. (1980). *The Narcissistic Pursuit of Perfection*. New York: International Universities Press.

ROTMANN, M. (1978). Uber die Bedeutung des Vaters in der 'Wiederannaherungs-Phase'. *Psyche* 32, 1105–1147.

SANDER, L.W. (1983). To begin with. Reflections on ontogeny. In J.Lichtenberg and S. Kaplan (Eds), *Reflections on Self Psychology*, pp. 85–104. Hillsdale, NJ: Analytic Press.

SANDLER, J. (1960). The background of safety. *International Journal of Psycho-Analysis* 41, 352–356.

SANDLER, J. and ROSENBLATT, B. (1962). The concept of the representational world. *Psychoanalytic Study of the Child* 17, 128–145.

SARTRE, J.P. (1956). *Being and Nothingness*. New York: Philosophical Library.

SCHAFER, R. (1976). *A New Language for Psychoanalysis*. London: Yale University Press.

SCHNEIDER, C. (1977). *Shame, Exposure and Privacy*. Boston: Beacon Press.

SCHWARTZ-SALANT, N. (1982). *Narcissism and Character Transformation*. Toronto: Inner City Books.

SEGAL, H. (1964). *Introduction to the Work of Melanie Klein*. London: Heinemann.

SMITH, D.L. (1985). Freud's developmental approach to narcissism: a concise review.

International Journal of Psycho-Analysis 66, 489–497.

SPENCE, D. (1982). *Narrative Truth and Historical Truth*. New York: Norton.

SPIEGAL, L. (1959). The self, the sense of self and perception. *Psychoanalytic Study of the Child* 14, 81–109.

SPILLIUS, E. (Ed.) (1988). *Melanie Klein Today*, Vol 1. *Mainly Theory*. London: Hogarth.

SPITZ, R.(1957). *No and Yes in the Genesis of Human Communication*. New York: International Universities Press.

SPRUIELL, V. (1975). Three strands of narcissism. *Psychoanalytic Quarterly* 44, 577–95.

SPRUIELL, V. (1981). The self and the ego. *Psychoanalytic Quarterly* 50, 319–344.

STECHLER, G. and KAPLAN, S. (1980). The development of the self. A Psychoanalytic perspective. *Psychoanalytic Study of the Child* 35, 85–136.

STEIN, C. (1984). Being alone with one's mother: the horror of incest. *Psychoanalytic Inquiry*, pp. 269–290.

STEIN, M. (1976). Narcissus. *Spring*. New York: Spring Publications.

STEINER, J. (1985). Turning a blind eye. The cover up for Oedipus. *International Review of Psycho-Analysis* 12, 161–172.

STERN, D. (1983). The early development of schemas of self and other and 'self with other'. In J. Lichtenberg and S. Kaplan (Eds), *Reflections on Self Psychology*, pp. 49-84. Hillsdale, NJ: Analytic Press.

STERN, D. (1986). *The Interpersonal World of the Infant*. New York: Basic Books.

STOLLER, R. (1975). *The Trans-sexual Experiment. Sex and Gender*. London: Hogarth.

STOLLER, R. (1976). *Perversion. The Erotic Form of Hatred*. London: Harvester.

STOLLER, R. (1977). Primary femininity. In Blum, H. (Ed.) *Female Psychology. Contemporary Psychoanalytic Views*. New York: International Universities Press.

STOLOROW, R.D. (1975). A functional definition of narcissism. *International Journal of Psycho-Analysis* 56, 179–185.

STOLOROW, R.D. and ATWOOD, G. (1992). *Contexts of Being. the Intersubjective Foundations of Psychological Life*. Hillsdale, NJ: Analytic Press.

STOLOROW, R.D. and LACHMANN, F.M. (1980). *Psychoanalysis of Developmental Arrest*. New York: International Universities Press.

STOLOROW, R.D., BRANDCHAFT, B. and ATWOOD, G. (1987). *Psychoanalytic Treatment. An Intersubjective Approach*. Hillsdale, NJ: Analytic Press.

STRACHEY, J. (1934). The nature of the therapeutic action of psycho-analysis. *International Journal of Psycho-Analysis* 15, 127–159.

STRAWSON, P.F. (1963). *Individuals: An Essay in Descriptive Metaphysics*. New York: Anchor Books.

TEICHOLZ, J.G. (1978). A selective review of psychoanalytic literature of theoretical conceptualisations of narcissism. *Journal of the American Psychoanalytic Association* 26, 831–861.

THRANE, G. (1979). Shame and the construction of the self. *Annual of Psychoanalysis* 7, 321–341.

TICHO, E.A. (1982). The alternate schools and the self. *Journal of the American Psychoanalytic Association* 30, 849–862.

TOPLIN, M. (1983). Discussion of papers by Drs. Stern and Sander. In Lichtenberg, J. and Kaplan, S. (Eds) *Reflections on Self Psychology*. Hillsdale, NJ: Analytic Press.

TRONICK, E., ALS, H., ADAMSON, L., WISE, S. and BRAZELTON, T. (1978). The infant's response to entrapment between contradictory messages in face to face interaction. *Journal of the American Academy of Child Psychiatry* 17, 1–13.

VAN DER WAALS, H.G. (1965). Problems of narcissism. *Bulletin of the Meninger Clinic* 29, 293–311.

VAN HERIK, J. (1985). *Freud on Femininity and Faith.* Berkeley, CA: University of California Press.

VINGE, L. (1967). *The Narcissus Theme in Western Literature up to the Early Nineteenth Century.* Lund: Gleerups.

WEISS, E. (1960). *The Structure and Dynamics of the Human Mind.* New York: Grune & Stratton.

WELLEK, R. (1960). Closing statement. In Sebeok, T.A. (Ed.) *Style in Language.* Cambridge, MA: MIT Press.

WHITE, M. and WEINER, M. (1986). *The Theory and Practice of Self Psychology.* New York: Brunner Mazel.

WILSHIRE, B. (1982). *Role Playing and Identity. The Limits of Theatre as Metaphor.* Bloomington, IN: Indiana University Press.

WILSHIRE, B. (1984). Paper presented to the Self and Identity Conference. Cardiff.

WINNICOTT, D. W. (1958). The capacity to be alone. In *The Maturational Processes and the Facilitating Environment*, pp. 29–36. London: Hogarth, 1965.

WINNICOTT, D. W. (1960). Ego distortion in terms of true and false self. In *The Maturational Processes and the Facilitating Enviroment.* London: Hogarth, 1976.

WINNICOTT, D. W. (1963). Communicating and not communicating leading to a study of certain opposites. In *The Maturational Processes and the Facilitating Enviroment*, pp. 179–192. London: Hogarth, 1965.

WINNICOTT, D. W. (1967). Mirror role of mother and family in child development. In *Playing and Reality.* London: Tavistock/Penguin, 1980.

WINNICOTT, D. W. (1971). Mirror role of the mother and family in child development. In *Playing and Reality.* London: Tavistock/Penguin, 1980.

WOLF, E. (1988). *Treating the Self* New York: Guilford Press.

WRIGHT, K. (1991). *Vision and Separation between Mother and Infant.* London: Free Association.

WURMSER, L. (1981). *The Mask of Shame.* Baltimore, MA: Johns Hopkins University Press.

WYLIE, R. (1974). *The Self-Concept*, Vol. 1. Lincoln, Nebraska: University of Nebraska Press.

YARDLEY, K. (1979). Social skills training. A critique. *British Journal of Medical Psychology* 52, 55–62.

YARDLEY, K. and HONESS, T. (Eds) (1986). *Self and Identity. Psychosocial Perspectives.* London: Wiley.

ZINKIN, L. (1983). Malignant mirroring. *Group Analysis* 16, 113–126.

Index